SECR

# Shaktipat

Awakening of Kundalini by the Guru

# SECRETS OF

# Shaktipat

Awakening of Kundalini by the Guru

**Ravindra Kumar**
**(Now Swami Atmananda)**
**Jytte Kumar Larsen**

**NEW DAWN PRESS, INC.**
UK • USA • INDIA

NEW DAWN PRESS GROUP
Published by New Dawn Press Group
New Dawn Press, Inc., 244 South Randall Rd # 90, Elgin, IL 60123
e-mail: sales@newdawnpress.com

New Dawn Press, 2 Tintern Close, Slough, Berkshire, SL1-2TB, UK
e-mail: sterlingdis@yahoo.co.uk

New Dawn Press (An Imprint of Sterling Publishers (P) Ltd.)
A-59, Okhla Industrial Area, Phase-II, New Delhi-110020
e-mail: sterlingpublishers@airtelmail.in
www.sterlingpublishers.com

*Secrets of Shaktipat*
© 2005, Ravindra Kumar
(Now Swami Atmananda)
Jytte Kumar Larsen
ISBN 978-1-84557-375-1
First Edition: 2005
Reprint 2009

PRINTED IN INDIA

*Dedicated to the loving memory of*
*Swami Vishnu Tirth*

# CONTENTS

# FOREWORD

*Shaktipat* is a secret path for the awakening of *Kundalini Shakti* in a disciple through the power of Guru, who is normally authorised to do so in the lineage. Only genuine seekers, who come to the Guru of their own, are qualified to receive the initiation. In the past the secret knowledge of *Shaktipat* has been passing as a word of mouth from Guru to disciple and never written in a book form. A seeker has only to find the right Guru to get the benefit of this direct method of awakening the *Shakti*. Since the symptoms of all self-effort methods, such as *Bhaktiyoga*, *Jnanayoga*, *Karmayoga* and *Tantrayoga*, etc, begin to appear automatically on the awakening and activisation of *Shakti* through *Shaktipat*, this method is known as *Mahayoga* or Great Yoga. The initiate experiences *Shakti* directly within him/herself and becomes conversant with it.

In the present book the authors have elaborated the various aspects of *Shaktipat* Initiation and have given a clear comparison with self-effort methods known as "aanvopaya." Through personal experiences of *Kundalini* awakening the authors have presented a complete guidebook for the purpose. A seeker on the path can prepare oneself very well before presenting him/herself before the Guru. This can save unnecessary time for the awakening of *Shakti*. Certainly the Guru is happy to accept such a disciple and the results are quicker than normal time.

Dr Kumar is a prolific writer, having already authored more than 15 books on *Kundalini* and other branches of occult sciences. The book is recommended to the seekers of *Shaktipat* Initiation as a preparation for receiving initiation in a short time and in a successful manner.

Swami Vishnu Tirth                          *Swami Shivom Tirth*
Sadhana Sevashram,
Indore, Madhya Pradesh
India.

# PREFACE

*Shaktipat* is the ancient method of being spiritually awakened by a Guru. The process awakens and activates the *kundalini* in the shortest time. This awakening has minimum or no risks or side effects, and in most cases is instant and effortless. Through the intuitive grace of the Guru one knows directly that there is no death, and as a result lives fully and awakes for the first time. Automatic movements in the body reverse the flow of vital fluids, which prepare the brain to receive enlightenment. Accumulated *karma* from several lives is thinned out and there is calmness, an inner contentment and a synchronicity with life. Living in two worlds becomes a reality.

I can make the above statements because of the awakening of my *kundalini* that took place in 1992. I have experienced *Shaktipat* through my Indian Guru, and I am reasonably versed with the Indian philosophy of liberation. Liberation of the East is the same as Salvation of the West.

The initiate surrenders to the Higher Consciousness in the Guru. The Guru being the vehicle of the Divine Grace, directs the passage of *Shakti* through him/her to the initiate to awaken his spiritually dormant *kundalini*. One's *kundalini* can also be awakened through self-effort, but this may take several years if not several lifetimes. *Shaktipat* Guru has transcended worldly attractions and lives a simple and dedicated life. Gurus initiate people for

Self-realisation as a service to God, and they do not
expect remuneration from the initiate, as they are self-
sufficient. But initiates are advised to offer the Guru
presents in line with the tradition for showing respect
and surrender. Some present-day gurus and Catholic
priests are found guilty, and even punished for abusing
children sexually; these are the ones who were forced to
live as celibates while not having risen above sex and
worldly attractions. Such pseudo-gurus have brought a
bad name to the real gurus, who have always existed and
will always exist. I have been having out-of-body
experiences and travelling in past and future. The
awakening of the *kundalini* enables these experiences.
*Shakti* brings these experiences according to the need and
education for the initiate. At times I have seen the figure
of Jesus Christ manifesting before me, and on another
occasion the figure of AUM has appeared large in the sky.
When this happens I am filled with feelings of bliss and
protection from God Almighty. Then there is the
knowledge that one is eternal as Soul or *Atman,* and the
fear of death is gone forever. It is the first time that one
lives life in a full way. I am convinced of the *Shaktipat*
method, and would recommend it safely to men, and to
women, like myself.

                                              *Jytte Kumar Larsen*

# ACKNOWLEDGEMENTS

I have been fortunate to have spiritual initiations from Gurus of outstanding reputation from time to time. I bow down my head to the lotus feet of these Gurus. Through my visualization of previous births, the first Master to mention is Pythagoras who was my Guru *circa* 600 BC and who has been helping me in different lifetimes too. In this life, I got simple initiation from Siddheshwar Baba at his ashram some 60-km from Delhi in the year 1986. He was formerly Dr B. S. Goel, author of the well-known book *Third Eye and Kundalini*. Next Eckankar Guru Sri Herald Klemp of Minnesota initiated me in the year 1987. After that I have been meeting some unknown saints in dreams and getting initiated by them. I was also given a *mantra* that stays with me till today.

Recently, I was lucky to get simple initiation from the popular lady saint Guruma at her ashram in Ganaur near Sonepat, some 80-km from Delhi. Soon after that I came in touch with Guru Deepak Yogi of Hapur near Delhi, who gave me *Shaktipat* Initiation with a touch and *mantra*. Eventually, I came to know about the Tirth lineage of Gurus and was initiated by Swami Parmananda Tirth of Indore. Parmananda Tirth is the disciple of the powerful *Shaktipat* guru Swami Shivom Tirth, who himself is a disciple of well-known Guru Swami Vishnu Tirth Maharaj. I have freely consulted the books written by the Gurus of this lineage and my sincere thanks are due to them. Thanks are also due to Swami

Parmananda Tirth for some important suggestions and thus improvising the text.

My disciple Advocate Harish Chandra Pradhan deserves thanks for dedicating the 10-acre ashram at Baharaich to the Academy of Kundalini Yoga and Quantum Soul for a noble cause. Through his efforts the management of the ashram is going so well that more and more people are joining it. Soon it might become an International Center for Kundalini Awakening through Shaktipat.

I'd like to thank Ms Kumud Mohan, a freelance writer from Delhi, for helping me edit the text to present it suitably for Western readership.

*Ravindra Kumar*

*jytteravi.kumar@mail.tele.dk*

We are grateful to our mothers late Mrs. Lakshmi Devi and Mrs. Allen Maria Andersen for their blessings and help at all time. Sincere thanks are due to Margaret Dempsey who first edited each chapter, as it was ready and then the whole book on completion. Without her help the presentation of the material may not have been proper. Thanks are also due to Jonathan Barber for some useful discussions and suggestions.

We would like to record our thanks to Advocate Suresh Chandra Singhal for legal help and advise from time to time; my brothers Rajendra Singh and Raghvendra Singh, my son Atul Singh and my daughter Seema Singh for their encouragement and interest in the spiritual work, and for their facilitations whenever we are in India.

*Jytte Kumar Larsen*

# INTRODUCTION

Impressions or tendencies formed in *chitta* or psyche from the past impel a person to continue in the same direction without any will on their part. This helplessness becomes the cause of further unhappiness. According to *sankhya* philosophy *sadhana* or spiritual pursuits should be such that the three types of burnings (physical and mental, spiritual, and calamities sent by heavenly beings) should be totally eradicated so there is no chance of them returning. Just as medication reduces fever to heal the body so the fever does not return, in the same way through spirituality we are healed so that unhappiness goes away and does not return. Yoga is the tried and tested permanent cure to unhappiness. *Kriyas* or automatic movements offer diagnosis, reason, treatment and elimination for the big disease. The big disease includes birth, old age, diseases and death. *Avidya* or ignorance is diagnosed as the reason, and Self-realisation is the treatment that eliminates the disease from its root.

Three mistakes prevent attaining *Atman*. The first is the belief that worldly pleasures enjoyed through the senses give happiness; the second is the desire to keep the body healthy and strong forever; and the third is the expectation that the cause of pleasures will always be available. Becoming attached to pleasures in this way keeps the cycle of re-incarnation continuing. The only way to end this cycle is to stop all mental modifications and by doing this to experience Self-realisation.

*Shakti,* on awakening and activation, onsets *kriyas* (automatic movements) in the initiate. This ends all mental modifications (past impressions and tendencies) and gives the experience of divine bliss to the initiate.

This joy surges from within, and is independent of the five senses. Enjoyment through the senses requires external objects which are not needed for inner joy, and the mind in inner joy does not become absorbed in external activities. The initiate is so absorbed in the bliss that he does not want to end the meditation. According to *Mundakopanishad* such a yogi is said to be dwelling within, attached to and active within the Self or *Atman*, and is said to be the best among those who know *Brahman*. In the *Bhagavad Gita* Lord Krishna describes such a *yogi* as being free from worldly activities, having achieved *nirvana* or becoming one with *Brahman*. Every *kriya* brings the joy of Self, and all pleasures of the world appear insignificant before it. Saint Kabir noted that when the mind is absorbed in the inner bliss, why should it wander around looking for other things? Omnipotence and omniscience of *Shakti* can be seen in all kinds of *kriyas,* such as shaking, rotating round or back and forth, singing, laughing, weeping, speaking in strange languages or advising like a Guru, which are done by *Shakti* herself. However, when *chitta* reaches the steady state within the *Atman* or Self, the *kriyas* become subtler, and having finished their job gradually disappear.

The initiate witnesses everything being done without his/her efforts. The main goal of *sadhana* is to control the mind through *kriyas*. Proper food, rest and other helpful activities are part of *sadhana,* while activities that hinder spiritual progress are called *obstacles*. Achieving the state of "unbroken inner contentment", where there is indifference to the pleasures and pains of the world, is *liberation* while still living in the body. This is the ultimate goal of *sadhana*. Once this point is reached there is nothing more to be done. According to Lord Krishna who says in the *Bhagavad Gita*, once reaching this state even the greatest sorrow cannot shake the person.

Most of the *kriyas* are such that the initiate through his own efforts cannot perform them. *Shakti* does everything. All *sanskaras* such as anger, fear and desire thin out and gradually disappear. Renunciation or disinterest in worldly affairs develops. After the quietening of *kriyas* a natural meditative state emerges in which *chitta* appears to have been dissolved, and the mind is empty of determinations and indifferences. Virtues of Self-realisation such as fearlessness, equanimity and compassion emerge in the initiate. Since yoga (oneness of *Atman* and *Paramatma* or Soul and God) takes place naturally, the process is known as *Sahajyoga* or *Siddhayoga.* Since it combines all the four major kinds of yoga—*Hatha, Mantra, Laya* and *Raja*—it is also known as *Mahayoga.*

*Shakti* motivates the initiate's interest in different kinds of yogic activities, according to what is needed. As the initiate realises that *Shakti* does all activities in him, the sense of doership dissolves naturally and of witnessing emerges. *Unmani avastha* or the state of "joyfulness beyond mind" sets in. The initiate should never fall prey to "doubt", and should maintain the state of faith and surrender to *Shakti* under all circumstances, until the final state of union with *Atman* is attained. I have discussed spiritual matters, including the awakening of the *kundalini*, in three earlier books – *Secrets of Numerology* (1992), *Destiny, Science and Spiritual Awakening* (1997), and *Kundalini for Beginners* (2000). In *The Secrets of Kundalini Awakening* (2002) I have attempted to harmonise the key points from these three books while elaborating on them, in order to present the reader with a shortcut "integral path" towards *kundalini* activation and enlightenment. Twelve mini books on various branches of occult science have also been published in the past three years. Up to now I have been presenting mostly self-help methods. In this book I present the shortest and most direct method of passing Cosmic Energy from Guru to initiate to awaken his *kundalini*. It is suitable to those who have faith in and can surrender to the Higher Principle in the Guru. Finding the true Guru, who has transcended sex and other worldly attractions, and who demands nothing from the initiate is rare. The only thing required from the initiate is to surrender to the higher principle embodied in such a Guru. A true Guru helps every genuine seeker only as a service to God and with no return in mind.

I was studying mathematics, having obtained my PhD from the Indian Institute of Technology, Delhi, in 1968. I taught mathematics in eight countries including India, UK, USA, the Middle East, the Far East and Africa. About six books and 30 research papers were published in mathematics. After experiencing *kundalini* in 1987 my interest shifted to spiritual and psychical research. More than a dozen papers have been published in the *Journal of Religion and Psychical Research*, USA. Presently I am a trustee of the Academy of Religion and Psychical Research, and founder president of the Academy of Kundalini Yoga and Quantum Soul. I eventually resigned my job as mathematics professor in 1994. Later I worked as professor of comparative religion at Belk Research Foundation, Charlotte, NC, and as professor of yoga philosophy and meditation at Hindu University, Florida for some time.

I studied by self-effort various methods of raising *kundalini* that exist in various faiths and traditions of the world. These methods are presented with details in my book *The Secrets of Kundalini Awakening*. In recent years I came across some genuine Gurus of the *Shaktipat* order and learned about the instant raising of the *kundalini* in an initiate by the grace of the Guru. Symptoms of arousal are seen within days or even within hours in an initiate who is well prepared through *sadhana* or spiritual practices prior to *Shaktipat* initiation. For others the *kundalini* first purifies the *chitta* by thinning out the *sanskara* or accumulated *karma* from several lifetimes. This process may take a few weeks, months or years, according to how much *karmic* debris has been stored. As the *chitta* purifies so the symptoms of active *Kundalini Shakti* appear in the initiate.

There are certain vocabularies related to the mechanism of *Shakti*, which are helpful for the reader to know. The next article, 'The Mechanism of Shakti', fulfils this need. References from each chapter are listed in the end. A comprehensive glossary of words in Sanskrit and a bibliography are given at the end of the book.

# THE MECHANISM OF *SHAKTI*

*Shakti* is Cosmic Energy that is behind everything, animate or inanimate. The Self is subtle and conscious or animate while the body is gross and inanimate. When *Shakti* manifests in the Self it becomes *Chaitanya* or Conscious Self. When *Shakti* interacts with inanimate *chitta* or mind-stuff it appears conscious because of the reflections of Conscious Self on the *chitta*. When *Shakti* interacts with *chitta* it is called *Chit-Shakti*. When *Shakti* interacts with the senses it stimulates their own consciousnesses known as *Chetna* or consciousness. Thus the same *Shakti* has three different names and performs three different functions depending on what it is interacting with: *Chaitanya, Chit-Shakti* or *Chetna*. This is the downward journey of *Shakti* called *Prasava-Krama* or the involutionary process. After birth the self becomes pre-occupied with phenomenal consciousness, senses and objects. This is known as involution. When *Shakti* withdraws its involvement from objects, senses and finally from consciousness itself, it is evolution and the process is called *Prati-Prasava-Krama* or evolution.

When *Shakti* projects outwardly through the senses, it is known as *Chetana* or consciousness, and when it turns inward it is *Pratyaka-Chetana* or Pure Consciousness. *Chit-Shakti,* on awakening, fights with *sanskara* and thins them out, making the *chitta* pure; and then, it is the Pure Consciousness that reaches the Conscious Self which enables the witnessing of *Atman* or Soul.

There are various methods of self-help that can awaken *Shakti*. However, a practitioner cannot depend solely on self-help for spiritual advancement. The person may be impatient and give up spiritual practices when there are not immediate results. Awakening *Shakti* through the grace of Guru is more authentic and certain. The Guru acts as a catalyst and accelerates the initiate's energy system. The Guru remains present until the goal is reached. He prays to God for *Shakti* to awaken inwardly in the initiate who has placed himself in His protection with full faith and surrender. The awakened *Shakti* of the Guru interacts with the spiritually dormant energy of the initiate, and stimulates it with force. The greater the power of the Guru, the quicker *Shakti* awakes in the initiate. Transmission of power in this way through the descent of *Shakti* is known as *Shaktipat*.

To meet the Guru, the *chitta* or mind should be calm, which is attained through good *karma* over several lifetimes. Doing *sadhana* (spiritual practices) and *satsang* (being in the company of evolved ones) while being absorbed in love for God and with a sense of service to God prepares one to receive the grace of the Guru. Surrender is to the Higher Consciousness in the Guru, which is the real Guru, and not to the physical form of the Guru, which is only the vehicle. Activation of *Shakti* induces *kriyas* (automatic movements) in the initiate, which thin out *sanskaras* (layers of impressions and tendencies, and accumulated *karma* from several lifetimes), and purify the *chitta,* eventually clearing the way for the initiate to witness *Atman.* Such a person is now liberated, the veil of *maya* (illusion) is lifted and the chain of further incarnations is broken.

The ultimate goal of spiritual pursuits is to realise that *Shakti* operates undividedly throughout the whole creation and to dissolve or merge the Self with the all-pervading universal *Shakti.* This goal is reached when a person's *Kundalini Shakti* is awakened. *Kundalini Shakti* on awakening introduces herself to the initiate through various symptoms, such as light, sound, and various other subjective experiences. She also makes her natural qualities of omniscience, omnipresence and omnipotence known to the initiate. The secret of *Shakti's* oneness with Self or *Atman* is also revealed. *Kriyas* gradually remove all limitations and illusions allowing the initiate to experience his/her real Self.

Although the activities of *Shakti* are self-propelled, nevertheless, each initiate must support the process by giving time and attention to the spiritual journey. This reduces any obstacles in the way of *Shakti* and increases the pace of progress. There are three major supports: firstly there should be full faith in the Guru and deity concerned; secondly, there must be total surrender to *Shakti* to give her the freedom she needs to work to annihilate the ego; thirdly, acts should be performed without attachment to the fruits of one's action, in the form of wanting particular results. This is *karmayoga,* and it annihilates any new impressions forming in *chitta*. To achieve this it is not necessary to take the vows of *sanyas* (renunciation) formally. Doing everything to the best of one's ability without being attached to results can attain the fruits of yoga. Giving up the fruits of one's actions is real renunciation. However, if a person really wants to take *sanyas* this is possible in order to have real detachment, that is, a total lack of hunger for worldly pleasures and attainments. One should remain in the world and fulfil one's duties, without the *chitta* being affected either by pleasure or suffering. This purifies the *chitta*, reduces the destiny and bodes well for the rest of the spiritual journey.

A common mistake is thinking that success in the spiritual world can be achieved alongside success in the material world. This is like having your cake and eating it too, which is not possible. To have one, the other must be renounced. Early in the spiritual path a choice is made between getting on in the physical material world or getting off the material to pursue the spiritual. This does not have to mean breaking away from the material and/ or conventional but it does mean being in the material/ conventional world in a different way. The initiate must be clear about two things in order to be successful: first, clear about the real meaning of service and surrender; and second, clear about the kind of commitment which is required to achieve the spiritual goal.

The Soul and *maya* (illusion) are so interconnected that their qualities reflect upon each other. The bliss of the Soul reflects on *maya* and the illusion of *maya* reflects on the Soul. When the initiate arrives at the causal body, which is above the physical and subtle bodies, then the Self is dealing with subtler levels of *chitta*. The bliss experienced at this level of the *chitta* is of the Self or *Atman*.

Although creation started with the wish of God, the cycle of death and rebirth came into being as a result of ignorance, and the *chitta* collected impressions and tendencies, which caused further incarnations. Spiritual liberation involves reversing the creative process of *Shakti,* from unfolding to infolding, and although self-efforts and long *sadhana* can do this, the most easy and direct way is through the grace of Guru or *Shaktipat*. Awakening of the *kundalini* is the point at which the initiate becomes the spiritual path instead of being a walker on the path. It marks the beginning of the process and not the end. After the *kundalini* awakes it is important to be regular with *sadhana* and have continuing reverence and service to God.

# *SHAKTIPAT* AT A GLANCE

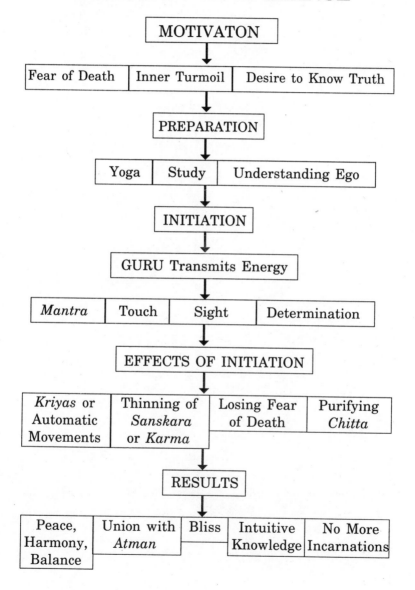

# 1

# *SHAKTIPAT*—THE ROYAL ROAD

The royal road of *Shaktipat* is little known about in the Western spiritual world. It is called the royal road because of its superiority in achieving Self-realisation. *Shakti* means "energy" and pat means, "flow". *Shaktipat* means the "flow of energy" from the Guru to the initiate. This is the easiest and most direct way of achieving Self-realisation. Grace from the Guru to the initiate flows from higher consciousness to lower consciousness, to raise the consciousness of the initiate. In *Shaktipat* the higher consciousness directed through the Guru raises the lower consciousness of the initiate and enables enlightenment.

As electricity flows from a point of high voltage to a point of low voltage, heat flows from a point of high temperature to a point of low temperature and water flows from a point of high hydrostatic pressure to a point of low hydrostatic pressure. In the same way, when a Guru with high spiritual energy touches the initiate, the energy flows from Guru to initiate, resulting in the initiate's 'awakening'. *Awake,* in this case means that the initiate recognises the formless, changeless, yet infinite nature underlying the universe of form. Having realised the nature of illusion and then awakening, the initiate-now turned-Guru may pass his spiritual energy into new initiates, adding to the world's spiritually advanced beings, and enriching the earth for evolving.

A Guru may transmit higher energy into the initiate in other ways. Just as a fish hatches its eggs by constantly looking at them, similarly a Guru by his looks can awaken the energy within the initiate and bring him to spiritual completion. And as a turtle by concentrating mentally on its eggs inside the ground hatches them out, similarly a Guru by mental determination and concentration on the initiate can awaken the power within him/her and bring him to spiritual realisation. The greatest gift a Guru can give an initiate is direct experience of the illusion of death. He does this by raising the consciousness of the initiate to a state of direct intuition or experience that he realises that death is an illusion. Most people are afraid of death and this takes away their joy in living. Fear destroys life. A Guru's way of living can be an example to others that fearing death and the unknown is not part of human nature. Rather, these fears are taught and conditioned. It is just as possible to learn of and experience infinite existence. First we need to be exposed to the idea that it is possible to focus on and experience living each moment instead of the fear of and experience of death in every moment. *Shaktipat* is this opportunity.

## Why is There Anxiety about Death, and How Can *Shakti* Relieve This?

*Chit-Shakti*, or conscious energy, forms the visible world. Understanding the nature of the conscious energy of *Shakti* can greatly relieve death anxiety. Anxiety about death arises from the transition we believe happens or fear may not happen when we die. This is the shift from physical being to non-physical being or the shift to non-existence.

Vibrations within *Shakti* create the rivers, mountains, humanity, animals, the sun and the moon. These exist and appear independent like waves in the ocean until they merge again with the ocean. The internal awareness of *Shakti* enables the objective world to exist and as *Shakti* withdraws her awareness, the objective world disappears and only *Shakti* remains. *Shakti* can be understood by thinking about electricity. A fan will run as long as electricity powers it; the moment electricity is shut off, all fans stop working. The same is true of humans. We are alive as long as *Shakti* powers us. The moment *Shakti* withdraws the life-force, we die. The *Shakti* connection is responsible for our everyday experience of the physical world. But science has no explanation for this phenomenon, and without this understanding, we suffer when our loved ones die, not knowing that they continue to live in another form, in another world or reality. *Shakti*, forming the seen world, also forms the unseen world. And, because of uncertainties about the death experience and the mysteries of our after-life, we are afraid of dying. Accordingly, "the fear of death" is a menace to humanity because it denies us the full enjoyment and experience of life. Our minds cannot focus on fear and joy at the same time. Life cannot be lived in fullness and joy as long as we believe in a death that separates us from life.

### How Does *Shakti* Take Away the Fear of Death?

When Cosmic Energy or Universal *Shakti* comes into contact with its latent *Shakti*, called *kundalini* that is lying dormant in the individual, *Shakti* awakens and activates the (spiritually) sleeping *kundalini*. The awakening of the *kundalini* is a sure sign of the active *Shakti*; although, even when inactive, it still supplies the energy that keeps us alive. The individual consciously feels the oneness of one's own *Shakti Kundalini* with the Universal *Shakti*, just as a drop of water feels union when it contacts the ocean. With the rising of the serpent power *kundalini*, comes the intuitive knowledge—that there is no death. When this happens the inner state of the aspirant quickly changes; there is calm, an inner contentment and a synchronicity with life not present before. This knowledge comes about through the grace of the Guru through *Shaktipat*. Accumulated *karma* from other lifetimes gradually loses its potency until all *karmic* debt dissolves. The practitioner then experiences *Shakti* active within him as an all-encompassing, expansive energy. The body of the practitioner becomes the entire cosmos, as the cosmos and the practitioner complement each other. He experiences a unified, eternal flow of life-force or energy circulating between him and Universal Consciousness. The physical limits of the practitioner now extend to the cosmic level, and all distances come within his reach; his third eye is opened, so that other dimensions can be seen and travel to higher realms becomes a reality. Not only is the "fear of death" gone for ever but also one begins to live fully and becomes totally awake for the first time. At this level the Self-realised person can do anything on earth except the divine processes of creation, preservation and destruction. A kind of "on-off switch" develops enabling him to be conscious of either this world or other worlds, if and when he chooses.

**Is Enlightenment Possible for Everyone?**
*Kundalini* energy is the vehicle for enlightenment, and because it is at the base of every spine, enlightenment is possible for everyone. It can be awakened through three main practices: (i) Yogic postures, *mudras* and breath control exercises, (ii) Grace of the Guru, and (iii) the accumulated results of devotional practices through several lifetimes. Awakening the *kundalini* through the grace of a Guru is often seen as an easy, natural way of stirring this energy. For the first method there are several rules to be adhered to in order for the energy to rise. One must learn the yogic postures, *mudras* and breath control practices of *Hathayoga*. These may not be easy for everyone, and having embarked on learning these postures and *mudras* there is no way of knowing how

long the person will need to practice before *kundalini*
rises and the person "awakens". For this reason finding a
Guru and receiving his/her grace is helpful.

When *kundalini* energy awakens through the grace of
the Guru, yogic postures, *mudras* and breath control
exercises need not be performed artificially as often
happens when *kundalini* rises through yoga practise;
rather, everything unfolds by itself according to the
individual's *karmic* history. Awakening through the grace
of the Guru is a sure and quick way, although finding
your suitable Guru may not be easy. When the
consciousness of the inner and the external Guru
integrate, an external or physical Guru is not needed for
awakening. Where it is not possible to receive grace from
a Guru then the first method can also work but may be
slower.

Using examples we can compare the three methods of
awakening. The first method is comparable to someone
who works very hard, tolerates the sun and heat of the
day, working relentlessly to earn his living. The second
method is similar to a person who receives great wealth
from someone rich through an act of compassion. The
third method is comparable to suddenly discovering
wealth on the way home or while sitting at home; it is
instant and without much effort. Whatever the method,
those who have had successful *kundalini* awakening can
be recognised by their good physical health, calm spirit,
appearance of "anahat-shabd" or the "inner sound" known
as *AUM* or WORD, beautiful, peaceful eyes, becoming an
"urdhvareta" or one in whom the reversal of the flow of
semen has taken place or the one who has attained the
power of retaining the semen, and whose body and nerves
have been purified. In my own experience when the
*kundalini* awakened I felt additional activity in my
testicles, a squeezing sensation that seemed to direct fluid
upwards to the brain. Sexual arousal passes on to other
parts of the body as sublimated energy. There is a cooling

down and an upsurge of pure love for everyone.[1] Swami
Muktananda[2] and Pundit Gopi Krishna[3] described similar
experiences in their books. Female practitioners also
reported similar experiences. In one case, a college
professor and Siddhayoga practitioner felt energy rocket
up from the first *chakra* (*mooladhara*), causing her whole
body to vibrate and shake. In the case of Beth, from
Arkansas, there was often a sucking sensation around the
cervix, as if vaginal fluid was needed by the energy[4].
Thus, whether the person is male or female, it seems that
vital sexual fluids are used to enrich and strengthen the
brain making it strong enough to receive enlightenment.

### Shaktipat—Kundalini Mahayoga

*Kundalini Mahayoga* is a self-proven and self-perfecting
spiritual practice. It involves *kriyas*. These are automatic
movements over which a practitioner has no control. The
power of *kundalini* can cause an initiate to perform *kriyas*
through the power of *kundalini* itself. The force of the
*kundalini* is such that the body performs these *asanas* or
yogic postures unconsciously. Another name for this is
*Siddhayoga*, or the self-proven path of meditation. In all
aspects, body, mind and intellect, *Shakti* uses *kundalini*
to perform the meditation. The initiate is drawn into
flowing with the energy and must surrender to the
process. When and how *Kundalini Shakti* manifests is the
work of the divine power (*Shakti*). To practise
*Siddhayoga* one must allow divine power the opportunity
to perform the meditation and yogic postures without
interference.

Without initiation it is difficult to realise the fruits of
knowledge, meditation, yoga, *japa* (chanting), *tapa*
(austerities), devotion, *karma* and *dharma* (religious
duties). *Kundalini Mahayoga (Shaktipat)* as a path of
initiation is different from other paths of meditation and/
or initiation, because on other paths certain tasks have to
be learned or specific techniques mastered. This means

that one maybe expected to meditate or may need to learn different stages in meditation. Ceremonies may need to be performed or different yogic postures or *asanas*, or one may be needed to free his/her mind of undesirable thoughts. In *Shaktipat* it is not necessary to do any of these things. All the person has to do is sit with complete surrender to the present moment and experience. To be warm and welcoming to all thoughts or emotions as they occur, saying 'yes' to their experience and allowing life to flow effortlessly through the body without interference. Then, according to the nature and state of the spiritual consciousness of each initiate, different meditative experiences—emotional, intellectual or creative in nature—will occur by themselves. *Shaktipat* initiation is successful to the degree that an initiate demonstrates the qualities of non-attachment and renunciation. Non-attachment and renunciation catalyse the whole process of *Shaktipat*; the initiate is advised to embody them before taking initiation.

**Non-attachment and Renunciation**
Building strong spiritual foundations generates two qualities. First, non-attachment, the state of controlled *chitta* (mind-stuff) that contains no movement toward anything desired or away from anything not desired, and second renunciation. This does not mean there is a physical dissociation with the world, but more a sense of detachment at the mental level that breaks the cycle of desire and attachment. When this happens renunciation follows. Discarding materialistic attachment completely is renunciation. A practitioner develops non-attachment first and then renunciation follows naturally. Non-attachment and renunciation are the result of a meditative and contemplative life. They are the pillars for the highest good and are called *parmarth*. They are important qualities for the initiate to possess, in order to experience successful and effective *Shaktipat*. To understand the above and the suffering that arises when

one doesn't have these qualities, look at people in general
and how they suffer because of their attachment to
worldly affairs. The physical body is everything for them,
and as a result "the fear of death" is paramount in their
thoughts. Little spiritual progress is made when the mind
is consumed with the fear of death or any other fear.
Nevertheless, by controlling the *chitta* (mind) through
making it dispassionate in gradual steps, non-attachment
can be achieved. Slowly, one understands that this world
is transitory, changing constantly and ultimately
decaying. The pursuit and satisfaction of desires cannot
lead to inner peace, since one desire leads to another in
an unending chain of craving and dissatisfaction.
Combining this understanding with the study of spiritual
literature, contemplation and meditation increases
detachment from the objective world, which results in
gain in spiritual advancement. An initiation at this stage
can produce direct experiences with *Shakti.*

**Path of Knowledge and Path of Yoga**
The relationship between the path of knowledge and the
path of yoga is also important. Those on the path of
knowledge experience yoga (joining the Soul with Supersoul, or Self-realisation), after many lifetimes. A yogi
acquires knowledge through the practice of yoga
becoming liberated in a single lifetime. Therefore yoga is
the only certain method by which results can be achieved
in a single lifetime. Just as the monkey jumps from one
branch to another to finally reach the desired tree laden
with fruit, so the yogi moves from one *chakra* to another.
He gradually crosses the first six *chakras* and finally
arrives at the seventh (crown) centre, where
consciousness and *prana* are anchored. At this stage the
yogi acquires intuitive knowledge and liberation at the
same time. An ideal way for spiritual advancement is to
pursue the path of knowledge and the path of yoga
simultaneously, as they complement each other. This may
also be the fastest. In some cases a devoted yogi may not

achieve liberation because of an inability to control the senses, and as a result, Self-realisation and liberation are not achieved before death. Lord Krishna, in the *Bhagavad Gita*, discussed the plight of such yogis. An unrealised yogi is never destroyed either in this world or in others. One who has worked for the good of all is never abandoned. One who has progressed but not completed the path of yoga because of the pull of the senses, after death, will live in heavenly worlds, because of the good deeds performed by him. When a dedicated practitioner of yoga dies before achieving the end result, he incarnates into a family of yogis. Such a birth is rare. The seeds of yoga sown in a past life are germinated again in this life and the individual is unknowingly impelled toward the perfection of yoga. (*Bhagavad Gita* 6, 40-44).

## How the Paths of Yoga and Knowledge Compare with Other Methods

In all other methods a sense of I-ness (or the doer) is present, whether it is the path of physical postures, devotion, austerities or *mantra*. All methods prepare for the awakening of the *kundalini*. After the awakening of *kundalini*, "action" is replaced by "automatic movement", and the original method should be given up as it has served its purpose. The sense of "I" is replaced by a sense of perception. In other words, "sense of the doer" is replaced by the "sense of the seer". One's body sings, dances, laughs and cries, and one experiences directly that one is not performing any of these actions, but that some other power is responsible. This is the reason that *Shaktipat-Kundalini Mahayoga* is known as a "self-proven system". To get to this stage of awakening by methods other than *Shaktipat* takes an unduly long time. However, by the method of *Shaktipat* this stage of awakening may be experienced in months or a little more than a year; in cases where the practitioner is advanced, this stage may occur in a matter of days. The state of "surrender to God", which is talked of so much in other methods and is not achieved even after long practice, is automatically attained in *Shaktipat*.

## Different Types of Yoga

*Bhaktiyoga* is known as *Gauni Yoga* or the "secondary path of devotion", which is like a staircase that is followed and then given up when the top of the stairs is reached. When the practitioner directly experiences the power of *kundalini*, an unbounded love is awakened. There is no longer pleasure in material objects. According to the *Narada Bhakti Sutra* a practitioner is not interested in acquiring the *siddhis* or yogic powers, such as *anima*, making one's body as small as one likes, *laghima*, making one's body as light as one likes, the physical disappearance of one's body, floating in the air and walking on fire. *Siddha* means natural, and when this natural state of absolute love for the Divine is attained, there is no desire for devotion. Gradually all symptoms and automatic movements disappear and one becomes a witness to whatever happens. Like a rock in the ocean where the waves may crash around it but it remains silent and steady, in the same way life events leave the initiate undisturbed. He becomes intoxicated with joy in this state of realisation. Instinctive movements, such as laughing, crying, singing, dancing, clapping, composing prose and poetry, performance of yogic postures, *pranayama* or breath control, *mudras*, seeing light and hearing sound internally, shedding tears and falling motionless on the ground take place by themselves. One is inwardly awakened to the happiness that is not found anywhere in the world. Complete withdrawal from the world and dependence on God is total in this state.

## Hathayoga

*Hathayoga* is the time-tested method for awakening the *kundalini* through performing yogic postures and *pranayama* or breath control. "Ha" stands for "moon" or the *ida* nerve to the left of *sushumna*, and "Tha" means sun or *pingala* nerve to the right of *sushumna*. The three currents of the three nerves originate at *mooladhara*. The aim is to make *prana* enter *sushumna*, and not *ida* or *pingala*; this done successfully is the awakening of the *kundalini*. Before this stage is reached one may theoretically say "I Am That", without understanding it—meaning, it being it, and by saying it may only be inflating the ego. A healthy body is important as well as controlled diet and right acting character, and above all an adept or Guru in awakening the *kundalini*. Unfortunately the right atmosphere for *Hathayoga* is not found in the present time because of the lack of right Gurus.

The Vedanta talks about *pragyan*, which is the virtual sense controller that allows the creation, procurement and enjoyment of the world, without itself getting involved. It is in the world but not of it, since it is not affected by opposites, such as pleasure and pain. *Sanskara* or the accumulation of *karma* by the individual continues until one realises the existence of *Shakti*. Then *pragyan* is awakened and the mind controls the senses. The veil covering the three elements of creation—*Sat* (pure and real), *Raj* (active) and *Tam* (inert)—is removed and *chitta* (mind stuff) is quietened. Thoughts and counter-thoughts occurring in the mind perish and the mind is no longer controlled by the senses. One realises that the power he thought was separate is within him/her. The five afflictions—greed, lust, anger, attachment and ego—are destroyed and one arrives at the fundamental truth—that the nature and knowledge of all truth lies within. It is now that the practitioner proclaims the great pronouncement, *SOHAM*, meaning "I Am That." This only happens when *pragyan* has completely lifted the veil of consciousness so that *maya* or the world of illusion is revealed. *Pragyan* cannot be understood theoretically no matter how much reading and thinking has been undertaken. The process can be understood by thinking about an orange. A person can explain the texture and juiciness of an orange but until the person actually tastes it he has no concept. The understanding comes only when *pragyan* itself has awakened the *Shakti*. In order that the veil of *maya* is lifted, reason and discrimination must be present. There is pleasure in studying scriptures and a clear understanding of their meaning and importance; detachment with materialism increases until total detachment is acquired, the Soul illuminates the mind and ideas arise from within.

*Tantra*, which is another form of initiation, is based on a graphic symbol called *yantra* that has a point within the circle. According to the *tantric* theory the whole universe expands from that point. The practitioner concentrates on that point, which symbolises the point of *mooladhara chakra* or the root centre in the human body, which is the seat of the *kundalini*. Eventually the *kundalini* is awakened and *kriyas* or automatic movements are manifested, and then the *yantra* has served its purpose and its worship becomes secondary. It is unfortunate that the real meaning of *yantra* worship has been lost in time and that practitioners devote more time to ritualistic worship. As a result there is no awakening of *Shakti* and hence no manifestation of *kriyas*, unless one has the guidance of an able Guru.

The purpose of external sacrifice is to induce the desire for internal sacrifice that is by the *kriyas* and surrender to the involuntary bodily movements caused by the rising energy. And if the *kundalini* does not awaken, this purpose is not served, and external sacrifice may continue endlessly.

Every spiritual method aims at awakening the *kundalini*, and the practitioner can choose the one he likes, depending on the body structure, habits, faith and tradition, and the availability of the Guru. As pointed out earlier, *Shaktipat* is the most direct and fastest method, provided one can find a Guru. Other methods can be pursued without a Guru, but *Shaktipat* requires a giver (Guru) and a receiver (initiate).

## Chakra Activity in *Shaktipat* Initiation

Everyone's backbone has seven sections. These are based on the seven plexus/glands of the sympathetic system, and are: coccygeal, sacral, solar, cardiac, cervical, pituitary and pineal. The seven vortices of energy are the seven *chakras* and are at the knots where the nerves from different directions meet. They are named as *mooladhara, swadhishthan, manipur, anahat, vishuddhi, ajna* and *sahasrar* or root-centre, sacral-centre, naval-centre, heart-centre, throat-centre, eyebrow-centre and crown-centre. Since the *chakras* belong to the causal plane, as does the *kundalini*, they can only be recognised by their activities, not seen by the eyes. The *chakras* are responsible for distributing energy from the universal *Shakti* to different parts of the body, to enable proper functioning. For details one can refer to my book on *kundalinis*[5]. As *Shakti-Kundalini* passes through these *chakras* specific *kriyas* are manifested in the body of the practitioner according to the different forms assumed by *Shakti*, such as heat, air and electricity. Thus, at *mooladhara* one experiences excessive heat, at *swadhishthan* one's sexual feelings are aroused and sublimated, at *manipur* the movements of the stomach are witnessed, at *anahat* one hears internal *naad* or sounds, at *vishuddhi* one begins crying, or laughing, at *ajna* there is entry into one-pointed concentration and meditation, and at *sahasrar*, as *Shakti* meets Shiva at the top of the head, there is the experience of *samadhi* or absorption with the Absolute. By watching the automatic movements it is possible to see which *chakra* has been activated.

Two authorities have varying views on these *kriyas*. The Vedanta says that everything is illusion, while *Yogadarshan* says that everything (the world as well as

the *kriyas*) is real. According to the *Yogadarshan* of
Patanjali the *kriyas* are important in the sense that they
minimise and eventually annihilate the *karma*. They are
purifying in nature. Also the world is real since the
embodied Soul gets the opportunity to experience the
afflictions—greed, lust, anger, attachment and ego—and
thus become purified and elevated. However, one should
gradually develop the sense of detachment from worldly
objects and relations since they are not everlasting and
are only stepping stones for achieving liberation. The goal
is to enjoy worldly objects without becoming attached. At
this point both the Vedanta and the *Yogadarshan* appear
to be saying one and the same thing.

**Liberation or Salvation**
*Shakti-Kundalini*, when awakened, transforms the seeds
of past actions into automatic movements, which reduce
passions. The thought currents of *chitta* (mind-stuff)
transform from disturbing to calm, and ultimately lose
their power. Similarly, the mind is also freed of desires.
The vices of lust, anger, passion, attachment, pride and
jealousy are transcended. These vices are the veils of
ignorance, which delude the mind. The awakened *Shakti*
destroys the veil of *maya* (illusion), which, when
shattered, returns and reunites with the Soul. Thus, the
identification of *chitta* with Soul is broken, and with the
destruction of the *chitta* activity, the state of Self-
realisation is attained. In this way the individual Soul
attains the state of super-consciousness.

As the automatic movements (*kriyas*) become
progressively subtler, the aspirant experiences greater joy
from these movements, though they may not be seen
visibly. For example, there may be intense jerking,
vibrating, rolling or rigorous yogic postures in the
beginning, with little or no peace and bliss. In later stages
the vibrations become rhythmic and soft, with the
aspirant experiencing light and sound and entering into

trance. The aspirant is inwardly absorbed in bliss and after his mind has been purified the movements disappear. He now experiences oneness with the Ultimate Reality.

## *Jivan-mukta* or The One Who is Liberated While Living

As the practitioner continues with the *kriyas* he experiences joy, but there is still an attachment to life. He may be talking of salvation intellectually, but the real state is achieved gradually. According to the purification of the mind and freedom from desires and passions, one attains deeper and deeper states of bliss that lead to the state of *samadhi* or inner absorption. The experiences of *samadhi* continue until they become recurrent and then the impressions of the world are washed out from the mind gradually. When intellectual consciousness is maintained this state of *samadhi* is called *sabij sampragyat* or "*samadhi* with seeds" by sage Patanjali. When the imprints of intellect are erased then *nirbij asampragyat samadhi* is achieved; that is the one without seeds (of intellect). This is the fourth stage of intellect out of a total of seven according to the *Yogadarshan* of Patanjali.

The first four stages depend on the efforts of the practitioner as he is affected by life and world events. The next three are independent and are related to freedom from life and the world. The person is not affected by actions in the world and is free from further accumulation of *karma*. Events still take place and pleasures come to the practitioner, but they are no longer through his efforts; they are automatic. At this stage he is called *jivan-mukta* or "the one who is liberated while living."

Self-realisation happens in three stages. Just as the lotus, although deep in the water does not retain a drop of it, the practitioner, also in the world, remains unaffected by its events. This is the first stage. Next he sees things as if he is dreaming or looking into the mirror.

The events appear to him like waves in the ocean and he remains as a witness. Thus there is an awareness of the causal vibration of the Self that is beyond the world of name and form. Now the *Chaitanya* or conscious Self is of primary importance while the world and its events with names and forms are secondary. This is the second stage. In the third stage the practitioner sees things and events as if they belonged to a dream world. The world and its events are lost, he is neither conscious nor unconscious about them, and there is neither bondage nor freedom, neither personal nor impersonal; he is conscious only of the conscious Self. There is always bliss, whether out in the world or in *samadhi*. This is the third stage after which the practitioner may live for a maximum of three weeks and then leave his body, according to *Mahayoga Vigyan*. The three bodies—physical, subtle and causal— are dissolved into the source later.

Such a person can understand the difference between *chitta* (mind stuff) and the Self. *Chitta* alternates between lust, greed, anger, attachment and ego at one time and tolerance, forgiveness, compassion at others; the Self is always pure, free and full of knowledge and bliss. The after-effect of seedless *samadhi* is transformation from the afflictions of *chitta* or mind to emerge into the Self. There is complete dependence on God for everything and the next higher stages are acquired automatically by the grace of God. *Shaktipat* initiation burns *karma* through automatic movements faster than any other method. The conscious Being in the practitioner is identified and *Shakti* merges one's consciousness in Self. This is the seventh stage that is free from the bondage of life, and there is no physical or mental activity.

**Different Kinds of Practitioners**
Practitioners can be divided into four categories, and the period of perfection or time required to achieve salvation depends upon which category a practitioner belongs to.

A practitioner of the first category is fully dedicated, has complete faith and surrenders to a Guru and God, every action is performed for God, not for his own self. His spiritual practices are regular and uninterrupted, as he/she knows that *initiation alone is not sufficient*. Non-attachment to materialism and worldly relations is also an important factor shown by such a practitioner, who is supposed to be the best amongst all. Non-attachment to spiritual materialism is also a powerful factor. *Shakti* acts immediately on such a disciple who has surrendered completely to her power. The practitioner does not interfere either physically or mentally in the working of *Shakti*, but cooperates with it fully. One has balanced one's mind towards the duality of pleasure and pain, friends or foes and sees all as a game of consciousness. Such a practitioner believes that every action is the play of *Shakti* and looks at everything as a witness. No exact time for enlightenment can be predicted but on average such a practitioner achieves salvation in less than three years.

Those practitioners who lack dedication, whose aspirations are not keen enough, who are affected by dualities, such as friends or foes and profit or loss, continue to accumulate, their minds are not purified and they do not truly possess renunciation. Some practitioners are attached to the fruits of their actions, and their pleasure depends on achieving success. Some of them consider *Shaktipat* to be one of many methods, and their faith is not complete. When practitioners in this category are initiated *Shakti* takes the responsibility of the practitioner and decides the particular *kriyas* that are necessary for him. When the practitioner does not have full faith in *Shakti*, the process of purification does not run the way it should. When the movements fall under the conscious control of the mind, the sense of doership remains and the witness or seer is absent. The desire for a particular *kriya* that caused happiness converts the *kriya* into action, which then creates *karma*, because the movement is not automatic. These are some of the factors why practitioners fall into lower categories. Accordingly they can be called average, poor and worst, depending upon the state of their *karma*. Thus there are four categories altogether: best, average, poor and worst; practitioners are expected to take on average three, six, nine, 12 and years from initiation to enlightenment. By analysing one's state of mind, i.e., how calm, torn between pleasure and pain, or balanced, a practitioner can decide for himself into which category he falls.

There is possibly another category that is above all these divisions. It is possible to meet someone who has been practising yoga, meditation and/or some kind of metaphysical practices very seriously and for a long time. Although he was not under the direction of a physical Guru, his process was almost complete already. A touch from a recognised Guru to such a person is all that is necessary and the symptoms of salvation will be displayed within days or weeks. To ensure that the awakened state continues, *kriyas* may be practised for a few months, but he is already a Guru himself and is ready to help others.

## References

1. Kumar, Ravindra, *Kundalini for Beginners*, MN, USA: Llewellyn Worldwide Ltd., 2000, p 83.
2. Muktananda, Swami, *Chitshakti Vilas (The Play of Consciousness)*, Maharashtra, India: Gurudev Siddhapeeth, 1972.
3. Krishna, Gopi, *The Awakening of Kundalini*, New York, USA: Kundalini Research Foundation, 1975.
4. Greenwell, Bonnie, 1990, *Energies of Transformation: A Guide to the Kundalini Process,* Cupertino, CA: Shakti River Press, 1990,. p. 203.
5. Kumar, Ravindra, *Kundalini for Beginners*, op.cit., 2000. pp 7-9.

# 2

# KRIYAS OR AUTOMATIC MOVEMENTS

**Recognising *Kundalini* Awakening**
Yoga is the most effective way of raising the *kundalini*, and because it is so widespread and produces results felt by everyone, it is not surprising that the personal experiences of hundreds are being recorded as their *Kundalini Shakti* awakens and becomes active. Through *pranayama* (breath control) or meditation or through *Shaktipat* of an able Guru the inner power awakens and the following symptoms are observed in the practitioner. However, no two practitioners experience the same symptoms. The symptoms are not permanent, and their intensity is proportional to the *karmic* debt of the practitioner. They fade away with acquiring maturity. A practitioner who has less *karmic* debt is likely to have milder symptoms than one who has more *karma* to work through. At the end of the process, only feelings of inner bliss and intuitive knowledge are left, all else vanishes.

I witnessed the manifestation of *kriyas* or automatic movements at the annual conference of Kundalini Research Network in Philadelphia in 1995 for the first time. The person was a male practitioner from Rishikesh, India. For almost one minute he called out the name of the holy River Ganges and began to move his hands, while sitting on the ground. Immediately his movements seemed to be taken over by an unseen force and he began to perform various yoga postures, one after another. Many of the postures he performed were not ordinarily possible and he demonstrated some pain while performing them. But the genuineness of the performance was felt and appreciated by everyone present. As has been said earlier, a practitioner will automatically go into those movements, which are necessary for his development. He has no control or authority over them; they take place automatically. After half an hour he came back to normal and reported feeling fine. The next demonstration I saw was in India by practitioners in the presence of their Guru.

There are many kinds of movements known to manifest in practitioners when the *Kundalini Shakti* is awakened. Below are some examples by which the wakening of energy can be identified. A movement of energy, sometimes subtle and sometimes intense, characterises all cases. When they occur they should be seen as an indication of purification and spiritual growth. The examples below give a sense of the variety of movement which the *kundalini* acting through the *kriyas* produces in those whose intentions and actions are concerned with raising the *kundalini*.

The body of the practitioner begins to vibrate. Due to *prana* (life energy) that rests in *mooladhara* (root centre) the Practitione becomes full of bliss and begins to dance. Since *Kundalini Shakti* resides in the root centre, it is where the base of creation is and one sees the whole world there. All gods reside in the base. On the left side of the base are the three nerves: *ida, pingala* and *sushumna*, which are united. Concentrating attention where the three nerves unite opens the mouth of *sushumna* and eventually frees the practitioner from bondage to the world.

If the root centre becomes activated the body begins to vibrate. There is a holding in or release of the breath, which becomes automatically strong. Inhalation and exhalation become forceful, and it may be difficult to keep the body still. This is evidence of an awakened *kundalini*, and one should sit quietly and observe the process.

When the body begins to vibrate, the mind is caught by an unusual pleasure, one may begin to laugh or cry without will, strange and unusual words may be spoken, one may suddenly ejaculate. There may be fear, and visions of fearful images may be seen, there may be the passing of urine without will, then the power of *kundalini* is at work.

If a person is sitting on the ground with crossed legs, the root, naval and chin lock applied automatically, the tongue turns backward forcefully, he finds it difficult to sit with the rush of energy, as the hands and legs are pulled forcefully by themselves. This is an indicator that the *kundalini* has been activated.

When the person is sitting on the ground and his sight is concentrated between the eyebrows; when the pupils in the eyes begin to rotate, the breath is held spontaneously, and thinking becomes free from worldly thoughts, then the *kundalini* is activated.

When one feels *prana* moving from the root centre to the crown centre, the chanting of a *mantra* begins automatically, and one feels bliss in different ways, then the *kundalini* is activated.

When the unstruck Sound or Word begins to be heard in different forms, the spinal chord appears to vibrate; feelings of numbness or non-existence are experienced with regard to the body; everything appears void; one becomes unable to open one's eyes even with sustained effort or the flow of electric currents may appear to be coming out of the body; then the *kundalini* has been activated.

When one feels an upsurge of energy and feels that someone else has entered the body, and is performing

various yogic postures, without there being any kind of
uneasiness (some practitioners experience pain, if they
have not practised *Hathayoga* earlier), rather one may
have a feeling of happiness or bliss, some *pranayama* may
also be accompanied with it, then the *kundalini* is
activated. When a person can create vibrations in any
part of the body solely by thought even when asleep, when
there is an experience of *pranic* movement in *sahasrara*
or crown centre, and there is activity in dreams, then it
indicates the awakening of the *kundalini*.

When a person sits and sees his subtle body by sheer
will, he may lose the sensation of the physical body. Even
with open eyes may feel the void everywhere, and the
sense of time may be lost, then the *kundalini* is awakened
and active.

When in the mornings and evenings, at a fixed time,
automatic movements begin to take place without
determination, which may compel the body, mind and
consciousness to move with it, then the *kundalini* is
awakened and active.

When the person is grounded just after sitting and
closing his eyes, the body may begin to rotate like a mill;
there may be no inhalation or exhalation; the body may
jump and fall like a frog here and there; the body may
move in all the places and may fall on the ground like a
dead person; it is not possible to lift the hands or feet. All
the nerves in the body may feel like they are being pulled
so hard that there is a chance of passing out. The body
may jump and feel tortured like a fish out of water, then
one should understand that the *kundalini* has become
active.

When sitting with closed eyes and willing for it,
various parts of the body may go into automatic
movement; the hands and legs may be thrown in different
directions and the words coming from the mouth may
have a twisted or unusual language; one may be uttering

words like animals, birds or frog or may roar like a lion, then this indicates an awakened *kundalini*.

When soon after sitting on the ground the body may appear to be going in easy and leisure postures, one may feel so happy that one may begin to sing, and the tune may be so pleasing that all around may be absorbed in it and appreciative; one may be composing poetry effortlessly and continually; one may be clapping in a professional manner, speaking in many kinds of unknown languages without knowing their meaning, and which nobody may be able to understand; but they still enjoy it, then one should know that the *kundalini* has been activated. When there is a feeling of intoxication without taking any kind of alcohol, the hands and legs vibrate in their own direction, there is exuberance but also an inability to do any kind of practical work. There is a lack of interest in talking or listening, then one may understand that the *kundalini* has become active.

When there is a feeling of flying in the sky while walking on the ground, there is the feeling of a body which is as light as a feather, and the person can travel any distance without getting tired. There is a feeling of being overwhelmingly happy, and pleasurably intoxicated even in dreams. One may not be disturbed either by good or bad omens, then one should know that activation of the *kundalini* has taken place.

When the person enters into a dreamy state immediately after sitting and on closing the eyes, and sees gods and goddesses, there is an experience of divine smell, beauty, taste, speech or touch, and instructions may be received from gods and goddesses, then these are the indications of an activated *kundalini*.

When there is concentration soon after sitting and getting ready for *sadhana*, there are conversations with gods and goddesses; prescriptions for medicines may be received from the gods, or *mantras* given for specific purposes. Adepts may give the person some knowledge of yoga, then one should know that the bestower of divine powers, *kundalini*, is active.

When soon after sitting on the ground and determining to go into *sadhana* there is the witnessing of the subtle body, there is a loss of the senses of the physical body. Even after opening the eyes all that is seen is a void and the person loses all concept of time, then *Chit-Shakti Kundalini* has been activated.

The following examples from people who have experienced an awakened *kundalini* are given below and show how the symptoms differ depending on the person. A large variety of cases have been collected and analysed by Dr Bonnie Greenwell in greater detail in her book, *Energies of Transformation* (1990).

Nan was a college student in the Midwest in the 60's. In the past she was a drug addict but later lived in an ashrama in India, where she meditated up to eight hours a day and ate little. She frequently experienced *kriyas* such as making sounds, humming, jerking her body, rolling around on the floor and falling over. She said: "I experienced twisting-snaking energy that was blissful, moving from the lower back or base of the spine upward, that caused my body to writhe around, moaning and groaning, twisting, swaying, falling forward or backward and then having a sudden backward jerk of the head which was accompanied by the sound of 'hum'. There was also an arching backward until falling over." Sometimes she fell over and rolled on the ground or moved into *asanas* or *mudras*, and once she danced in a trance of ecstasy[1].

Chris was born in California in 1941 and raised as a Catholic by a devout mother and non-Catholic father. Once while meditating she felt intense awareness of a column of brilliant light running through her. She would go into intense *kriyas* during the sessions, shaking, jerking, doing *asanas* (yogic postures), and feeling a loss of conscious awareness.

Karen, a college professor, slim and graceful in her 40's, studied Self-realisation Fellowship courses of Yogananda and practised kriyayoga. She began Jungian analysis, and had lucid dreaming. One night she began spontaneous rapid breathing and felt like jumping into an abyss. She saw an image of a door opening and some kind of energy passing through her. Another time, vibrations and tremors passed through her legs, spine and face, and she performed yoga asanas (postures) spontaneously for about three hours. Energy streamed upwards and vibrations shook her entire body. She felt that the energy wanted to do things with her body that she was unable to do, and her body felt like clay. She was pulled into extreme postures—underneath, backward and curled forward—and then began rocking. Then she fell backwards and upside down, her fingers rigid. Next she performed a headstand against the wall with her head between her knees. Then she stood up with a full body vibration and went forward to the ground. She heard the words "siddha-yoga" and her head jerked from side to side. She did not know if she was laughing or crying. She had a sense of a butterfly body living within her as if her body was its cocoon. It seemed to break out as a new body through her back with still wet wings beginning to unfold. She began laughing and crying at the same time. An unusual breathing pattern took over. Then she had phlegm in her throat and began growling and pawing at the floor. She found herself saying, "I am a leopard; I'm a South-American leopard." She felt completely embodied as this animal, growling and moving to clear her energy. Her body went into postures, some of which choked her, and she felt like vomiting but held it back[2].

These examples demonstrate how the *kundalini* energy varies according to the individual and their *karmic* history. The kind and intensity of the *kriyas* experienced by the practitioner depends on the category they fall into. To be more precise the practitioners can be divided into four categories, as in Chapter 1.

Every experience, whether pleasant or unpleasant leaves its impression in the *chitta,* (mind). Unless the consciousness is cleared of these past impressions and sensual attractions, *sadhana* (yogic practices or *Shaktipat* initiation) cannot achieve completion.

*Prana* is the life energy experienced by practitioners who have cleared their *chitta* from the past. *Kundalini* carries *prana,* its quality depends on the body of the practitioner, and it is stored according to the four elements of earth, water, fire or ether (*akash*). Following *Shaktipat, prana* will work differently in different practitioners. When the practitioner's body is solid, *prana* dwells in earth and the practitioner sits firmly on the ground with legs crossed. If the body is of water then the person experiences a flow of tears; in the state of fire there is the experience of surprise; and in the state of ether (*akash*) one experiences catastrophe, *samadhi,* senselessness, trance or sleep. By observing these symptoms in daily practice, it is possible to know how much *prana* there is in the practitioner. By this the Guru knows how committed the initiate is.

**Order of Experiences**
When the awakening of the *Kundalini* is first experienced, the practitioner feels that the body, mind and *prana* have become powerless, since all activities are stilled. Next when the *kundalini* receives light from *Shakti,* he feels the active energy of *prana* in the consciousness. Later, he hears an internal Sound but cannot find the origin of the Sound. When the *kundalini* assumes the form of *nada* (unstruck continuous sound) then he begins to hear its form very faintly. Next he begins to see divine lights that gradually take the form of a fine flame, whereupon the *nada* takes the clear form of

sounds from the violin, flute, humming of bees and other similar sounds. Finally, the nada takes the form of *OM* or *AUM*, which is *Brahman* Itself, and then whatever the person thinks happens. The subtle form of *OM* eradicates sin, and the deeper form of *OM* provides liberation. All other forms of automatic movement cease and only the sound of OM remains. One is sightless, only the state of peacefulness and single-pointed concentration remains. On physical death one attains the *Brahma-lok* or the plane of the residence of *Brahman*, the final achievement.

The Divine Light is seen in various forms and colours, such as the lustre of electricity, lightning, stars, moon, sun, fire and the flame of light. The Divine Light is also seen in the form of points of light and diamond-like groups, such as glow-worms. The subtleties of this Light are seen in proportion to the quality or fineness of one's consciousness.

As the consciousness becomes pure one sees the Guru, *Brahman* and various demi-gods or saints clearly. Visions of the spiritual identities one is most familiar with, such as Krishna, Buddha, Jesus, Mother Mary, formless Light, or any other representation of pure and compassionate energy is also possible. The practitioner sees them either in dreams, visions or in trance states. Their appearance indicates successful spiritual practice. These may be witnessed while walking, sitting or in spiritual practice.

Sounds too have various forms, such as the sound of blowing a conch shell, ocean waves, a waterfall, a burning fire, peacocks, buzzing of bees, a flute, the humming sound of a high tension wire, singing voices and crowd noises. There are ten sound forms of the unmanifested *OM*: *chin* sound, *chin-chin* sound, bell, conch, violin, a pair of striking metal pieces, flute, drum, pipe organ and clouds. On the first appearance of the *chin* sound the body experiences fine vibrations. The second *chin-chin* sound produces feelings that the body is breaking down. The third bell sound produces feelings of giddiness. The

fourth sound of the blowing conch produces vibrations in
the head. The fifth violin sound produces nectar that
trickles down from the palate in the mouth. The sixth
sound of striking of metal pieces produces the taste of
nectar. The seventh sound of the flute brings intuitive
knowledge of deep subjects. The eighth sound of the drum
brings the power of speech. The ninth sound of the pipe
organ produces physical beauty, paranormal powers and
divine insight, and the tenth sound of clouds brings the
state of *samadhi* and oneness with *Brahman.*

One experiences divine flavours, divine smells and
divine touches also.

**Awakening with or without a Guru**
The results of awakening through a Guru have been
described in detail. Awakening can often happen for
practitioners of *pranayama* or breath control, without the
aid of a Guru. Even if one cannot find a Guru one should
continue with *sadhana* or spiritual practices. When the
time is ripe the Guru will appear. Spiritual practices are
never wasted. Everything bears fruit at the right time.
Even after finding a Guru liberation does not happen
immediately. It is necessary to practise *sadhana* anyway.
The best spiritual practice is that which is done without
having any expectation or desire for awakening, to do the
practices out of love and service.

The *Kundalini*, after awakening, induces *kriyas* or
automatic movements, which opens the practitioner to
various experiences. Unfortunately, if he fails to complete
the process of *sadhana* or fails to perform his duty
towards the Guru properly, the experiences remain
incomplete. After finding the Guru every effort should be
made to earn the grace of the Guru. He should preserve
devotion, seminal fluid, memory and capability. He should
always speak the truth and make decisions through
vigour, zeal and subtle knowledge. In order to reach the
state of "perfection in yoga", he should be vigilant.

Many people's experiences remain incomplete even after finding a Guru, because of their *karma*. Unfortunately bad (negative) *karma* is already present in the consciousness of the initiate because insufficient attempts may have been made to purify *chitta* or mindstuff. When contact with the Guru is made the power of *Shakti* is suddenly awakened. This is the beginning of good (positive) *karma*. However, the residual negative karma that has not been cleared becomes an obstacle. It is important in these cases to continue practising with determination, which will increase good *karma* and decrease bad *karma*. A time will come when the good will influence the bad. Scriptures mention that the initiate should be "qualified" to receive the initiation. With the awakening and activation of the *kundalini*, the doors of divine realms open up, but one cannot go there yet. Before this one has to witness oneself as the Soul or *Atman*.

*Shakti-Kundalini* causes the *kriyas* or automatic movements, so that the body, mind and *prana* can become healthy and unified. This process is important since a weak body and mind prevents the witnessing of oneself as *Atman*, which is why the *kundalini* induces *kriyas*. The *kundalini* will make one store enough essentials to enable liberation in this lifetime. *Mahayoga* results in liberation and has the following four stages.

**From Awakening to Completion: Four Stages**
*Stage 1*: The *kriyas* following the awakening of the *kundalini* is stage one. Real yoga begins here. The *kundalini*, on awakening, begins with *Hathayoga* or the performance of yogic postures. This includes various *asanas*, *bandha* or locks, *mudras* or gestures, *pranayama* or breath control and purification of nerves. *Asanas* give stability to the body, *bandha* and *mudras* give strength, *pranayama* gives subtlety, and the purification of nerves gives perfection and balance in everything. *Hathayoga* is essential since it is the only way to strengthen and control

the body. Without *Hathayoga* it is not easy to get intuitive knowledge. This stage of *Hathayoga* is called *arambha-avastha* in Sanskrit.

*Stage 2*: The second stage begins when the body becomes purified and is full of *sattvic* (pure and spiritual) qualities; greed and lust have been destroyed; remembering God becomes continuous; *Hathayoga* and *Layayoga* (yoga of absorption) becomes easy and smooth. The practitioner remains purified and happy; renunciation increases every day, and there is a hunger for a meeting with God and a discomfort because of the perceived separation from Him. The first two stages run together as stage one unifies the body while stage two unifies the mind. As both body and mind become purified and strong, *kundalini* finds its path unobstructed and travels easily and smoothly to the crown centre. This stops the entry of *prana* in the nerve that is to the left of Sushumna making the prana static and bringing "stability in the mind". This stage of "stability of mind" is called *ghatavastha* in Sanskrit.

*Stage 3*: The third stage begins when *prana* is absorbed in the inner-*akash* or sky. *Shakti Kundalini* establishes *prana* in the *anahata chakra* or heart centre and here it unites with Shiva in the *sahasrara* or crown centre. Then as long as *prana* remains static, the practitioner's body becomes motionless and gives the appearance of being lifeless, although he is fully alive internally. This stage is called *parichaya-avastha* in Sanskrit.

In this stage the power of *Atman* becomes united with *prana* that is considered to be important in *Mahayoga*. The practitioner who has reached this stage is called a *siddha* or adept, and is supposed to attract powers from beyond. Such a person is now able to pull *prana* from all over the body and concentrate at *mooladhara* or root centre, the centre that provides the most indescribable bliss. All other parts of the body appear lifeless. One achieves this stage through the grace of *kundalini* and the persuasion of a Guru. *Prana* crosses all the seven *chakras* and rests in the crown. Semen converts into energy and the practitioner finds intuitive knowledge flows to him. The practitioner becomes *siddha* or adept, and can then pass power to others and awaken their *kundalini*. *Karma* is burnt and the knot at the level of heart is opened by the grace of God Almighty. He is absolved and has the power of absolving others too. Even if such a person appears without morals outwardly, his knowledge cannot be camouflaged by anything whatsoever. Those who criticise him take these sins with them, and those who praise him take these virtues with them. He has seen the way to the realm of *Brahman* and when he leaves this world he will arrive straight into the realm of *Satya* or Truth.

*Stage 4*: Stage four begins when the practitioner-turned-*siddha* or adept witnesses himself as the Soul or *Atman*. He has reached the level of Shiva-ness and is known as *jivan-mukta* or liberated-while-living. Such a person enjoys all pleasures and bliss through his *Atman*, which is in reality oneself.

**My Own Experiences**
Details of my experiences are given in my books from time to time according to the situation; see, for example, *Kundalini for Beginners*[3] and *The Secrets of Kundalini Awakening*[4]. In this book also the experiences are referred to at different places, the ones relevant here are as follows.

I experienced death and paradoxically, in death I awakened to a new life. I was living in Zimbabwe in 1987.

At 5 am on a balmy October morning, while praying to God, I asked Him to help me on my path toward enlightenment. Feeling despair at my inability to access Him, tears flowed from my eyes. My rosary beads had

fallen from my hands and I no longer sensed the world
outside. Suddenly, I saw my dead body being carried on
the shoulders of four people as they repeated the words,
"Ravindra Kumar is dead." Emerging from this all-
engrossing and miserable situation, I felt relieved,
peaceful and happy. A new horizon had opened before me.
I felt that something had shifted in me. I did not know it
then but this was my spiritual rebirth. My state of bliss
and cheerfulness was overwhelming as I got up from my
chair and left the room. The sunrise at Zimbabwe was
beginning to blossom as I went out for my usual long
walk, bringing new-found happiness with me. Going to
the mathematics department later that morning, my
heart was no longer in my work. Telling others about my
experience, I found they could not comprehend it. From
that day on, I began losing interest in mathematics, and
my profession.

Continuing to chant *mantras* and meditate as I had
in the past, I was about to take tea in the evening about
two weeks later, when suddenly my body began to twist
like a snake. My tongue felt like it was coming out of my
mouth, and there was immense heat coming from the
crown of my head. Running out of the house, I took a
brisk walk for half an hour, and then cycled on an indoor
machine at home for another 20 minutes. I then had a
cold drink and rested. The next day, the university doctor
examined me and listened to every detail of my
experience. He said clearly, if I had not been so healthy
and physically fit I would be paralysed today. He advised
me to discontinue all meditative practices and not to
lecture at the university for two weeks.

On that day in October 1987, after discontinuing all
types of chanting and meditation, a wonderful series of
experiences began to unfold. While continuing to pray
each morning, on three occasions in the period of two
months, I witnessed the Mother Goddess clad in a red silk
sari (Indian dress) with shining silver bangles. She sat

smiling at me. Oh, what a beautiful face and shining eyes! I saw myself dressed in white, bowing down to her as She was blessing me with Her right hand touching my head. Following these visions, I was very cheerful and content. My focus shifted from mathematics to religion and parapsychology. I started writing articles based on my experiences. They were published in *The Journal of Religion and Psychical Research*, USA.

All faiths and traditions have talked about the primordial or unstruck Sound, which one hears internally in the successful states of meditation. It is this Sound which takes the Soul towards God. My experiences with Sound began in the middle of the night when I got up to answer the call of nature. At around 2 am I heard a constant sound, like the blowing of a conch shell. I asked everyone in the house if they heard something unusual, like an aeroplane flying over the house or the blowing of a conch shell. They denied hearing anything. In the morning, I went to the university hospital where the doctor examined me. The doctor said there was nothing wrong with my ears. He had heard of cases where people hear internal sounds that either subside or continue, but in my case there was nothing to worry about. I still live with that sound today. It has become more clear and pronounced over the years.

My experiences with outer light started in 1984 while practising meditation. I was teaching at the University of Port Harcourt, Nigeria at that time. Suddenly, on hearing a lightning sound, as if electricity had jumped between two poles, my eyes opened and I saw a six-inch-high and four-inch-wide column of white Light standing four feet from my head. Amazed at seeing it, I looked around to find the source, but could find none. Shortly, the Light began to flicker and move left as it diminished in size and vanished completely after traversing about three feet. This Light was cool and bright and did not hurt my eyes, rather it felt soothing. After that event my faith in the

Divine increased and I remained happy, becoming less concerned with the external activities around me, and more interested with my thoughts and feelings of God.

An experience with Inner Light came two months after my awakening in 1987. In the early morning, as I was about to leave my bed, I saw a blue Light through my inner eyes. Unusually attracted to it, I kept my eyes closed and continued to concentrate on the light. After a while, I opened my eyes and found the light still there. Whether my eyes were open or closed, the blue Light stood there, remained 10 to 15 minutes and then disappeared. Now when I close my eyes, the first thing I see is the blue Light.

I had experienced what in the East is known as *kundalini*, a spiritual awakening from within. The *kundalini* is the spiritual energy that lies dormant at the base of the spine. It is in the form of a snake, sitting with three-and-a-half coils, with its mouth closing the opening of the central nerve along the spine, called *sushumna*. Most of us are only using 15 to 20 per cent of our brain. When the *Kundalini* awakens, sleeping parts of the brain begin to open, and the person acquires unusual powers. This makes the person a genius in his field of work. Outstanding achievements in any worldly field, and spiritual awakening or enlightenment, are the natural consequences of the arousal of the *kundalini*.

I can vouch by my own experiences that it is not necessary to cut oneself off from life to achieve them. One can be successful in yoga while living a practical conventional life. These two things are inclusive and they do not interfere with each other. On the contrary, practices generate the energy necessary for success in the world while also enjoying life more fully. By enjoying life's experience in full one achieves liberation and breaks the cycle of death and rebirth, once and for all. I have received a number of initiations from respected Gurus by the grace of God. I worked as a professor of mathematics for more than 30 years. After experiencing *kundalini* in 1987, I eventually retired in order to devote myself completely to my spiritual path in 1994.

My first initiation was from Siddheshwar Baba (Dr B.S.Goel, author of *Third Eye and Kundalini*) in 1988 at his *ashrama*, some 60 km from Delhi. He told me that my *kundalini* had already awakened but I should continue with *satsang* (company of devotees to God) and sing religious hymns. The second initiation I got was a *Shaktipat* initiation from the lady saint known as Guruma at her *ashrama* some 80 km from Delhi. The third initiation was the most effective one in the order of *Shaktipat* from my Guru, Deepak Yogi. I have seen the manifestation of *kriyas* or automatic movements in practitioners in the presence of this Guru. This same Guru initiated me. This I am going to describe in more detail in the following paragraphs. I had two initiations in dreams also, one from an unknown saint whose charming face and figure I can never forget and, another from Sri Herald Klemp, leader saint of the religion of Light and Sound, known as Eckankar, who has his headquarters in Minnesota.

One of my numerology students brought me a book written by Deepak Yogi. I quickly finished reading his book and decided to meet him at the earliest moment possible. Jytte and I made an appointment and spent four days at his centre. We discovered he was a *Shaktipat* yogi of the lineage of the well-known Swami Vishnu Tirtha, and the first person to convince me with his silent power. We chose to become his disciples and receive his initiation.

During my first stay with the Guru, which lasted three days, we discussed on matters related to *kundalini* awakening and related symptoms. Later in the afternoon of the first day he invited practitioners to partake in *sadhana* for about an hour, during which he touched each person. I went into a trance after about half an hour.

Experience of bliss and a readiness for my consciousness
to leave my body was felt by me, which I told the Guru
about when he asked. During discussions we talked about
those practitioners who were engaging in *sadhana* on
their own for some time. He said that such initiates could
reach the goal faster although he expected them to take
longer as *Shakti* would first purify them. On the second
day also we had *sadhana* in which I experienced yogic
sleep and bliss. However, I felt through my talks with
him that he found some traces of *ahankara* or ego in me
and that my surrender to him was not total. I thought
about this, and when we met the next day I put my head
on his feet and took his blessings. He told me that talking
about the books I had written showed that my ego was
still active. He advised me to forget about books and
surrender myself to *Shakti* for a few months and live fully
as an initiate. He then declared that the next day he
would give me the proper initiation, and told me about
the preparations I was to make.

As he advised, flowers, garlands, sweets and fruits,
and some items for worship were gathered and made
ready. The Guru appeared in his saffron robes and the
whole ritual took about an hour including *sadhana*. He
gave me a *mantra* to chant, if and when I wanted, but
that the main emphasis should be on the *kriyas*. I
experienced a passage of power from him into me as he
touched me I went into "vibratory meditation" under his
supervision for 45 minutes, and then I had to lie on the
ground in a state of yogic trance. My concentration was
beautiful. I felt I might leave my body when some figures
appeared, in addition to the indigo colour on my mental
screen. I asked him why I needed further initiation as I
had already experienced the awakening of the *kundalini*,
resulting in the manifestation of the Divine Light and
Sound, and the soul travel to subtler realms. He said the
*kundalini* needs further modifying for its full activation.
Also, it is better to be a "Shaktipat Yogi" of a "lineage of

the tradition of saints," than to be an independent one, in order to be effective and of service to others. Being in the lineage attracts the power of all other saints in the lineage, even after they leave for higher realms.

He asked for me to stay one more day so he could watch the effect of initiation. The Guru noted the symptoms of stage-3 *Mahayoga*, such as rhythmic *kriyas* or automatic movements and going into the "sleep of trance" soon after the *kriyas*. He told me later that he was looking for a person to give Guru powers to his successor, and that he recognised that potential in me. He asked me to meet him again after a week or ten days, before leaving India. On this meeting he was very satisfied with my progress in *sadhana*, which was gratifying to me. I burst into tears and wept for about ten minutes before him. He later told me that crying was the sign of *vishuddhi chakra* or throat centre that was now open.

I had two specific experiences after receiving this Guru's initiation. One, my back grew very hot, with strong itching sensations behind my spinal column for a few days. I rubbed my back against the wall for relief. Two, I had a recurring dream of a huge chimney with smoke pouring from it. The dream appeared to rightly explain my burning sensation in the back with the passage of the *kundalini*. I also dreamed of horses running in all directions. The *Brhadaranyka UpanishadI* says that horses are related to cosmic meaning. I have been seeing blue to violet colours both in dreams and on the internal screen. Dreams have come as friends over the years, conveying the information in a subtle and regular way.

For some time I experienced breath control after inhalation and sometimes after exhalation during my one-hour practice; these are the inner and outer "kumbhak". Sometimes my breath would be violent, signifying "bhastrika pranayama". On a few occasions I found "uddiyan bandha" or navel lock taking place by itself. One day when I was in bed, preparing to sleep, I felt something crawling up my back, from the base of my spine, up the length of my back, in repeating wavelike motions. In trance, I would sometimes see birds taking off from the ground, heading toward the sky. Sometimes I flew in the sky. During that time I felt bliss and a connection with the Infinite Void. During the day I felt the happiest with closed eyes, not wanting to open them and reconnect to the outside world.

When the *kundalini* is both awakened and active for some time, and the *Shaktipat* becomes stabilised in the practitioner, he becomes a Guru himself and begins to help others their *kundalini*. My Guru wanted me to help others and to spread this knowledge so that his efforts are multiplied. I hesitated a little, as I was not sure of my effectiveness. However, once I saw that some practitioners who had spent time preparing themselves would go into yogic-trance when I touched their third eye, I was reassured that continuing the *Shaktipat* lineage was what I should be doing. Another day an Australian couple came to see me after reading the book *Kundalini for Beginners*. The man had been practising *Hathayoga* and *Pranayama* for several years. In the morning he came for lessons. I gave him instructions in performing *asanas* and touched him. He began to perform several yogic postures perfectly and effortlessly, which he could not do earlier. His eyes were closed all the time, and he did not see what he was doing. After about half an hour he became still and normal, and was looking very peaceful and happy. He told me that he had some *kriyas* in the past but not as intensely as that day. I began to have some confidence after this.

Although the art of *Shaktipat* is the easiest and most direct method of awakening the *kundalini*, its use is uncommon and rare in the present age. This is because practitioners do not prepare themselves well enough in detachment, renunciation and *Hathayoga* practices; and, because of a lack of faith and surrender to Guru and God. The Guru chooses only a few practitioners as his disciples. Also, the teachings of *Shaktipat* have been oral and hence, they are lost in antiquity. It is not easy to find the real master, but when you do, you are enchanted by his simplicity, completely demandless nature and force of *Shakti* in him. One is more than willing to surrender to such a Guru for one's own benefit, if and when one finds such a master.

## References

1. Greenwell, Bonnie, *Energies of Transformation: A Guide to the Kundalini Process,* Cupertion, CA: Shakti River Press, 1990, pp. 189-90.
2. Ibid., pp. 208-9.
3. Kumar, Ravindra, *Kundalini for Beginners*, MN, USA: Llewellyn Worldwide Ltd., 2000.
4. Kumar, Ravindra, *Secrets of Kundalini Awakening,* New Delhi: Sterling Publishers Pvt. Ltd., 2002.

# FINDING A GURU OR INITIATE

## Guru and Initiate

A person who can awaken the *kundalini* energy in another is called a Guru. A Guru is important for spiritual awakening because of the transmission of consciousness from an open point of awareness to a narrower point as mentioned in Chapter 1. The person receiving the transmission from the Guru is the initiate. The initiate uses a Guru to understand, recognise and dissolve the ego through a process of self-surrender.

The Guru is there to show the initiate the principle of surrender. The danger comes when instead of surrendering to the principle of higher consciousness (which the Guru mirrors to the initiate), the initiate surrenders to the physical form and characteristics of the Guru. He confuses the impersonal with the personal, and in identifying with the personal, sabotages further understanding and self-realisation. The greatest indicator of success in the Guru-disciple initiation is the level of awareness, which each have of the dangers caused by attachment.

A person in whose presence or by whose touch there is a feeling of inner awareness and bliss is a Guru. In fact, one's *Atman* or Soul is the ultimate Guru; there is no one above *Atman*. This is a very abstract concept. A Guru's guidance can be very helpful in exploring this spiritual path, which is why some seek one. A relationship with a Guru may be adopted until the realisation of *Atman* (the inner Guru) takes place. Sometimes there is dissatisfaction with the results coming from the relationship with the Guru. If this happens another can be chosen, but this should only be done when following that Guru doesn't feel intuitively correct any longer. A Guru is there to reveal and dissolve the ego. This is never an easy task. Awareness on the part of the disciple as to why there be dissatisfaction with the Guru is vital, because when the ego feels threatened it will find excuses to leave the Guru in order to stop any further spiritual advancement. Just as a bee goes from one flower to another in search of honey, a practitioner may also go from one Guru to another in search of knowledge, but he needs to be aware that superficial flitting holds back the process of spiritual unfoldment.

During initiation, if the initiate does not feel inner awareness or bliss, and certainly if within one year after initiation when instructions have been followed and there has been vigilance with the ego, there is no experience of bliss or the receiving of intuitive knowledge, then it may be time to look for another Guru. Finding a Guru authentic to your needs will be the direct result of what you are truly seeking for in a Guru. Not everyone looks for a Guru with the same goal in mind. Some want a Guru for worldly achievement, and if they take initiation from someone who is known for leading to liberation, then worldly achievement will never be gained. Similarly a Guru known for worldly achievement cannot lead a disciple to liberation. Service to a wrong Guru goes in vain. In both cases both the Guru and the initiate will lose out. It follows then that they should leave each other. One should adopt a Guru according to one's requirement. Practitioners desiring liberation can achieve Godly virtues; and then they should remain with the Guru through whom the Godly virtues have been achieved.

Normally practitioners look for a Guru for knowledge, because it is only knowledge that provides peace and liberation. Self-examination and the honest appraisal of the motivations for finding a Guru will have a great deal to do with the Guru you find and the results of your work with that Guru.

Just as a bee gives up a flower that has no honey and sits on another with honey, in the same way the initiate should give up a Guru who cannot lead to knowledge and take refuge with another who can. If someone has taken a Guru who does not know things, is devoid of knowledge and is doubtful, he has the right to go to the right kind of Guru, without feeling any guilt. Thus if he does not experience the symptoms of *Shaktipat* to some extent within a year, he should change his Guru. However, the former Guru and his relatives and other acquaintances should never be disrespected even after the change has been made.

**Recognising a True Guru**
A genuine Guru is one whose dress is clean and pleasing; whose body is attractive and in good health. Someone who is in possession of subtle scriptural knowledge, who can talk about the procedures described in the scriptures, attracts visitors, please everyone coming close to him, see whether the visitor has the feeling of a deity, wear a pleasing countenance, is well versed in thoughts in favour and against the principles of scriptures, one who can make others understand subtle knowledge easily, whose explanation makes others understand difficult subjects easily and in whom doubts are removed, such a superior person alone is fit to be a Guru for initiation into the subtle knowledge; because, with these qualities comes a high level of consciousness which can be transmitted to the initiate. However, these are only ideal conditions described by the lineages of Gurus.

One whose goal is within even if the sight is outside, who has the necessary knowledge and has the proper approach to *siddhis,* who has the power in his words, the capacity of bestowing power and also taking it away, who is established in the *ajna-chakra* or the eye-brow centre, who can generate *Shakti* in and provide intuitive knowledge to another person through his energy, who is peaceful and compassionate to everyone, who has achieved victory over the base desires, whose senses are controlled, who normally leads in most activities, who is quite serious, who knows the difference between a deserving and a non-deserving person, who has equal devotion to all deities, who is in possession of the virtues of a *sadhu* or the saintly person, such a superior person alone deserves to be a Guru to initiate others into yoga.

Just as the Guru must be suited to you, so the initiate needs to be prepared for the initiation. This means the mind and body must be made as stable and strong as possible. This is to support the *Kundalini Shakti* when it rises. If cement is placed on mud, its use as a supporting foundation is no stronger than the mud. Set on bedrock the cement becomes as strong as stone. When practitioners prepare themselves through *Hathayoga* and understand the nature of material and spiritual attachment before *Shaktipat* initiation, they will develop spiritually soon after initiation. Gurus normally do not insist on prior preparation. In cases where the initiate is unprepared, after initiation some of the *Shakti* is used for purifying and transforming the initiate, to strengthen the body and stabilise the mind. After being initiated, solid foundations should be built for spiritual advancement by making life an ongoing spiritual practice. Yoga provides physical stability, *mudras* strengthen the body, and *pranayama* or breath control provides subtlety, cleans the nerves and turns the focus onto the inner world. Determination and meditation provide single-pointed-concentration on consciousness, and *samadhi* (inner absorption) provides the final absorption of consciousness. The Vedanta says that knowledge without practical application in the form of spiritual practice is insufficient for Self-realisation. According to the Vedanta, "One whose consciousness has become quiet and single-pointed through *sadhana*, who has controlled one's senses, whose karma has been burnt through *tapas* or austerities, who is ready to act and serve according to one's *dharma*, who is virtuous and willing to follow the directions given by the Guru, such a one alone deserves the teachings of *Brahmajnana* or the knowledge of *Brahman*." In actuality everyone deserves these teachings and knowledge. What this text points out is that desire, discipline, action and integrity are necessary to benefit from the teachings.

**About the Guru**
When the practitioner lets go of his attachment to worldly objects or when the bondage to *maya* becomes weak in a practitioner and one experiences the flow of *Shakti* within, then that person generates enthusiasm and passes energy into others. A practitioner (Guru) whose *chitta* has been cleared of worldly desire and who has experienced the inflow of *Shakti* can be accepted as Guru. All the *kriyas* or spiritual activities mentioned in *Hathayoga-Pradipika* are dependent on *Guru Shakti*. Whatever individual effort the practitioner does without the *kriyas* that are blissful and known for the annihilation of *karma* they are not effective without the grace of the Guru. Also in the *Goraksh* system, the one originated by Guru Gorakhnath during the medieval ages, the importance of a Guru has been mentioned. When the Guru is not physically present, it is helpful to have the Guru-element present before the initiate, in some form, when spiritual practices are performed. This could be a photograph of the Guru. In this way the *Guru Shakti* spreads to every part of the practitioner's body and the

person experiences bliss everywhere, within as well as out in the world. A practitioner, who cares only for the physical closeness of the Guru and does not care for mental or intellectual closeness, and distrusts the principle of surrender, will not experience the awakening of *Guru Shakti* within him, and loses the benefit offered by the presence of the Guru. Yogi Gorakhnath would respectfully prostate before his Guru before beginning his practice. Scriptures have also clearly mentioned that all experiences are dependent on *Guru Shakti*. I believe this because of my own experience over the years. It is possible to awaken one's own *kundalini* through self-effort and tell others how to do it, but it is not possible to raise another's *kundalini* by touch or other ways of *Shaktipat*, unless one belongs to the lineage of *Shaktipat* Gurus. When one belongs to the lineage, *Shakti* from all Gurus of the line and not the present Guru alone acts in raising the *kundalini* of the initiate. And that is why it works.

*Samadhi* is essential in realising *Atman*. Maharishi Gherand tells his disciple Chand that *samadhi* is the greatest in yoga, and it is achieved with the accumulation of good *karma*, and through devotion to and the grace of the Guru. The authentic Guru is the Guru-element that has awakened within the physical Guru. The same Guru-element or *Chaitanya-Shakti* awakens in the *chitta* of the initiate and remains present within him. It purifies him of greed, lust, anger, attachment, covetousness, and pride and establishes him in *Atman*. Prior to this, *Shakti* and *chitta* or mind appeared to be the same, but after awakening, the two separate and *Shakti* is clearly seen or witnessed by *chitta*, and has its own awareness. All these experiences take place with the grace of the Guru, the outer Guru or the inner Guru.

Knowledge spoken by the Guru brings success. A practitioner who experiments with something without knowing it from the Guru does not achieve success. But the knowledge received from the Guru after satisfying him in all ways leads to success. Being in the company of worldly people and/or doubting Guru does not bring success. Those who do not revere the Guru and enjoy the company of like-minded people are also not successful. Telling lies and speaking hard words to the Guru also takes one away from success. It should be remembered that God manifests before practitioners through the Guru. The Godly-*Shakti* that manifests through the Guru and helps the practitioner is the real Guru. Thus the physical Guru is the vehicle of real Guru. When one meets such a Guru one is more than willing to surrender to the Higher Principle in one, with proper reverence to the physical Guru too. There are authentic Gurus, who exist even today and will always exist. It is one's luck, nay one's earning through good *karma* over several lifetimes, that one meets the true Guru. Others fall into the clutches of the wrong Gurus. I can make this statement through my own experiences and those of others whom I know personally. True persons have always existed; one only needs good *karma* to meet one.

This world is full of misery for the ignorant, but for the knowledgeable it is the playground of God, full of bliss when seen through the eyes of Self-realisation. As long as *Kundalini Shakti* is lying dormant, any kind of spiritual practices or paths of liberation cannot lead to success in the form of purifying *chitta*. But either by the grace of the Guru or through one's own efforts, if the *kundalini* awakes then all effort, even right or wrong (not according to the prescribed rules of a faith or tradition) kinds of worshipping will begin to bear fruit. This world that looked like a prison soon feels like heaven. Someone who can transmit this bliss of being in the world to you in a short time is the Guru. It is through the Guru, inner or outer, that God can be met. It is also possible to achieve this through individual effort, but it may take years if not several lifetimes. Finding a Guru depends on how clear the mind is. Just as one has to work hard to get the real Guru, or to earn a meeting through good *karma*, in the same way the Guru has to do a lot of research to find the right kind of disciple. The research the Guru does is to test practitioners who come to him to find the deserving initiate.

Almost all those who have been recognised as a Guru have been renunciates living ascetic lives. They have normally given up worldly desires. Those who have achieved the supreme state of *Atman* do not desire the lesser pleasures of the world. Paradoxically, even though physical pleasures follow them automatically, their hearts are no longer attracted to them. They enjoy pleasure as it comes, as part of living but not as a result of their own will. Those who possess more are seen to renounce more, and in this lie their greatness.

## How an Initiate Becomes a Guru

There are two ways which a practitioner becomes a Guru. The first is through one's own effort and spiritual practice, becoming devoid of desire and afflictions such as greed, lust and attachment. When this happens *Shakti* awakens and becomes active. One should have experienced *Shakti* and should have received a clear and uncontroversial direction from within saying that the position of the Guru should be assumed and efforts made to guide disciples. This job has to be performed with the utmost honesty and wisdom. This is because a practitioner may want to assume the position of Guru to be worshiped. When this is done out of spiritual materialism they may not possess the authentic qualifications and capabilities of a Guru.

The other way to become a Guru is to be permitted by the Guru-tradition to perform the role of a Guru. The original Guru may permit an initiate to continue one's spiritual practices for him and at the same time authorise him to act as a Guru for the benefit of others. In this situation even if the practitioner is not capable of Guruhood, the original Guru operates through the practitioner using his will power. The Guru wills the disciples of his Guru-designate to be initiated and awakened. In this way *Shakti* awakens and activates in the disciples of the Guru-designate, who continues to work in this manner. In this position, if the Guru-designate is not afflicted by the ego of being a Guru and serves others as a service to his own Guru, then he is able to help others and at the same time his own position remains safe. However, if the Guru-designate feeds the ego with the authority of the Guru and initiates others through this ego, then pride dissociates the will power of the original Guru from the designate; and he becomes ineffective while initiating others, and will eventually lose all power.

Both the Guru and the disciple should test each other before accepting the relationship. The Guru should test the practitioner through knowledge of yoga and spiritual discipline and *kriyas* for at least three months, may be more, depending on his acquired ability, before accepting the practitioner. When a practitioner, who engages in impure activities, lies and is devoid of virtues such as devotion and reverence, is given knowledge he becomes more impure. Just as butter given to a dog makes the dog sick and it loses its hair, in the same way knowledge given to an undeserving person produces catastrophic situations. Giving initiation to a wrong person may result in harm to him and to society. Similarly, initiating the right practitioner fulfils many aims and objects described in various faiths and gradations.

The lineages of Gurus have been prescribing rules for judging the Guru and the initiate, see, for example, *Mahayoga Vigyan* by Yogendra Vigyani[1] and *Kundalini Siddha Mahayoga* by Shivom Tirtha[2]. What follows is based on the findings of the various lineages.

## Recognising a False Guru

One who has had tuberculosis or a skin disease, one whose nails have been spoiled by blood disorders, who has blue or black teeth, who is deaf, whose eyes are red due to some defects, whose eye sight has become defective, who is blind, who is bald because of disease, who has either a deficient or an extra part of the body, whose eyes are naughty like those of a cat, whose nose gives bad smell, whose testicles have become enlarged, who is extremely short in size or is a dwarf, who is devoid of the manly strength and is impotent, such a Guru who is in possession of any of the above symptoms is said to be defective and false as he cannot really awaken the *Shakti* in another, and should not be accepted as a Guru.

Someone who is not familiar with the scriptures and does not follow prescribed rules, who does not know the Vedas, or perform Vedic duties, who speaks dry, unsocial and rude language, who earns money by worshipping deities in the houses of people, who poses as a holy person, sells medicines to make profit and even becomes a Guru to impart knowledge to people for profit, who is full of lust, who remains under the control of the spouse for sex, who eats too much, who is rude, egoistic and deals in illegal trade, who is a liar, a thief, cheat, and consumes liquor and other intoxicating materials like drugs and opium, who is ungrateful and harmful to others, who has an animal-like nature, who keeps bad company, who does not believe in God, is fearful, who is in possession of serious diseases as a result of bad *karma* in the previous life or the current life, such a person should never be accepted as a Guru.

One who is not versed in the worship of deity, fire and Guru, who does not pray and/or chant *mantras* according to the requirement of the yogic scriptures, or who has given up these pious activities, who does not want to be active in anything and is lazy, who is engrossed in sense enjoyments, does not perform religious duties, depends on others for everything, such a lustful and defective person should never be accepted as a Guru for initiation into yoga or knowledge of *Atman*. Someone, who is possessed of diseases, has no family, or whose mind has been spoiled by unwanted thoughts, such a Guru should never be accepted for initiation. A Guru who attracts disciples on false pretexts, takes their money and is not capable of helping them to achieve spiritual goals, should be immediately given up.

Someone who is defective as described in the above paragraph, may be capable of leading practitioners to *siddhis* or paranormal powers, or to some success through chanting of a *mantra*, yet this kind of person should never be looked upon as a Guru. Those having physical, mental and behavioural defects should not be accepted as Guru, even though they may possess *siddhis* in the fields of *mantra* and medicine. Such people cannot provide liberation in this lifetime. However, if someone through greed has taken initiation from such a Guru, then he should withdraw himself immediately and go to a true Guru for fresh initiation.

## Recognising a True Guru
A Guru is someone who is not interested in the opposite sex and material possessions, who is not inclined towards bad company and bad habits, who is beyond confusion, observes daily activities in routine and remains satisfied in oneself, who does not will for desires, who never segregates, who is such a desireless void and has witness of oneself as *Atman*, who is religious, who experiences praise and condemnation equally, who always contemplates, who does not discard anyone, who can control others through his will power if necessary, such a person possessing good symptoms is fit to provide initiation for the knowledge of *Atman* as a Guru.

## Guru is Lord Shiva in Form

No one can worship Lord Shiva, who is infinite, everywhere and subtle; it is only through the Guru in whose form Lord Shiva presents that can be worshipped, and the initiate receives worldly enjoyments and liberation simultaneously from Him. According to Lord Shiva an initiate cannot perceive Him as He is. Therefore He assumes the form of the Guru through whom to speak to initiates. Lord Shiva ventures in the world in His formless state and follows His devotees. Through the physical Guru He helps His devotees and appears to be living the life of an earthly person. Those who do not have good *karma*, see the Guru as a human being; while those who have good *karma*, see the Guru as Lord Shiva. A true Guru never exploits his disciples or initiates either physically or financially. The Guru has lived a full life earlier and he is now beyond worldly requirements. His only desire is to help the initiate reach Self-realisation in the service of God. I have met such Gurus and I know they will always exist. A Guru helps the initiate to realise the *truth* that would otherwise be very difficult through individual effort alone.

Even though Lord Shiva is present before others in the form of a Guru, the people with negative *karma* do not see Him, just as the blind cannot see the sun. It is true that Guru is Shiva Himself, otherwise how can the initiate receive worldly enjoyments and liberation? There is no difference between the Guru and Lord Shiva, and those who see any differences are mistaken. A Guru assumes the form of the preacher to cut from the very root the constraints of the individual and lead him to the supreme position, since, God, the ocean of love and mercy, Himself assumes the form of the teacher through the Guru, and liberates the individual Soul through initiation. There itself Lord Shiva accepts the prayer and worship of the initiate in the form of the Guru and liberates him from the clutches of *maya*.

*Maya* or confusion results from a will to do and withdrawal from doing. The great illusion of *maya* is maintained when we are fooled into thinking that we are the 'doers'. Liberation from *maya* comes when we realise that we are just witnesses. Confusion in the form of being a "doer" is the cause of involvement into *maya*, while its disappearance leads to liberation. This is because the sense of doership creates *karma*, while seeing things are done automatically (i.e., witnessing). Even through oneself, one stops *karma* accumulating. Thus one should always be ready to do (say, for God), but without the sense of being the doer, believing that God Himself is doing through everyone. Thus seeing God as the doer and for Himself, and seeing oneself as the witness, even if involved in the act, is liberation. Therefore, a person who can lead the *chitta* of the initiate to the state of *samadhi* and remove all confusion and illusion is the real Guru. A Guru is virtuous as a speaker of truth, a follower of truth, devoted to one's own Guru, determined, charitable, meditates on *Atman*, and, is devoid of lust, greed and cheating, and is born in a family with virtues. The practitioner should be able to find and recognise such a person and adopt him as Guru. Only then can he find peace of mind and attain the supreme position through his grace.

One who has the power to pierce the *chakras* through the central nerve *sushumna*, who can talk at length about *Kundalini Shakti* and *Para Brahman*, who knows the secrets of *mantra* and *tantra* together with the knowledge of their awakened state, who knows the motion of the awakened *kundalini*, who knows the method of awakening a *mantra* properly, such a person alone can be a Guru and none other.

**The Initiate**
There are two views regarding the fitness of an individual for receiving initiation. In one view each individual can

be initiated, without considering his or her physical
fitness. Another is that the decision about the fitness
rests with the Guru. In the first case, even if the
practitioner is not well qualified, the *Shakti*, after
initiation, purifies the *chitta* or mind of the practitioner.
In practice both views are found to prevail; however, it is
advised that the person who wants to become initiated
should work tirelessly towards self-improvement. The
affect of the initiation is proportional to the purity of the
*chitta* of the practitioner. My personal view as a Guru is
to accept anyone who is really sincere and serious in
following the path of spirituality and who is willing to
follow the instructions given to him.

A Guru normally has his own way of judging whether
a practitioner is *sat* (pure) or *asat* (impure). I would judge
a practitioner by his will to enter the path with
dedication, since *Shakti* can turn impurities into purities.
A person who may appear impure and immoral outwardly
may still be acceptable to the Guru because of
preparedness and sincerity. Conversely, a person
appearing pure, spiritual and moral outwardly may not
be prepared for initiation, and hence is unacceptable to
the Guru.

There is a story of an individual who was well versed
in rituals and scriptures, and a scholar of Sanskrit who
kept asking the well-known saint, Swami Narayan Tirth,
for initiation. But the Swami was indifferent and kept
postponing the initiation. After some time a Muslim
gentleman approached the Swami very humbly, and to
the surprise of all he was accepted for initiation
immediately. The scholar was surprised and unhappy to
see this. When he asked for the reason, the Swami
replied, "In a building which is wired properly and is
ready for power, the electricity can be provided
immediately. You, being much too proud of your
scholarship and gentlemanliness, have shut yourself up
in the darkness of your knowledge. The cave of your heart

is now difficult to light, even by *Shaktipat* initiation."[3] We can judge from this event that an individual is not the best judge of his own preparedness.

## Symptoms of an Impure Initiate

Those who do not possess the virtues described in scriptures, their *chitta* cannot be lighted with the knowledge of *Brahman*. Symptoms of such practitioners can be described as follows.

One who is born in a family of bad characters, and has bad character, devoid of virtue, a person who has the pride of knowledge, who is a disciple of another Guru, who likes to have many Gurus, the Guru should not accept such an unworthy person as a disciple. Such a person does not deserve the knowledge of the Self or *Atman*. One who is deficient in or possesses an additional part of the body, where some part of the body has been spoiled or destroyed, a person who is lame, blind or deaf or who is always sick, such a person is not fit to become a disciple. One who has been expelled from the house or from society, who has been given up by the Guru, his parents or the community; one who generates sorrow or fear in the hearts of others, one who alternates between being a renunciate and a householder, one whose talks or appearance are displeasing or fearful, such a person does not deserve initiation.

One who is inactive because of excessive sleeping, inertia or laziness, one who is a gambler, does not believe in charity, engages in dirty sense enjoyments, one who is having relations with another person's wife, who earns money through illegal means and poses as a clever person, such a person should not be accepted for being a disciple. One who constantly finds faults in others, who appears naïve but actually engages in heinous acts, one who is unable to keep a secret and speaks out about things that should not be said, such a destroyer of work does not deserve initiation into knowledge. However, if such a person sincerely and seriously wants to take the spiritual path, I would personally encourage and help him.

One who diplomatically cheats others, deceives and returns a charitable act by selfishness, one who is known to create differences between others, and one who is engaged in sinful activities, such a person is not fit for discipleship. One who is known to create terror, who is known to create problems for others, who is known to be a wrongful witness and thinks oneself to be right, such a proud person is not fit to get initiation. One who is a liar, who is merciless, who talks senseless things, who creates nonsensical situations for others, who is in possession of bad thoughts and brings differences between others without any reason, such an individual does not deserve to know the Truth and the knowledge of *Atman*.

One who is foolish and a non-believer of God, creates knowledgeable things simply by imagination, criticises others for no reason, appears as a well-wisher in front of people but speaks badly about them behind their back and tries to harm them in their absence—such a person does not deserve any kind of help by the Guru. One who talks about *Brahman* without having any real knowledge, steals knowledgeable writings and teachings from the Guru and talks good about oneself, remains unhappy for not tolerating virtues in others, destroys his own peace by his own anger—such a person does not deserve an initiation into the knowledge of the subtle. One who talks aimlessly, who keeps friendship with wrongdoers, is criticised by everyone, troubles others for no reason—such a person who keeps enmity with knowledge and with those who are followers of the path of knowledge is not fit for an initiation.

Someone who talks only about his own problems to others, opposes his own master, finds pleasure in the tastes of the tongue, who is either a thief or deceives self, behaves without the consideration of what is proper or improper—such a person who is disconnected with *Atman* does not deserve an initiation. One who keeps enmity without reason, laughs, fights and angers without reason, dares to do any heinous act, enjoys troubling others without a reason—such a person who plays adversely with the sentiments of others is not fit to become a disciple. The Guru should not accept such a person as a disciple who tries to act in an unsocial manner for no reason, who is in possession of ego and anger, who indulges in lust and is shameless.

A person whose heart is full of envy, unforgiveness, cheating, ungratefulness, anger, and, one who is restless, unhappy, fearful, weak, surprised and eager, such a person should not be initiated for the knowledge of *Atman*. One who is completely devoid of knowledge, devoid of wisdom and is inert and foolish, who is surrounded with worries, who is possessed by greed and is dissatisfied, who shows one's poverty and non-possession of things to others and keeps begging—such a person is not fit for the subtle knowledge.

A person who eats too much, cheats others and confuses them, is devoid of devotion, dedication, compassion, peace and religious behavior—such a person should not be given initiation. Someone who makes fun of mother, father, Guru and knowledgeable persons, such a person is equipped with bad characteristics and should not be accepted as a disciple. Such a person does not deserve knowledge.

## Symptoms of a Pure Initiate
A person who is well versed in the rules and requirements of *samadhi*, *asana* or yogic postures and *pranayama* or breathing practices, who has virtue and humility, such a practitioner alone deserves an initiation into the knowledge of the subtle. Someone who has a pure heart, devotion and the kind of dedication mentioned in the

scriptures, who has a beautiful body and who puts on neat and clean clothes, such a practitioner alone deserves to become an initiate and receive the knowledge of *Atman.* One who thinks before one speaks, who is charitable, serious, has a small appetite, who is expert in most work and does not have an ego, who is brave and ready to serve others without expecting any return, such a superior person alone deserves initiation into yoga.

A person who accomplishes all jobs with expertise, who does only good to others, who is fearful of sinful acts, who is pious with acts of virtue, who is grateful to others and behaves nicely with virtuous persons, such a superior practitioner deserves initiation into knowledge. Someone who believes in God, in charity and who is constantly engaged in helping everyone, who does not deceive anyone to extract valuables from them, who is dependable, humble, such a person alone deserves initiation into knowledge. One who dares to undertake Herculean tasks, and is dedicated to one's favourable activities and yogic practices without being distracted, such a zealous and brave person alone is fit for initiation into the knowledge of *Brahman.*

A person who lectures for the benefit of others in a truthful, unadulterated, limited and blissful manner, who is intelligent and clever, who doesn't need to be told twice to understand meaning such a wise practitioner deserves initiation into the knowledge of *Brahman.* A person who does not like to listen to praise for the self or listen to somebody speaking ill of others, who is very happy, and always ready to do the job the way others like it to be done, who has control over the senses, is satisfied, intelligent and celibate, such a disciple is fit for initiation into yoga. One who is not in possession of any mental and bodily ailments, who is free from greed, sorrow, delusion and doubt, who is eager to contemplate on the Guru, and worship the deity, such a practitioner alone is fit for the knowledge of the subtle.

Someone who is constantly near the Guru, and tries to make the Guru happy, who is devoted to the Guru and deity and thus is expert in worshipping the Mother *Kundalini*, such a person alone is fit for initiation into yoga. A person who is ready to serve mentally, emotionally and physically, and who carries out the orders of the Guru, who promotes the name of the Guru, such a practitioner deserves initiation into yoga. One who takes the words of the Guru to be truth, who is dedicated to the service of the Guru, who acts according to the mood of the Guru, such a superior person alone deserves the knowledge of the subtle.

A person who does not boast about his caste, honour and riches before his Guru, who does not expect to get the riches of the Guru, who depends on the grace of the Guru, such a superior person alone deserves to become an initiate and receive knowledge of the subtle. Someone who prays constantly and undertakes austerities and contemplation, whose desire is solely for the liberation of others, the Guru should accept such a person with good symptoms to be an initiate. He alone deserves initiation into the knowledge of *Atman*.

Someone who dedicates himself mentally, emotionally, and physically to the service of the Guru and then learns yoga, he alone is known as an initiate. The above qualities of the ideal initiate emphasize on care, kindness to others and an attitude of service. This is because concern for others is the key to enlightenment as there is no separation between Self and others. Separation is the greatest obstacle to enlightenment.

Due to the negative publicity that Catholic priests have given some Gurus, i.e., Mother Meera and Sai Baba, and the cases of sexual abuse of children, some shame has been brought to Guruhood. People who are forced to live celibate lives, have not transcended sex, and so suppressed sexual desire, seek release through them and as a result many have abused children. A true Guru has transcended sex and other worldly attractions and is a sincere person to guide the initiate to Self-realisation. He makes no demands on the initiate, except true surrender to *Shakti* and to the Higher Principle that the Guru represents. Unfortunately or fortunately, the Guru is the most direct method of reaching God in the shortest time. It is a person's choice as to whether to take a self-help method without a Guru or to take the direct method through the Guru. In the book *Secrets of Kundalini Awakening*[4] we have presented a large variety of methods from various faiths and traditions, from which a practitioner can select one suited to him as self-help to Self-realisation. However, for those who are convinced of the direct method through a Guru, the method of *Shaktipat* initiation is open to them. There have always been true Gurus, there are true Gurus at present, and there will be true Gurus in the future too.

## References

1. Vigyani, Yogendra, *Mahayoga Vigyan,* Rishikesh, India: Vigyan Bhavan, 1938 and 1997, pp. 100-15.
2. Tirtha, Shivom, *Kundalini Siddha Mahayoga,* Devas, India: Sri Narayana Kuti Sanyasa Ashram, 1984 and 1997.
3. Ibid.
4. Kumar, R. and Larsen, J., *The Secrets of Kundalini Awakening,* New Delhi: Sterling Publishers Pvt. Ltd., 2000.

# 4

# *SHAKTIPAT* INITIATION

**Initiation**

The principle of all initiation is 'surrender.' The symbolic surrender given to the Guru at initiation represents the surrender of the ego self to the Higher Self or *Atman*. All faiths and traditions, such as Vedanta, Yoga, *Mantra*, *Tantra* and *Bhakti* or Devotion, have always had a system of initiation. The process involves the transmission of *Shakti* from Guru to initiate. On receiving *Shakti* or energy through initiation the initiate easily receives and understands knowledge about deeper subjects.

Initiation has two effects. It destroys sin and *karma* gradually, and it provides intuitive knowledge over time. *Karma* that has been accumulated through mind, speech and action is destroyed at its root. The system of initiation comes directly from Sri Maheshwar as an unbroken lineage from Guru to initiate, and dates from ancient times. In modern times it has become almost extinct, nevertheless the seed of knowledge continues. Like the touchstone converting lead into gold, the Guru converts the initiate into another Guru like himself, and the process can go on for ever. We have not heard about a person outside the lineage of Gurus to have the same power.

Awakening through a Guru is called *Shaktipat*. In this method "Divine energy" passes directly from the Guru to the initiate. The initiation can be performed in four ways: through touch, sight, mental concentration and a *mantra*.

It is the duty of the Guru to determine the ability of the practitioners, in terms of their prior preparation with Hathayoga and the degree of faith and surrender they have before initiation. The desirable effects in the practitioner are brought forth through *Shaktipat*. Once activated, *Shakti* will first purify and transform the practitioner, and then the automatic movements will begin. Sometimes *Kundalini Shakti* is activated but its manifestation takes time. Activation and manifestation are two different things. To make *kundalini* manifest either the Guru has to impart additional *Shakti* or the practitioner has to engage himself in additional spiritual discipline.

Inactive *Shakti* in an initiate can be caused by a number of reasons, eg:

  i)  Nervous disorders or the continuous loss of seminal fluid can cause inactivation. Energy activates quickly in a sound body.

 ii)  Since the organs and senses become weak with age, activation is faster among younger practitioners. Since women are more emotional they have a greater chance of activating the energy.

iii)  Indifference or annoyance on the part of the Guru towards the disciple can impede the process.

 iv)  High spiritual values and a pure heart trigger activation. Impurities of any kind slow down the process.

  v)  Evil deeds or impure thoughts such as, theft, murder or a determination to harm someone in any way will impede the process of activation.

However, the practitioner has no reason to worry if he has truly surrendered to the Guru, since the Guru's additional supply of energy will guide him through. Ultimately he is responsible for his/her own actions and intentions. A Guru can only act as a catalyst for what is ready to be reborn, given the initiates *karmic* history. No Guru can short-circuit *karma*, and for this reason each person who is intending to awaken *Kundalini* either with or without a Guru must take the responsibility and *karmic* consequences of such actions.

Sometimes *Shakti* may manifest more intensely, which may affect how a person behaves in public. There may be imbalances in walking, trembling or perhaps crying at holy places. When this happens the Guru should be consulted. He can regulate slower as well as faster automatic movements. The practitioner should continue to practise yoga and avoid going to public places since the transmigration of energy into non-initiates can result in automatic movements, which may become manifested in others and may require hospitalisation.

If the Guru dies, the grace of the Guru is not lost, since the activation of *Shakti* in the practitioner is permanent and will always be a part of his experience. The power comes from God since the Guru, inner Guru, Universal Consciousness and God are one. If the practitioner dies before achieving the final result, the activated *kundalini* continues in the next incarnation, and the process continues as explained earlier, until the achievement of *samadhi*, that is, oneness with Ultimate Reality. The spiritual force then merges into the cause, that is, the Soul. In some cases the successor of the Guru, usually appointed by him before his death, continues to help practitioners unfold towards enlightenment.

### Types of Initiation
There are five main disciplines for initiation: Vedanta has *Shambhavi* Initiation, Yoga has Yoga and *Shakti* Initiation, *Tantra* has *Vedh* Initiation, *Mantra* has *Mantri* and *Anavi* (atomic) Initiation, and *Bhakti* or Devotion has *Vaishnavi* Initiation.

**Shambhavi Initiation:** Here the initiate has to do nothing; the power of Guru brings Self-realisation to the initiate. The process works very fast. The initiate comes to the level of Shambhu or Shiva, which is why it is called *Shambhavi* Initiation.

**Yoga Initiation and Shakti Initiation:** The established yogi creates a variety of *chitta* or mind-stuff in the initiate, through his will power or determination, and the created *chitta* creates a variety of *kriyas* in the initiate. The yogi joins the *Atman* of the initiate with his own *Atman* to provide knowledge and *samadhi* to the initiate. This is *Yoga* Initiation.

When the Guru and the initiate are not at the same place but both desire initiation, then the Guru uses his power of the "divine eye of knowledge" and awakens *Shakti* in the initiate through this power. *Shakti-Kundalini* passes through the central yogic nerve called *sushumna* and becomes one with Shiva in the crown of the head. This is *Shakti* Initiation.

**Mantri and Anavi Initiation:** The Guru connects the deity of the *mantra* with the initiate by passing his own power of *mantra* to the practitioner. The *mantra* triggers the awakening of the *kundalini*. There are certain rituals and formalities to be completed. Through the energy of the deity the initiate enters into *samadhi*. If the initiate is immersed in the world he receives the enjoyments of the world, while if he has renunciated the world then liberation is given. Thus *Mantri* Initiation provides both worldly pleasures and liberation.

Any initiation which includes *mantra*, worship, *asana*, ritual, concentration and other formalities is *Anavi* Initiation. Either by the grace of Lord Shiva or because of good *karma* or through intense prayers to Lord Shiva, when the *karma* of the practitioner is balanced, then he receives the *Anavi* Initiation and arrives at the same level as Lord Shiva. Thus initiations received when there is the highest good in mind with no expectations of results, in accordance with the scriptures and by pleasing the Gurus who have spiritual powers, finally lead to unbroken liberation.

*Vedh Initiation: Vedh* literally means piercing. It is an initiation where *Shakti Kundalini* pierces the six *chakras* on the central nerve *sushumna* and merges into Para-Shiva in the crown centre. The Guru should contemplate on the subtlest and extremely powerful divine *kundalini* in the triangular region below the spine of the initiate and raise the *Shakti* through his own power, thereby giving the initiate direct experience of the truth of Lord Shiva and establishing him in that truth.

Due to the *Shaktipat* given by the knowledgeable Guru the initiate becomes free from sin and *karma*, forgets the concerns of the material world and falls down devotedly on the ground. The initiate experiences extreme bliss and reaches the level of Lord Shiva Himself. One is not born again since the extremely powerful *Vedh* Initiation destroys the veil of *maya* and all constraints of the physical world, once and for all.

During initiation the initiate passes through six states in order: bliss, vibrations, rising, rotation, sleep and trance. When these six states have taken place then *Vedh* Initiation has happened. Thereafter, wherever the initiate may be living, he is certainly liberated. Such a Guru as well as the initiate is rare. Therefore, Sri Maheshwar says that *Vedh* Initiation should not be given indiscriminately.

Where the *Shakti* does not flow for whatever reason, successful initiation cannot be achieved. Every path of initiation involves *Shaktipat* leading to the knowledge of *Atman*. The working of this *Shaktipat* is extremely surprising, effective and gives immediate results.

According to the well-known scripture *Yoga Vashisht*, in initiation all ignorance of the initiate is removed by the Guru just as darkness is removed with the sunrise. Thus the grace of the Guru is necessary. One is liberated and he cannot be born again. However, not every practitioner is at the same level of spiritual advancement. All practitioners can be categorised into either fast, medium or slow. Results are achieved according to one's category as described in Chapter 1.

### *Shaktipat* in Bhakti Marg or Path of Devotion

Like other spiritual disciplines the Path of Devotion has *Shaktipat* too. This results in awakening the *kundalini* either through individual effort or, through the grace of the Guru or through the accumulated *karma* of past lives. On awakening the practitioner displays outer symptoms, such as dancing, singing, falling and turning on the ground, twisting and turning of the body, yawning, shouting different names of God or deities, deep inhalations and exhalations, indifference towards talking good or bad about the world, laughing loudly, getting hiccups and throwing hands and legs about. However, this state stabilises gradually as *chitta* enters the *prana,* resulting in *pranayama* or the control of breathing. *Sattvic* or pure symptoms by which this state can be recognised are holding the breath and body, excitement, pleasant vibrations in the body, the flow of tears and entering into sleep or trance.

*Shaktipat* produces blissful states in *chitta* or mind, *prana* and the body. *Prana* is associated with different states, such as earth, water, fire and ether. The goal of every path is the same—the rising of the *kundalini* leading to enlightenment that in turn results in liberation.

### Essentials of *Shaktipat* Initiation

*Shaktipat* produces immediate results if the time is right for the initiate, otherwise spiritual practices have to be continued for longer. However, the *kundalini* automatically chooses a path for the practitioner, such as Vedanta, yoga, devotion or knowledge; and continues the process. Not all practitioners have to continue spiritual practice and discipline immediately after initiation. Following initiation there are changes in the body. Just as a woman on becoming pregnant does not deliver the child immediately, but feels the symptoms of pregnancy, in the same way, the initiate feels that changes have occurred because of *Shaktipat*. There is no fear associated with these mental and physical changes, just a knowing that the process is resulting in physical and mental changes. And just as the woman can destroy her pregnancy by being neglectful, in the same way the initiate can destroy those achievements bestowed through *Shaktipat*, if it is not honoured and protected from bad acts or unscriptural behaviour. Until the "knowledge of truth" has been achieved one has to be vigilant and careful with all speech, thought and action.

Concerns that cannot be destroyed any other way are completely destroyed by initiation from the Guru. A *Shaktipat* initiation should produce feelings of love, faith and *Atman* immediately; only then is it the real initiation, otherwise not. The fire of initiation will burn one's *karma* and bring one to the level of Shiva, just as the touchstone converts iron into gold. The process of worshipping God is complete and daily activities are no longer necessary. Practices of *japa* (chanting), *tapa* (austerities), fasting and pilgrimage are necessary for non-initiates only, however, these practices do not produce results where the initiate does not have the right qualities for initiation, just as a seed planted on stone does not bear any fruits.

**Place, Time and Method of Initiation**
The proper place and time are important to ensure that the initiation is successful in achieving liberation. Some of the most auspicious places for initiation are where the Guru lives, the abode of the deity, the place where there

are cows, secluded place in the desert, a place of pilgrimage, a garden, bank of the river, the sacred tree of the fruit *anwala*, the top of hill or a cave. On the bank of the River Ganges is always one of the best choices. In any case a place chosen by the Guru himself is unquestionably the best.

Whenever the Guru is available, whenever he is pleased to give the initiation, is the best time for it. Otherwise, whatever time the Guru and the initiate decide together is also good. The initiate should be guided and abide by the time and place identified by the Guru. A Guru with spiritual capacity is beyond social rules and regulations, and whomever they initiate also goes beyond social rules and regulations. Such Gurus will only be found where *karma* is good. In most cases people take initiations from Gurus who are only concerned with external rules and regulations, such as taking a bath, worshipping the deity, being at a place of pilgrimage, fasting and making sacrifices in the fire. Having found the true Guru with spiritual capacities external formalities are not necessary. External formality or the position of stars does not matter when the Guru and initiate are ready for initiation.

The practitioner should worship the Guru with respect, faith and surrender, give him presents according to ability, serve him according to his capacity and then take the initiation in whatever way the Guru chooses to do so. It is not necessary to give expensive presents because the Guru does not need or want them. Presents are only necessary to prove the selflessness of the initiate. The Guru wants only pure love, devotion and surrender with whatever flowers and fruits one can afford. The initiate must be without any assumptions or falsehood. This pleases the Guru and then the *Shakti* can flow unhindered from him to the initiate. One should look at the Guru as God in the real sense, never disrespect him and should never see him as a human being, but a divine representation. Even after the initiation the same kind of feeling must continue towards the Guru.

After initiation the person should remain with the Guru for three, five or seven days, and do spiritual practices until the *kriyas* or automatic movements begin. When the Guru allows the initiate and when the initiate is satisfied and knows the Guru *Shakti* through personal experience, then permission should be asked to leave. If one does not do so then the *Shakti* returns to the Guru. After leaving the Guru the daily spiritual practice as recommended by the Guru should be continued, and there should be no pessimism towards the Guru. If there is, then the *kriyas* begin to lose their potency and may cause disease in the body. The intellect can be also affected and may result in different kinds of 'bad luck.' The initiate should fix the time of the next meeting every time one meets the Guru. Staying with the Guru for a month or a fortnight or at least a week in a year is good for one's spiritual progress. The Guru should be remembered every day through prayer and constant contact maintained through letter or telephone. Keeping contact in this way saves the initiate from unnecessary obstacles.

**Presents for the Guru**
It is not necessary to give presents beyond one's capacity. Flowers and fruits offered with love and respect show the initiate's devotion to Guru. And those who can donate large sums of money and material things will help others through Guru, and in this humanity can be served. If one is rich and can afford to be generous then one should not behave as a miser, since in the spiritual world like other worlds one gets what one pays for both financially and in terms of commitment in terms of time and intention. Withholding such actions can also lead to unhappy situations, as nothing can be concealed from nature or God. If the Guru has a family then one should present garments, jewellery or other useful items to his wife,

children or other dependents. It is the duty of the initiate
to serve the Guru in all possible ways since he is the one
providing liberation to the children of God. It is similar to
serving one's own parents. Thus serving the parents and
the Guru according to one's capacity is natural and
essential, and those who avoid doing so deliberately are
likely to face bad luck indefinitely. Therefore, if one does
not have devotion to the Guru, then even if one donates
all material possessions good results for one's spiritual
practices cannot be achieved. Such practitioners
ultimately find that their *japa* (chanting), *tapa*
(austerities), fasting and other spiritual practices have
not borne any fruits. Thus getting everything from the
Guru and not returning to him whatever best the initiate
can according to his capacity results in spiritual practices
being wasted.

A *brahmin* who methodically arranges the offering
ceremony to the holy fire, called *yagya,* is offered presents
in the form of food, garments and money for him and his
family by the practitioner, since this is the only way for
the *brahmin* to earn his living. Although a Guru with the
capacity to provide liberation is not as needy as a
*brahmin*, nevertheless, donations and presents help
humanity in the broader sense. This is because there is
no separation between others and us. We are all
sparks of the divine flame of *Atman.* So paradoxically
when presents and kindness are given to another they
are also given to the person who gave them. When a
practitioner withholds such giving he is withholding
growth for himself. What is important is not so much the
giving but the awareness of the importance of giving. It
is this awareness together with the actual giving
that enables spiritual results. Since nature and God all
know, any religious or virtuous act performed without
return or remuneration in a sense does not succeed in the
long run.

## Taking Initiation

The practitioner should continue with his spiritual practices, firm in faith and religious beliefs until initiation. Worship of the chosen form of the Divine, which is cherished, should also continue. Morning prayers, worship of deity, chanting of *mantra*, austerities, yogic exercises and *pranayama* prepare the body and mind for initiation. *Sanskara*, good or bad, will affect the initiate accordingly, both before and after initiation. Other factors that can be useful are the purity of thoughts, practices, way of living, and the kind and amount of food eaten.

It is advisable to get up before sunrise, take a bath, put on clean clothes, take flowers and other worshipful offerings, and come to the Guru a little earlier than the time fixed for *diksha* or initiation. One should use the *asan* or the piece of rug for sitting such that it is a bad conductor of electricity, for example, wool, so that the energy after initiation does not pass into the earth. Details of *asan* have been given in a later section. One should face either north or east or as directed by the Guru. The *mantra*, which is given by the Guru, should be chanted. The initiate should worship the Guru with flowers, fruits and/or sweets and leave the body, mind and intellect free, with a sense of surrender and reverence to *Shakti*. There must be complete openness and acceptance of whatever is going to happen. After receiving initiation it is likely that some kind of *kriyas* will take place in the body and mind, according to one's *sanskara*. No efforts should be made to restrict the automatic movements, and there should be no fear of the *kriyas* because they are benevolent. One may feel that some power has taken over, and control over the body and mind have been lost.

Watches, glasses, caps or anything that is restrictive should be removed so that one feels comfortable. One should not sit leaning against a wall, because this may restrict the *kriyas*. One should sit freely and comfortably to allow the movements to flow freely, and one change the position from sitting to standing or lying on the carpet and/or to stretch one's legs and arms as one feels comfortable.

The initiate is normally required to stay with the Guru for three or four days. During this period only spiritual or religious books should be studied, so that the attention is always towards God. One should spend as much time as possible in the room for spiritual practices, and spiritual exercises should preferably be done in the presence of the Guru. One should not be concerned if the *kriyas* do not take place immediately, sometimes it may take up to five days. Furthermore, the type of *kriyas*, whether gross or subtle, depends on one's *sanskara*. Some *kriyas* may not be noticeable externally. Sometimes manifestation of *Shakti* may not take place for months, which is when *Shakti* first takes over to clear the blockage or some *sanskara*.

After initiation the Guru experiences a reduction of spiritual strength, just as a snake loses its strength through the loss of poison when it bites and a man loses his strength by losing semen. This happens because the strength of the Guru attacks the accumulated *karma* of the initiate and burns it off which in turn attacks the Guru. Although the Guru regains the lost strength after some time, he can become weak and experience problems. In these cases if the initiate does not serve the Guru, then the Guru may think that the initiate is not true to him, which can lead to unpleasant consequences for the initiate. The Guru also begins to feel pessimistic about initiating practitioners in general. There are Gurus who have renounced everything and are continuously moving. They do not normally need any help or service. However, there are Gurus who have families and are householders. They need help and service. Both kinds of Gurus have existed since time immemorial. The famous Gurus Vashisht and

Yagyavalkya both were householders. In the modern times it is difficult to find a Guru who is a full renunciate, and hence help and service to him is highly recommended. There is further discussion in Chapter 11.

**Duty of the Guru**
Just as the initiate offers physical, emotional and financial service to the Guru and becomes free from material obligations, the Guru must follow and take care of the initiate in his spiritual progress, otherwise he can earn bad *karma*. The responsibility of the Guru increases enormously once an initiate has been accepted. It is the duty of the Guru to supervise and help the initiate until he achieves liberation from *maya* and gains knowledge of the Truth. Simply giving initiation is not enough; the initiate should be helped through all difficulties that will be experienced when the ego feels its existence is in danger. For this the Guru should have spiritual energy to protect the initiate.

The Guru should observe whether the initiate is experiencing *kriyas* and bliss after the *Shaktipat* or not; if not, then he should ensure that the initiate experiences these things which are essential and which provide scriptural proof of *Shaktipat*. This should be tested repeatedly to make sure that *Kundalini Shakti* is operating in the initiate. It should also be observed that the initiate is receiving enough knowledge and purification through the *kriyas*. Until and unless the knowledge emerges from within the initiate and *kriyas* begin to operate automatically, the Guruhood of the Guru is not proved. A Guru who leaves the initiate without achieving these goals loses his own power, and may inherit a miserable life as a result.

The basic property of Cosmic Energy is intuitive knowledge and bliss, and the initiate should experience this. In this way the initiate can know whether the Guru has spiritual power or not. Although intuitive knowledge may take time to manifest the initiate should experience some *kriyas* and inner happiness immediately. The experience is a combination of knowledge and bliss, which the initiate should feel like an electric shock. Inhalations and exhalations can become faster and deeper. There may be rotations and throwing of hands and legs, a feeling of sleep and thoughtlessness, a feeling like movements of ants in the body, a feeling of voidness, the mind and body becoming inactive, and an entering into a trancelike state. There may be a feeling of headache, feeling intoxicated and energetic. These are some of the symptoms the initiate may go through in the beginning. Chapter 3 has described the symptoms in greater detail.

These inner and outer symptoms appear in the initiate during the first, second, or third day; in some cases the symptoms may appear after five or seven days. The variations are so because both the Guru and the initiate belong to different categories. Even if full-grown experiences do not take place in the initiate, a changed feeling can indicate that *Shaktipat* is working, and there is no reason to get disappointed. In fact, one should wait for a period of one year to see whether *Shaktipat* has worked or not.

When the amount of devotion the initiate has for the Guru increases the effect of *Shaktipat* becomes more obvious. But in some cases he may be carrying a backlog of accumulated *karma* from previous lives, which prevents the awakening of the *kundalini* in spite of the efforts made by the Guru. It is important to be prepared for such situations, and not to be down-hearted because repeated efforts by the Guru could bring positive changes later. The intention and desire for initiation, where the heart is pure, can do much to dissolve former negative *karma*. However, if the Guru feels that the *karmic* history is such that no efforts are likely to dissolve it then he should not accept him as an initiate. Accepting a practitioner for only financial or material benefits can lead to unhappy situations for the Guru.

## *Asan* for Spiritual Practices

A cushion is essential for all yogic or spiritual practices. Cushions made of cotton, blanket pieces, the skin of lion or deer are normally recommended. A cushion made of cotton helps to remove troubles or problems of the material world. A cushion made of blanket removes miseries. A cushion made of lion's skin leads to achieving liberation, and a cushion made of deer's skin helps to achieve intuitive knowledge. Spiritual practices without the use of a cushion lead to misfortune. A cushion made of bamboo results in poverty, and spiritual practices on stone lead to pain and disease. A cushion made of grass results in the loss of power and position. A cushion made of leaves brings confusion in the mind, and a cushion made of cloth destroys the good effect of yoga and meditation.

Yoga and meditation should be carried out in a neat and clean room. It should be decorated with the pictures of yogis, saints and deities, and should be provided with flowers and incenses. The room should not contain containers of materials such as water or milk, and it should be free from cooking and fire equipments. The cushion on the ground should be big and facing eastwards when doing yoga and other spiritual practices. One should pray to God and pay respect to other saints through their pictures in the room before starting the practice.

# 5

# YOGA THROUGH INITIATION: A SELF-PROVEN PATH

## Understanding, Knowledge and Initiation

It is important to distinguish between understanding and knowledge. Understanding which is gained by studying scriptures is not knowledge because it is unstable; it can be lost or changed, and because it changes does not provide satisfaction. Understanding received through experience after spiritual practices like yoga is stable. It results in unshakeable knowledge. It appears before the initiate as proof does not change and satisfies the *chitta* or mind. The Vedas believe that any knowledge gained without experience cannot liberate. Knowledge received through yoga cannot be explained or passed to others; it can only be experienced in person. People who only have theoretical knowledge cannot have real satisfaction either as bliss or as the intuitive knowledge of *Brahman*. Too often the emphasis is put on spiritual understandings through theoretical books, at the expense of practical experience. This has led to widespread spiritual dissatisfaction in the world today.

Four requirements lead to the actual knowledge of *Atman* or Self: study of scriptures (for initial understanding), practical exercises, accepting a Guru and personal experiences. Any subject understood through personal experience eliminates all kinds of arguments and uncertainties. The smallest experience is more powerful than the grandest thought or idea.

There are two kinds of initiations possible through which *Atman* can be experienced—outer and inner. Outer initiation involves *japa* (chanting), *tapa* (austerities), sacrifices in the holy fire and other rituals. However, *Shambhavi, Shakti, Anavi* and *Vedh* Initiations, which have been described in Chapter 4, are inner initiations which only need the Guru and the awakening of the *kundalini*; they do not require any external efforts like those required for outer initiations. Outer initiations are directed towards achieving depth in religion, material gains and to satisfy other desires. An inner initiation will provide inner bliss and liberation, and, is accomplished through the communication made between the Guru and the initiate. *Shakti* flows from the Guru to the initiate without the need for anything external. After receiving *Shakti* the initiate works according to the will of the Guru, and does not use his own will in anything. The process of inner initiation is one of complete surrender to the Guru. The word of the Guru is the highest for the initiate, and the experiences which result are so extraordinary that grasping for an explanation through words is inappropriate; it is only the Guru who should be approached for an explanation. This kind of initiate experiences the *kriyas* or automatic movements through the awakening of the *kundalini,* and witnesses the subtle body of God in the form of "Light" one day.

### Development of the Initiate

As the initiate continues to surrender to the Guru, and continues with the prescribed spiritual practices new *kriyas* are experienced which manifest by themselves. There is an increase in the number and quality of intuitive insights and notable accelerated spiritual knowledge. Soon the body and its organs become inactive, the movements of *prana* almost disappear and the *chitta* or mind achieves one-pointed-concentration. Regular practice of yogic *asanas* or postures, *bandhas* or locks, *mudras* or gestures, *pranayama* or breath control and purification of nerves is helpful in achieving *samadhi* or inner absorption at this stage.

Two kinds of *mudras* or gestures are important in achieving *samadhi: Shambhavi mudra* and *Khechari mudra. Shambhavi mudra* is characterised by the "goal being inward and the sight being outward." *Khechari mudra* is characterised by the tongue reverting back and sticking to the palate in the mouth. With this *mudra* one experiences the flow of a nectar-like fluid inside oneself. *Khechari mudra* which allows the initiate to realise the truth and *Shambhavi mudra* which makes him realise the form of Shiva take place by themselves. The elements of *Atman* or Self are lit within the initiate, hence the meaning of enlightenment as "inner light". When these two *mudras* are practised and experienced, all physical, mental and other *kriyas* become minimised, leaving only the *kriyas* of *prana. Prana* enters the central nerve *sushumna; Khechari* and *Shambhavi mudras* remain firm, and the initiate witnesses *Atman* or Self, an experience that is indescribable. At this stage the initiate has no memory of anything external and is totally absorbed in the element of *Atman* or Self; and, the bliss that comes with it. This bliss can only be experienced, not learned or described. But those close to the initiate will be able to see physical and mental changes as a result of the awakened *kundalini.*

Only the initiate knows the deep inner changes that result from an awakened *kundalini* in an initiate. Nevertheless, there are some external signs that others can see. Since the body, mind and *prana* assume *sattvic* (pure) mode and the organs are quietened, these people appear cheerful and happy at all times. At the thought of meditation they turn their attention inward and their life becomes mindful and meditative. Their eyes appear intoxicated. They speak politely and their whole body shivers with the internal bliss of *Atman*; inhalation and exhalation appear to have stopped. If you find such symptoms of *Brahmic* concentration in someone then you can believe that his/her meditation is deep, and intense and new spiritual insights and intuitions are arising in each moment. This is because the awakened *Kundalini* fills the body, mind and *prana* with zeal, and the person is so happy and absorbed in inner attention that the outer attention appears ineffective. Physical and mental stresses are no more, and the knowledge of *Atman* comes through in this relaxed and bliss-filled state. Yet externally the person appears grounded and enjoying each moment of physical existence. In the Sufi tradition such a state is described as being of the highest spiritual development, being inwardly drunk with divine essence while remaining outwardly sober—always in touch with and deeply wounded if one is separated from the inner bliss of meditation for even a second.

Experiencing *kriyas* is a necessary stage for achieving this state. Their speed varies from mild, medium and strong depending on the individual. When the *kriyas* are mild they can be controlled by will. If they are of medium strength then interfering or trying to control the flow of bodily and mental movements may create pain, and if the *kriyas* are strong the body and mind are forced to perform the positions without any control. Those who feel devoted towards Lord Shiva because of the awakening of the *kundalini* by the Guru are not ordinary. Just as iron on the entry of fire does not remain iron any more, in the same way, these people are transformed because of their closeness to Lord Shiva. They do not remain human; they have moved from being human to being spiritual. From here on they are in the world but not of it.

Transforming yoga happens when *kriyas* begin after the awakening of the *kundalini*, and this is known as natural yoga, *Siddhayoga* or *Mahayoga*. *Kundalini*

*Shakti* induces automatic movements that produce a "chanting of *mantras*" and the desire to study various spiritual sciences. Then the initiates see visions of their deities and know the secrets of many occult sciences, Vedas and other scriptures. The *kundalini* controls the experience of six elemental properties in the initiate: palace, element, art, division, position and *mantra*. After the *kriyas* have eased, the initiate receives knowledge of subtle or divine realms (palace), is given the knowledge of thirty-six elements like earth (element), receives the knowledge of the working of *Shakti Kundalini* itself (art), and finally the subtler knowing of division, position and *mantra* begins. Different kinds of *kriyas* are associated with all these properties. The *kundalini* pierces the *chakras* and enters the path of *sushumna*, which carries the initiate to various stages of *samadhi*. Initiates pass through such astonishing *kriyas* at times that they cannot be even imagined. According to one's *sanskara* or accumulated *karma* the initiate passes through the *kriyas* corresponding to *hatha* (physical), *mantra* (mental), *laya* (emotional or absorbing) and *raja* (pranic) kinds of yoga. It is difficult to describe all kinds of possible *kriyas;* many have been described in Chapter 2 earlier.

**Cleansing of Nerves**
Before *samadhi* can be experienced the nerves of the body must be cleansed. This is necessary because *prana*, the food of enlightenment which results in liberation, travels in the nerves that connect with the *sushumna* nerve in the spinal cord. Before the *kundalini* awakens all the nerves in the body are clogged with *karmic* dirt, so *prana* cannot enter *sushumna* easily. When this happens *pranayama* or breath control cannot produce the elevating results, which is possible when the nerves are clean. So cleaning of the nerves is the first step taken by the *kundalini*, and hence the initiate experiences

corresponding movements. There are many kinds of *kriyas* done for this purpose. They can be divided into three: *neti*, *dhoti* and *basti*. These *kriyas* involve *purak* (inhalations), *rechak* (exhalations), *kumbhak* (holding of breath) and *pranayama* (breath control). In other words, Mother *Kundalini* puts the mouth, nose, anus and *lingam* (male) or *yoni* (female) into specific use through automatic movements.

In addition to the *kriyas* described in Chapter 2, there are other symptoms that can be seen in initiates. Less urine and stools may be passed. There can be insomnia, feeling of being very cold or very hot, with sometimes a high temperature, the onset of dormant diseases in the body, pain in various parts of the body, pain in the stomach, intense sexual desire and/or ejaculation of semen or vaginal fluids, having dysentery or passing urine. The person may experience continuous hiccups. All these bodily manifestations are performed by the *kundalini* to eradicate disease in the initiate, which will be mild or severe depending on the accumulated *karma*.

Sometimes the initiate may speak with different words or utter sounds by the mouth, nose or throat, such as growling roaring like a cat, dog, lion or other animals, speaking strange words and strange languages, weeping, laughing, singing, producing sounds like a stringed-instrument, clapping, lecturing and creating prose or poetry—all intended to cleanse the related part(s) of the body by the *kundalini*.

### Hathayoga: Asanas and Mudras
*Asanas* and *mudras* are the tools of yoga. There are four kinds of yoga: *Mantra, Hatha, Laya* and *Rajayoga*. While the *Shakti* remains dormant these four are different, but after *Shakti* awakes the four kinds of yoga become united into one, called *Mahayoga*. The initiate recites certain *mantras* automatically sometimes, while at other times there is a memory of a past *mantra*, which had been

forgotten. At other times the initiate experiences the *kriyas* of *Hathayoga*, while at other times there is absorption in the Cosmic Sound. Sometimes the initiate becomes absorbed in a particular subject, while at other times concentrates without any subject.

The *kriyas* in *Hathayoga* are divided into three parts: *asana*, *mudra* and *pranayama*. Initially the person takes on these practices voluntarily, and may practise for a very long time without noticing any changes, but after the awakening of the *Shakti* these take place automatically as part of the *kriyas*. For example, *Khechari mudra* is important since the tongue turns inward, sticking to the palate and its tip presses against a point from where nectar begins to flow and rejuvenates the yogi. Due to the automatic application of *Khechari mudra* the tongue reverts and presses against the palate deep inside in the mouth which results in the release of nectar from *sahasrara* or the crown centre. This is how yogis always look younger than their age. The taste of the nectar is somewhat salty, then it is acidic and sharp in the beginning; as it progresses it tastes like butter, ghee, milk and yogurt; at the end it tastes like honey and grape juice. The saltish juice eradicates general diseases; the sharp juice cures otherwise incurable skin diseases; the acidic juice removes the slackness of the skin and the maturing of hair before time; the honey-like juices provide the secret knowledge of the scriptures; and the butter-like juices provide immortality through liberation from falsehood. Some people cut the thread that attaches the tongue to allow the tongue to produce nectar. But this does not really work. Real *Khechari mudra* works by itself when *Shakti* awakes. All kinds of *asanas, mudras* and *pranayama* are performed through effort before *Shakti* awakes, and they are experienced automatically afterwards.

*Asanas* make the body fit to practise yoga. The word *asana* means a way of sitting. It is believed there are

840,000 forms of life on earth, and as many ways of sitting. However, only 84 of them are the main ways of sitting. When these *asanas* are performed through personal effort the purpose is to keep the body healthy and free from disease. *Sanskaras* carry the memory of how the person was sitting in different life forms. When *Shakti* is activated and turns inward, it gives practical shape to these *sanskaras* by way of *kriyas* or automatic movements. The initiate performs various *asanas* with ease like a perfect yogi, even if he does not know some of them, since he only witnesses them taking place through *kriyas*. If such *asanas* are performed by his efforts alone there may be a sense of frustration at not being able to perform them. When the initiate performs *asanas* or yogic postures automatically, the purpose is to provide stability to the body, to maintain the digestive fire in the stomach, and to free the body from diseases; also to destroy the *rajo-guna* (property of being active) and *tamo-guna* (property of being inert) in favour of the *sato-guna* (property of being pure and devoted).

Some yogic postures are like animals and carry the name and qualities of the related animals. For example, *bhujangasana* or the cobra-posture requires the initiate to put his body in the shape of a rising cobra, which makes the spine young and strong. This arrests the ageing process and directs the seminal fluid to the brain. Other postures imitate a lion, ox, fish, peacock, frog, cock, turtle, *garuda* (a big holy bird), crocodile and others. There are also postures in the form of a bow, a dead person, a circle and other shapes, each one designed for the care and growth of a particular part of the body. For more details one can refer to my books on *Hathayoga*[1], *Kundaliniyoga*[2], *Kriyayoga*[3] and *Chakras and Nadis*[4].

Different *asanas* correspond to different kinds of life. So postures belonging to "plant life" are *taal* (pond), *padma* (lotus) and *vriksh* (tree) *asanas*. Postures belonging to the "life in water" are *kurma* (turtle), *matsya* (fish) and *makar* (crocodile) *asanas*. Postures belonging to the "insect life" are *bjujang* (cobra), *shalabh* and *vrishchik* (scorpio) *asanas*. Postures belonging to the "bird life" are *mayur* (peacock), *garuda* (a big holy bird), *hansa* (swan) and *kukkut* (cock) *asanas*. Postures belonging to the "animal life" are *singh* (lion), *vrashabh* (ox) and *ushtra* (camel) *asanas*.

As far as *sadhana* or spiritual practice is concerned, the initiate, after the awakening of *Shakti*, does not need to practise or sit in one particular form such as *padmasana* or *siddhasana*. Sitting in a comfortable position is enough. However, there is no harm in practising some *asanas* to keep the body fit. It is important to understand that *sadhana* (the way of doing) achieved through surrender and that achieved through effort by yoga are different and should not be practised together. After achieving *sadhana* any *asanas* performed through personal effort should be done as a service to God; otherwise this can create impurity in the mind that can result in more *karma* being accumulated.

*Mudras* are the outward signs of inner experience. If a person is happy then happiness is seen through outer bodily gestures or *mudras*. Similarly, when there is unhappiness or worry there are gestures or *mudras* that will reflect this inner turmoil. There are nine forms of gestures or representations or *mudras*, which are explained later in this chapter. There are some yogic *mudras* which involve contracting the nerves. Contracting nerves or putting the body in special positions affects the flow of blood and activates certain dormant or inactive nerves. Thus these yogic *mudras* have a special place in *sadhana*. They are called locks and provide an important defence to the body against ageing and death. The initiate performs *bandha* (lock) and *mudra* (body-gesture) in different forms, such as *moola bandha* (root-lock), *uddiyanbandha* (navel-lock), *jalandhar bandha* (chin-lock), *maha mudra, maha bandha, maha vedh, khechari, viparitkarani, vajroli* and *shaktisanchalan*. There are about *bandhas* and *mudras*, which are performed along with *asanas*, and they help in achieving *siddhi* or success in spiritual practices.

In the same way as *asanas* stabilise the body, *mudras* strengthen the body, and distribute and stabilise *prana*, to assist the mind to concentrate. So *ashwini mudra, mool bandha* and *maha bandha* belong to the anus and genitals; and, contraction and expansion of the anal muscles is the related exercise for them. *Uddiyan bandha, taragi mudra* and *sarangi* concern the navel and stomach; they fill the air in the stomach and empty it. *Jalandhar bandha* or chin-lock results from the squeezing of the throat region which helps to open the throat *chakra* and provide strength there. *Tratak* or one-pointed-concentration and *shambhavi mudra* relate to the eyebrow region which opens the third eye in the eyebrow centre. *Naad* or Cosmic Sound, *shravana, bhramari* and *pashnamukhi mudras* relate to the ears. *Khechari, nabho mudra* and *manduki* relate to the tongue. *Bhujangi, kakai* and *yoni mudras* relate to the mouth; *vipareetkarani* to the head; and, *maha mudra, maha vedh* and *taran* relate to the body as a whole. Thus, *kundalini* follows the scriptures and exercises, and strengthens all parts of the body through *kriyas* or automatic movements of the related areas. Different *bandhas* and *mudras* provide bliss and zeal to the initiate; and, regular practice maintains the digestive fire, and eradicates diseases related to breathing, coughing and throat ailments.

## *Pranayama* or Controlled Breathing

*Prana* travels in the nerves of the body, and is the synonym of *Shakti* or *Chaitanya*. Not only do the nerves have to be purified but also the *prana* has to be disciplined. Disciplining *prana* is called *pranayama*. Gross or outer manifestation of *prana* is inhalation and exhalation or what we know as breathing. Therefore, one tries to discipline *prana* by controlling inhalation and exhalation. *Pranayama* or controlled breathing is one of the main means of awakening the *kundalini*. Once the *kundalini* is awakened through *pranayama*, the need for *asanas* and *mudras* become obsolete. Now the efforts of the individual have ended and self-proven-*sadhana* takes over. There is no more *sanskara* or *karma* accumulated; the old accumulated *karma* begins to thin out. Spiritual practices of previous lifetimes surface by themselves, which the initiate performs effortlessly. All these *kriyas* purify the *chitta* or mind.

There are three categories of controlled breathing: low, medium and high. With low breathing attention from materialism is withdrawn and the person becomes interested in religion. Medium breathing produces vibrations, and high breathing raises *prana* and awakens the *kundalini*. Initially these practices are performed through personal effort, but when the *kundalini* is activated and it induces *kriyas* then the breath is controlled automatically. This results in experiences of bliss, rotations, yogic sleep and pleasant sensations. There is an absorption in blissful happiness. The initiate begins to utter the sound of *OM* or *AUM*. He may experience bodily twisting and turnings, vibrations and blissful tears flowing through the eyes. There may be entry into a knowledgeable trance that explains the meaning of yoga. This is the best form of *pranayama* induced by the *kundalini* and is made possible because of the union between body, mind and *prana*. Just as the broom removes the dust from the house, in the same way *pranayama* removes the dust from all the nerves of the body. After cleansing, life-air moves freely into the nerves. This gradually removes disturbances and fickleness from *prana* and mind, resulting in one-pointed-concentration and *samadhi*. According to Sage Patanjali, the covering of knowledge and wisdom is destroyed by *pranayama* and the illusion that covers the *sato-guna* (virtue of purity and devotion) is gradually thinned out. There is no better *tapasya* (chanting and austerities) than *pranayama* to wash away the dirt of mind and reveal the shining light of wisdom. To perform *pranayama* normally the nose is closed with a finger and thumb. But in the automatic system *pranayama* takes place without having to touch the nose.

## The Process of *Pranayama*

*Pranayama* has three ingredients: *purak* or inhalation, *rechak* or exhalation and *kumbhak* or holding of the breath. This activity stabilises *prana*, that is why it is called *pranayama*. *Kumbhak* stabilises life-air, which in turn stabilises intellect and *chitta* or mind. There are three forms of *kumbhak*: inner *kumbhak*, outer *kumbhak* and *stambhvrati* or natural *kumbhak*. Inhaling the air fully and holding it as long as possible is called inner *kumbhak*. Exhaling the air completely, and holding it out as long as possible, and then inhaling slowly to breathe normally is outer *kumbhak*. Stopping the air or *prana* suddenly in whatever position it is, so that the amount of air inside remains inside and the amount of air outside remains outside, and holding this position for as long as possible is natural *kumbhak*. Any kind of *pranayama* occurring in the initiate, who has awakened *Shakti*, comes in the category of a *kumbhak*.

There are different kinds of automatic *pranayama* or *kumbhak* induced by the *kundalini* that have different results. When air is inhaled through the right nostril the *pingala* nerve is activated, and the person holds the air as long as possible, then exhales through the left nostril, which activates the *ida* nerve gradually. This is called *suryabhedan kumbhak*. If the initiate has been practising it earlier in past lives and it is in the memory store as a *sanskara*, then this *kumbhak* comes to the surface automatically. It will continue as a part of the *kriyas* until the *sanskara* is burnt off, and then it will stop. There should not be any interference. While inhaling through the *pingala* one inhales with a jerk in one go, but while exhaling through the *ida* the process is slow and gradual. The *kumbhak* purifies the mind and makes it fit for concentration.

In *shitli kumbhak* one observes *kaki mudra*, that is, one pushes the tongue out of the mouth and between the lips, looking like the beak of a bird or *kaki*, and draws air in through the tongue and holds it; everything is happening by itself, the initiate is only an observer. This *kumbhak* eradicates indigestion, coughs and diseases related to *pitta* property of ayurveda. In *bhastra kumbhak* one inhales and exhales through the nostrils with great speed like the ironsmith pushes the air hard to generate fire with his *bhastra* or leather instrument. This *kumbhak* eradicates *vata*, *pitta* and cough, the three diseases mentioned in ayurveda. The bodily fire is increased and the *kundalini* activation accelerates. The dirt in *sushumna* is removed and the three *granthis* or knots along *sushumna*, known as Brahma, Vishnu and Rudra *granthis*, are pierced. The movement of the *kundalini* becomes swift and makes its way unimpeded to the crown centre. In *sitkari kumbhak* inhalation takes place from both sides of the tongue making a sound of "sit" when the breath is held; later, exhalation takes place through the nose. These kinds of *kumbhak* make the body lustrous, and, sleepiness, laziness, hunger and thirst are eliminated. Sometimes the sound during inhalation and exhalation resembles the *bhramar* or bees, and there is a feeling of pleasure as the attention is completely absorbed. This is called *bhramari kumbhak*.

In *ujjayi kumbhak* the mouth is closed and inhalation is so forceful that the air along with the sound of it passes through the throat and reaches the heart straightaway. This kind of *kumbhak* eradicates coughs and other throat problems and increases the fire of the body. It removes the diseases related to the nerves and semen, and those where water collects in the stomach. In *murchha kumbhak* inhalation takes place sometimes through the mouth and sometimes through the nose, and then the breath is held to produce *kumbhak*. Later one experiences *jalandhar bandha* or chin-lock, and after a while exhalation takes place through the nose. There is concentration between the eyebrows and a feeling of being comforted. Since the mind goes into *murchha* (absorption or trance) through this *kumbhak*, it is named as such.

In *bahya kumbhak* deep exhalation takes place through the nose, and it is held similar to the *kumbhak*. After some time the inhalation and normal breathing are established. The time of *kumbhak* is decided by nature according to *karmic* requirements. This *kumbhak* stabilises *prana* and moves the *Shakti* upwards; the *Shakti* pierces the *chakras* and arrives in the crown centre. This results in the initiate entering into *samadhi*. Since bahya means outer, the holding of the breath outside names the *kumbhak* as such. The most effective *kumbhak* is *keval kumbhak* where *prana* becomes stabilised while the initiate is performing *sadhana* or spiritual practice, without any inhalation or exhalation. The initiate feels greatly comforted and peaceful. Due to the entry of *prana* into *sushumna* this *kumbhak* takes place again and again. An initiate who can perform this *kumbhak* is an adept, having achieved success in yoga. With regular practice the duration of this *kumbhak* can be increased and *prana* begins to move in the *sushumna* nerve only, and not in the *ida* or *pingala* nerves. Success in this *kumbhak* takes away desire for all sensual involvements; the *prana* becomes established in the highest position, and *samadhi* is achieved.

All initiates do not experience the same kind of *kriyas*, since everyone has a different nature and upbringing, and a different accumulation of *karma* and *sanskara.* However, the end result of all kinds of spiritual practices is one and the same—*samadhi* or wisdom/ knowledge and liberation.

**Different Forms of Representation**
The initiate remains cheerful and happy because of having acquired the hidden meaning of scriptures and intuitive knowledge within himself after the awakening of the *kundalini.* Sometimes the inspirations are subtle and at other times they are intense. The initiate should allow them to emerge without any hesitation in whatever form the feelings want to come out. Gratitude should be expressed each time a new insight or intuition has been received. It is only by being grateful and humble in the little that the great can come.

There are nine ways a person can express himself following awakening. When the mode is *intense* the initiate expresses feelings with anger and rough language. In *strange* mode there is surprise in whatever one says and a sense of disbelief that such knowledge and insights were even present to be said. In the mode of *beauty and decoration* one either looks at one's deity as one's husband or gets absorbed in one's *Atman* as the cherished beloved. There is a seeing of the divine essence in everything, both the profane and the profound. When the initiate passes through the mode of *fun* there is laughing for a long time. In the mode of *bravery* the initiate begins to shout or say clever things with zeal; and, there may be great acts of courage performed or heavy things moved with ease. There may be crying or weeping if he is in the *compassionate* mode, whilst in *fear* he may be afraid of something and make fearful sounds. In the mode of *hate* he may denounce someone or talk in abusive or hateful language and show body gestures to confirm the same. In the *peace* mode he may sit quietly with the attention turned inward, absorbed in the connection with *Atman*, and may experience great peace and bliss. Thus he experiences various *kriyas* of the body, mind and *prana.* The secrets of nature are revealed and there is a new friendliness and familiarity with all of nature's changing forms. Those who know such people should not be surprised by the different kinds of behaviour shown by them during their spiritual practice. It is important that there is no interference in what is happening in order to allow the process to deepen and unfold according to nature and its laws.

At this stage any kind of *japa, tapa,* worship or rituals done by the practitioner are fruitful because of the power of the awakened *Kundalini.* All gods and goddesses are happy with him at this time. Inhalations, exhalations, *pranayama* and *kumbhak* act as sacrifices, sins are washed, and past *karma* is burnt in the fire of purification. Association with the *kundalini* results in liberation, speaking at *sadhana* acts like reading scriptures. Food eaten at this time acts like the sacrifice in fire, and looking at anything acts like meditation. Whatever activities the initiate does at this time, all lead to spiritual knowledge and are always beneficial. Such is the effect of initiation and awakening of *Kundalini.*

When the *kundalini* awakens all kinds of *japa, tapa,* worshipping, rituals and pilgrimage are given up, and the initiate becomes free from all of them. According to Sri Maheshwar the initiates who have been purified in this way are not supposed to observe any kind of rules or regulations of the scriptures, since they have become akin to Sri Maheshwar himself. There are no constraints for these people any more.

It is easy to analyse the effect of wisdom that makes the initiate free from scriptural formalities since he has become desireless towards the material pleasures of the world. Nothing is done for self-gratification. Material desire is replaced by the desire to show others how to alleviate the suffering arising from *karmic* existence. There is a realisation of the truth that everything is inter-connected, and there is no separation between Self and others. All kinds of *karma* or duties become unimportant for such a person. Achieving wisdom frees him from daily duties prescribed in the scriptures, and he gives up even the division of the society he belongs to. The whole world becomes like a family for him. Achieving the wisdom of non-duality he becomes akin to Lord Shiva. No constraint of *karma* can bind him now.

### References

1. Kumar, Ravindra, *All You Wanted to Know About—Hatha Yoga,* New Delhi. Sterling Publishers, 2000.
2. ———, *All You Wanted to Know About—Kundalini Yoga,* New Delhi: Sterling Publishers, 2000.
3. ———, *All You Wanted to Know About—Kriya Yoga,* New Delhi, Sterling Publishers, 2000.
4. ———, *All You Wanted to Know About—Chakras and Nadis,* New Delhi: Sterling Publishers, 2000.

# 6

# THE ORDER OF EXPERIENCES

When the initiation is complete, *Kundalini Shakti*, who
has her own intelligence and only wants the best for the
initiate, shows herself to him through different wonderful
properties. After awakening and becoming active, the
*kundalini* draws energy from the Cosmic Sound, and the
initiate experiences many different experiences. Due to
virtues in the initiate *Kundalini Shakti* creates the desire
for discipline, wisdom and *kriyas*. The meaning and
utility of letters and words in scriptures on one hand, and
the power of speech on the other, emerge in the initiate.
Only the initiate knows the depth and kind of activities
that *Kundalini Shakti* is manifesting.

*Mantras* are a tool used by *Shakti* as part of
awakening. A *mantra* contains the subtle seeds of
divinity, and is not just a combination of words or letters.
The divine power of *mantra* is realised when it passes
from the Guru to the initiate. *Shakti* creates the world of
*mantras* within the initiate, and he begins to chant a
"seed *mantra*" from the Vedas or other scriptures. A seed
mantra is a mantra that is related to a particular deity
who will manifest to the initiate in a subtle form. The
arrival of the *mantra* takes place subconsciously or
unknowingly, and the *japa* goes on unceasingly in the
background even when the initiate is busy doing other
things. When this happened to me I began to chant the
*mantra*, "Om Namo Bhagawate Vasudevaya",

unknowingly and intermittently. Several *mantras* that the initiate may not have heard of arise and give him power. Certain *mantras* that may not even be part of his culture become successful at this stage. Before the *kundalini* wakens certain rules are followed to ensure that the *mantra* given to a person is suitable, but after *Shaktipat* initiation rules lose their importance and are not necessary. This proves the oneness of *Kundalini Shakti* and the world of *mantras*.

**The Cosmic Sound of *AUM***
The first or basic seed *mantra* from the Vedas is *OM* or *AUM*, and all other *mantras* related to different deities are formed later. The first *mantra* that manifests in the *chitta* or mind of the initiate is *AUM*, from which come all others. The word *AUM* itself is *Brahman*, and is the most superior. Successful yogis know the manifestation of *AUM* within their consciousness and its power to provide all they desire after its manifestation. *AUM* ultimately leads the initiate to the plane of *Brahman*. Due to this the Vedas have declared *AUM* and *Brahman* to be one. Just as the form of *Brahman* cannot be described in words, *AUM* can only be understood within oneself in the subtle form. The pronunciation of *AUM* does not depend on any words; it is created by the power of the *kundalini*, and is self-proven. Mental repetition of *AUM* softly eradicates sin, repeating it loudly liberates, while repeating it in the subtle form leads to unification and the synchronisation of body, mind and *prana*.

The pronunciation of *AUM* has to pass through various stages where it is not recognised before it takes a form that can be heard by the initiate. In the first stage *AUM* vibrations are felt in the *mooladhara chakra* or root centre and the base of the palate in the mouth. *Kundalini Shakti* provides inspiration to the initiate and he begins to chant *AUM* loud enough to be heard by others. The person is half conscious at this stage and hears the echo of many other sounds within himself, but cannot direct the sound properly and begins to chant *AUM* in a loud voice. This chanting of *AUM*, is heard far away and with pleasure other listeners become absorbed in it. When the loud form of *AUM* completes its time and fades away, practitioners often try to imitate it by their efforts, but then it is not the same thing. It does not provide satisfaction, and the effort of trying to re-create the sound is given up gradually. However, the sound of *AUM* continues in its mild and pleasing form with some initiates, who may perhaps be called lucky. In such cases it is like the automatic and continuous chanting of a *mantra*, which provides manifold bliss and peace. This chanting continues even when dreaming. It has no beginning and no end. I have described in my book *Kundalini for Beginners*[1] the onset of this pleasing sound of *AUM* in my own experience that started in July of 1987 and exists in the same form today.

*AUM* of the Vedas became *HUM* of the Tibetans, *AMIN* for Moslems, and *AMEN* for Egyptians, Greeks, Romans, Jews and Christians. It is known as WORD in Judaism/Christianity, KALMA-I-ILAHI in Islam; Pythagoras called it the MUSIC OF SPHERES, the Sikhs of India call it SHABAD, the followers of Eckankar call it AUDIBLE SOUND CURRENT, and parallel words can be found in different faiths and traditions. Some people approximate this sound by "the humming of a swarm of bees,"[2] some by the "blowing of a conch,"[3] some by the sound hear on opening the door of the refrigerator[4] and yet others by the "hissing sound of a serpent."[5]

The automatic chanting results in the initiate turning the attention inward. The desire for sensual pleasures is eradicated. There is a similar absorption as if in a trance. Lust and anger are not present. Inhalations and exhalations are never forceful during spiritual practice. One does not experience other *kriyas* so much because this sound is the main *kriya*. Other sounds are heard, but one does not see any scenes on the inner screen of the mind, rather his mind remains quiet, and concentrated on the void. He does not desire any other advantage or privilege resulting from yoga. Nevertheless, he possesses the capacity to enjoy the pleasures of the world whenever the opportunity arises. The mind is mostly engrossed in contemplation, and as a result laziness and sleep are transcended. The mode of *satogun* or the state of purity becomes firmly and permanently established.

*Brahman* can be represented in written form by various names, such as Krishna, Christ, Allah, Void, but the single representation in sound form is uniquely one *AUM*. The "automatic chanting within" and the "unstruck cosmic sound" have a connection with each other. The "automatic chanting" can be called a "name" of the Absolute, and "unstruck cosmic sound" the "entity" representing the Absolute in person. Thus the actual representation of the Absolute is the *unstruck cosmic sound* heard within by the initiate through the inner ears, and it cannot exactly be written in words. However, it is written by the word *AUM* or its synonyms to give an approximate representation to the real entity. Hearing the actual sound form of *AUM* is the aim of yoga, which is successfully accomplished through *sadhana* or spiritual practices. This *naad* or sound of the word *AUM* is called *Shabd-Brahman*. It is this "sound" which deserves salutation and which is the source of all paranormal powers. By knowing its science the initiate breaks the cycle of death and rebirth.

The cosmic sound manifests through *Shakti*, which is situated in point-form at *mooladhara chakra*. Just like the germination of the seed, the sound of *AUM* begins at *mooladhara*. All the letters are created by this sound, which then creates sentences and *mantras*. An initiate who experiences this sound-energy within oneself gains the power of speech and becomes the creator of literature akin to Vedas and other scriptures.

## Seeing the Divine in Different Forms

The initiate witnesses the powerful Light-form of the Absolute in the subtle, astral and causal bodies. During meditation, on the dark inner screen of the mind, he sees God in the form of the "flame of the light". The flame can be white, red, yellow, black or in the form of the various colours of the rainbow. That flame is visible between the eyebrows on the inner screen like the sun rising in the morning; this is seeing the divine form of the Absolute takes place naturally.

Working through the *kriyas* induced by the *kundalini* the body, mind and *prana* become involved in spiritual exercises of the highest order. To prevent initiates getting involved in sensual pleasures and to obtain stability of the mind, the Divine Flame appears by itself. When the Divine Flame appears the mind naturally becomes involved in it, and leaves behind the desire for any benefits from spiritual practices. At this point yoga and related things are done out of love and devotion, and not for any benefit which may result. After seeing the bright Divine Flame the mind of the initiate finds the highest pleasure in this alone.

The Divine Flame is seen in various forms, such as the lustre of electricity, lightning, the constellation of stars, moon, sun, fire, flame of fire or wild flame that is brighter than several suns. The Flame may also be seen as points of light, bright glass, diamond-like groups, groups of glow-worms or the top of the flame of burning fire. Each one can be white or in different colours. Sometimes he may see the sky full of stars, a blue sky, smoky, dark or deep dark sky. The subtleties of the Divine Light are seen in proportion to the quality and fineness of one's consciousness.

Another way of seeing the Divine is in the form of visions of one's Guru, specific deities, Brahma, Vishnu, Maheshwar, celestial males and females, gods and goddesses known as *gandharv, vidyadhar, yaksh, raksh, pannag* and *kinnar*. Devotees on the path of yoga, knowledge or devotion, who have acquired a *sattvic* (pure) mode and are adept in meditation, see saints, Shivalinga or statues of Lord Shiva. Celibates devoted to *Brahman* see other gods and goddesses during meditation, during twilight period between sleeping and waking, as visions when fully awake, or as dreams while sleeping. However, such forms are especially—though not necessarily—seen by practitioners who are on the path of devotion to God who has form. Other visions, such as Shiva, Krishna or Buddha, virgins, boys, chariot, lamp, temple, lobby, palace, lotus, river, horse, trees, ox, trees laden with fruits, fire, mountain or hills, burning fire, flag, aeroplane, throne, ornaments, jewels, precious stones, sun, moon, stars, house, raw meat, coronation, white seeds of sesame, honey, clean, specially, white clothes, sandalwood, king and a group of ladies may also be seen. These are all auspicious things, and are seen by the initiates either in dreams or in trance during meditation. They are strong indicators of success in spiritual practice.

Other auspicious indications of success in *mantra yoga* or similar spiritual practices, seen in dreams or meditative trance, are a pigeon, swan, cow, peacock, deer, frog, a *brahmin*, beautiful ladies, musical instruments, milk, curd, grains, fruits, rice pudding, new utensils, flowers, good quotations, a pitcher full of water, mirror, fish, dead body, recitation of the Vedas, hunter, soldier, one's dear ones, sunrise, solar or lunar eclipse, big houses, houses of respectable persons, mounting of a horse, ox or elephant, of a climbing mountain, entering fire and entering a palace or place of worship. There may also be fearful dreams, such as being slashed or beaten by a hunter, rubbing vomit on the body, taking a bath in blood, drinking blood, drinking alcohol and eating raw meat, eating cooked meat and eating with many ladies. Many initiates, especially the ones on the path of devotion, see the statues of deities, functions of gods, hearing the singing of religious songs, conch, bell, other sound instruments, places of pilgrimage, hearing about the virtues of God and flying in the sky towards the void. All these symptoms appear when the mind turns inward after the awakening of the *kundalini*. The initiate may be sitting, walking, engaged in other works, awake or asleep.

### *Naad* or the Divine Sound

There is no fixed rule as to whether one sees the Light or hears the Sound first, as the order of experiences varies from case to case. Sound that is heard and recognised clearly like the sound of a watch or a bell is said to be "expressible", while a sound that can only be recognised by comparing it with another is "inexpressible". Sound that manifests by itself within the initiate, without the striking of two objects or without any external pronunciation, is the benevolent unstruck (*anahata*) sound called *Shabd Brahman*. When *prana* arrives in *sahasrara* or crown centre, the sound of the clouds or a conch is heard. But when *prana* is in the *chakras* below the crown, the sound of bells is heard. Hearing one of these sounds ensures success in spiritual practice.

Sounds can take the form of blowing a conch shell, ocean waves, a waterfall, a burning fire, ox, peacock, buzzing of bees, chattering of insects, sounds of sitar, violin, flute, a moving vehicle, humming sound of a high tension wire, drum, bell, singing of voices and noises of the crowd. There are ten sound forms of the unmanifested *AUM* which progress from gross to subtle – *chin* sound, *chin-chin* sound, bell, conch, violin, pair of striking metal pieces, flute, drum, pipe organ and clouds. Each of these stages shows itself in the initiate in a specific way. When the first appearance of the *chin* sound appears, the body experiences fine vibrations. The second *chin-chin* sound produces feelings that the body is breaking down. The third bell sound produces feelings of giddiness. The fourth sound of the blowing conch produces vibrations in the head. The fifth violin sound produces nectar that trickles down from the palate. The sixth sound of the striking of metal pieces produces the taste of nectar. The seventh sound of the flute brings intuitive knowledge of deep spiritual truths. The eighth sound of the drum brings the power of speech. The ninth sound of the pipe organ produces physical beauty, paranormal powers and divine insight, and the tenth sound of clouds brings the state of *samadhi* and oneness with *Brahman*. All these forms relate to the inexpressible *AUM*.

Once the expressible unstruck sound of *AUM* manifests inside the initiate, he does not need to align with any of the inexpressible sounds described in the above paragraph. All forms of inexpressible sounds and all forms of-divine-flames or lights become absorbed in the real sound of *AUM*. There fore, he is advised to rely only on *anahata shabd* or unstruck sound of *AUM*. It is this that can lead one to the highest realm of reality. The wise person concentrates and depends on the expressible *AUM* alone as the provider of liberation who takes him to the realm from where there is no return to the lower worlds.

**Divine Touch, Taste and Smell**
Just as a needle touches and pierces the cloth and goes on binding together, in the same way *Kundalini Shakti* pierces the *chakras* in *sushumna* beginning with *mooladhara* or root centre and arriving in *sahasrara* or crown of the head. The initiate feels the touch of *kundalini* like the cloth feels the touch of the needle. Just as the bee moves around the lotus, touching it here and there, in the same way the *kundalini* induces *kriyas* in the initiate, to give wisdom and the feeling of the blissful divine touch. Sometimes this touch is soft and at other times it is hard, according to the *karmic* requirements of the situation.

When the initiate reaches the stage of *kewal kumbhak* after the cessation of inhalations and exhalations, the *prana* is stabilised and he hears various sounds internally. A kind of nectar begins to flow from the "point chakra" in the head. The flow of nectar takes place when continued *sadhana* or spiritual practice absorbs the mind in the eyebrow centre and witnessing of the Soul begins.

Divine smells also manifest and emerge from the region between the eyebrow centre and the tip of the nose. When this happens there is astonishment and absorption in these smells.

In normal circumstances human beings are trapped by the five attractions of speech, touch, beauty, taste and smell, and by losing the self in them are led to destruction. They lose their morality, and become destined to remain at the lower levels of evolution. This happens because the five attractions are strong, and easily possess the mind that leads to sorrow. But, if the same five kinds of attractions are enjoyed after the completion of yoga practices, then they do not lead to destruction, but become vehicles for higher spiritual evolution. Thus, the enjoyment of worldly pleasures by people without divine knowledge leads them to grief and suffering, while the spiritually perfected individuals, while needing nothing, receive everything to enjoy without longing and attachment, and remain ever happy.

**Some Obstacles on the Path**
The spiritual path more than any other path is beset with obstacles for the unwary initiate. The further one progresses the subtler are the obstacles. This is why vigilance in thought, word and action is so important. Similar to the sky in the physical world, we have sky in the inner world of the heart and mind. The physical, astral and mental planes lie between the outer and inner sky. In the same way the initiate experiences the divine objects of light, sound and other manifestations during

the course of his *sadhana*. Their appearance however, indicates how well the initiate is doing in acquiring subtle and para-elements of spirituality. These divine signs show that the initiate is getting close to the knowledge of *Atman* and the realisation of God.

However, having gone through all the experiences described above one should not cling to bliss, rather *sadhana* or the spiritual practices towards achieving one's goal should be continued with a sense of equanimity and non-attachment. Until and unless one has witnessed one's real Self or *Atman* one should continue to move like the hands of a clock and not give up the seriousness of the *sadhana*. Just as attention has to be kept on the bait while fishing, so that a fish may not eat it and go away, in the same way, the initiate has to keep his attention on getting the mind absorbed with the indivisible *Chaitanya* or Supermind, through *nirvikalpa-samadhi* or absorption without fluctuations. At this stage there are four obstacles that can befall the initiate:

1. *Obstacle of Absorption*: While engrossed in his *sadhana,* instead of his mind following the way to *Atman* or *Brahman,* the initiate falls asleep. This is the obstacle of absorption, which can be corrected by standing up and singing or chanting the names of God for some time, so that inertia and laziness can be encountered and transcended.

2. *Obstacle of Diversion*: Instead of the mind being absorbed in *Atman* or *Brahman,* it begins to think and worry about some worldly object. This is the obstacle of diversion that can be countered by bringing the mind back to the right goal over and over again. In whatever material direction the fickle mind runs, one should pull it from there. One should think that there is nothing real except *Atman*, and then direct the mind towards *Atman* or *Brahman*.

3. *Obstacle of Stagnation*: At times when the mind wants to pull itself from the first two obstacles, it is attracted by some sensual or material pleasure, and falls into surprise or stagnation. When this kind of stagnation takes place one should stop *sadhana* for a while and partake in some religious singing or recitation. When the mind becomes peaceful and stabilised, *sadhana* can begin again.

4. *Obstacle of Pleasure*: When the initiate concentrates on the mind pleasure results. Then the mind tries to enjoy the experience of pleasure resulting from *savikalpa-samadhi* or absorption with fluctuations. This is the obstacle of pleasure that prevents the mind from entering *nirvikalpa-samadhi* or absorption without fluctuations. One should think at this stage that this pleasure is nothing compared to the immense bliss experienced on achieving *nirvikalpa-samadhi*. Thinking like this the initiate should withdraw his mind from that pleasure and concentrate on furthering *sadhana*.

**State of Yoga and Related Facts**

Just as the flame placed in an undisturbed and quiet atmosphere does not flicker, in the same way thoughts of sensual or material pleasures do not disturb the mind of the yogi who has one-pointed concentration. His mind is always still and absorbed in *Atman*. The kind of immense bliss that the yogi experiences at this stage is above any lower kind of pleasure received through any sensual, worldly or even heavenly activity. A yogi so absorbed in his *Atman* is not affected by heat, cold, pain caused by wounds or mosquito bites. The state at which the yogi arrives and does not consider any other benefit to be greater, the state in which one is unmoved by the deepest grief, such a state of synchronisation with grief and detachment with everything is called "Yoga".

As stated earlier, it is extremely difficult to achieve three things without the help of the Guru: freedom from attractions of sensual pleasures, witnessing the indivisible and infinite entity called *Atman*, and achieving the natural state of yoga called *Sahajayoga* or becoming liberated while living—known as *jeevan-mukti*. To fulfil the needs of a worthy initiate many times the directions or Guru appear in visions, trance or dreams as follows:

Sometimes the person feels that there is a big mirror in the front and his whole body is reflected in it. But when he looks again he finds there is no mirror, but the image was real at that time. He may just see his own shadow without any mirror. Seeing his own form in this way purifies the body and indicates success in yoga. Although such an experience takes place by itself, he can look at his shadow in the sun for a while and look into the sky and see the image of his body. Practising in this way for a few days may result in seeing his image automatically. It is understood that one who sees one's image regularly has come through many lives and will achieves success in *sadhana*. This is another way of getting close to God and becoming absorbed with Him. After some time one sees one's image within oneself. Witnessing one's own image in this way is known as *Chhaya-darshan*.

Sometimes the initiate is given a *mantra* in *yoga-nidra* or yogic-sleep following *sadhana,* or in dreams, which is given to him by an elderly person or a saint. Here one should remember that a saint, Guru and God are one. The Universal Guru appears in the dream in some form and gives the *mantra* that the initiate most needs. The initiate should accept such a *mantra*, remember it and keep it secretly with him, and, should chant the *mantra* regularly until there is success in yoga.

When these things happen there is an experience of bliss. Sometimes one feels that energy is rising up in

one's body, and after piercing *sahasrara* or crown centre
it rises in the form of a flame. The flame is thumb size
and the initiate feels that the flame is nothing but
himself; the physical body is forgotten at that time. This
flame is his *Atman*; it resides in the heart. This flame is
the divine *Purusha* (man) who should be separated from
the physical body through regular practice and under the
direction of the Guru. The same flame is known as
*Paramatma* or Supreme Soul. Just as the sun and its ray
of light are not really different from one another, in the
same way *Atman* and *Paramatma* are not different from
one another.

### Gross, Subtle and Causal Bodies
Both gross (physical) and subtle bodies keep burning/
dying regularly due to the heat of spiritual, physical and
heavenly fires. Being internally connected through *Atman*
or Spirit, the body, sense organs and mind are spiritual,
and the grief caused by them is said to be "spiritual heat
or grief"—which is physical and mental. *Vata, pita,* and
cough are the body properties by which ayurveda divides
humans into three categories. Grief or heat which result
from the impurity of *vata, pita* and cough is said to be
physical. Grief arising from lust, anger, greed,
attachment, fear, envy, pessimism and not getting the
desired thing is mental. Grief caused by humans, animals,
birds, creepers and the elements of earth and water is
"physical heat or grief". Grief caused by the beings of
subtle realms, demons, troublesome gods and goddesses
and stars of the planetary system is "heavenly grief or
heat".

The physical body and its parts are well known. The
subtle body has seventeen components—five organs of
knowledge, five organs of senses, five *pranas*, mind and
intellect (that includes ego). The five organs of knowledge
are eyes, ears, nose, tongue and skin. The five sense
organs are mouth, hand, foot, anus and *linga* (penis) or

*yoni* (vagina). The five *pranas* are *prana, apana, samana, udana* and *vyana*. *Prana* spreads over the heart, *apana* over the anus, *samana* over the navel, *udana* over the throat and *vyana* spreads over the whole body. *Prana* goes out, *apana* travels downwards, *udana* moves upwards, *samana* is used to digest food, and *vyana* distributes the juices made by food in the body. There are also five sub-airs: *naag, kurma, kruckar, devadatta* and *dhananjaya*. *Naag*-air acts in releasing air through the mouth, *kurma*-air opens the eyelids, *kruckar*-air acts in spitting, *devadatta*-air acts in yawning, and *dhananjaya*-air nourishes the body. Mind works towards the formation and dissolution of thoughts and will, while intellect acts in decision making.

Apart from the gross and subtle bodies there is the causal body. The triune of gross, subtle and causal bodies is divided into five outer bodies or covers, called *koshas*: *annamaya kosha, pranamaya kosha, manomaya kosha, vigyanmaya kosha* and *anandamaya kosha*. *Annamaya kosha* is the gross (physical) body that arises from the semen and vaginal fluids of the parents coming together; and, the semen and vaginal fluids are made from the grain (*anna*) eaten by the parents. Hence the name, as this *kosha* contains the defects of the grain (*anna*). Just as the cover of a sword covers the sword and the hymen covers the womb in the virgin, in the same way the *annamaya kosha* (the cover made from grains) covers the Soul or *Atman*. Due to this covering the indivisible and faultless *Atman* became divided and gathered some faults that obscured its true identity. *Pranamaya-kosha* comprises the five sense organs and five *pranas*. The defects from *prana* allowed *Atman* to speak, to give, to move, to be thirsty, and so on; while originally the *Atman* was free from all these actions. Since this *kosha* has the power to act it is active. *Manomaya kosha* is made of the five senses of knowledge and the mind. Gathering the defects of the mind, this *Atman* became doubtful, and possessed of sorrow and attachment, and began to see things, while originally it was free from these properties. Since this *kosha* comes from the mind it possesses a will, and it is the cause of many happenings.

*Vigyanmaya kosha* is made of the five sense organs and intellect. Carrying the defects of *vigyan* (science) and intellect this *Atman* became a doer and accumulated *karma*. Not needing to know anything it began to gather knowledge; not needing to determine anything it began to determine; and not interested in the divisions of society and having an ego it began to take interest in divisions and acquire an ego of superiority. This cover of science and intellect has provided the *Atman* with the defects of being a doer, sufferer, happiness, sorrow, divisions of society and family, and acquiring an ego accruing from these. This *kosha* is the main source of ego. The collection of *vigyanamaya kosha*, *manomaya kosha* and *pranamaya kosha* is the subtle body with its seventeen components. *Anandamaya-kosha* is the inner self that is ignorant, and possesses the instinct of happiness, pleasure and entertainment. Carrying the defects of *ananda* (bliss) this *kosha* has provided the *Atman* with a desire for entertainment and acquiring artificial happiness, while originally the *Atman* was blissful and did not need artificial happiness. This cover of ignorance in the form of *anandamaya kosha* is called the "causal body".

The "inner self" has four components: mind, intellect, *chitta* and *ahankar*. Mind is responsible for willing and unwilling things, intellect for decision-making, *chitta* for research and *ahankar* for the pride in doing. Normally *chitta* is taken as a part of mind and *ahankar* is taken as part of the intellect. Thus "inner self" is represented by mind and intellect only.

Ignorance alone is the cause of the gross and subtle bodies. It is the first cause of *Atman* and the cover that obscures it by assuming a body. Just as a foolish person, seeing the sun covered with clouds thinks that the sun is powerless and invisible, so also, because of ignorance, he may think that a rope is a snake. Not only does this ignorance obscure the rope but it also distorts the true nature of the rope. In the same way humans losing themselves in materialism think that *Atman* is the doer, sufferer, happy, unhappy and attached. The purpose of ignorance is to cover the truth. Ignorance can only be destroyed by the combined wisdom of the individual Soul and *Brahman.*

## References

1. Kumar, Ravindra, *Kundalini for Beginners,* St. Paul, MN: Llewellyn Worldwide, 2000.
2. Krishna, Gopi, *The Awakening of Kundalini,* NY: Kundalini Research Foundation, 1975.
3. Goel, Dr B.S., *Third Eye and Kundalini,* New Delhi: Third Eye Foundation of India, 1985.
4. Woodroofe, Sir Joh, *The Serpent Power,* Madras, India: Ganesh & Co., 1981.
5. Bhattacharya, Dr B, *The Way of Tantra,* New Delhi: Sterling Publishers Ltd., 1985.

# 7
# ELEMENTS OF *MAHAYOGA*

There are four kinds of yoga: *Hatha, Mantra, Laya* and *Raja*. Before *Shakti* awakens they are different. After awakening they merge together as *Mahayoga*. *Hathayoga* has been described in detail in Chapter 5. Other branches of *Mahayoga* are:

**Mantrayoga**
The aim of *Mantrayoga* is to achieve one-pointed concentration and absorption by mentally repeating a collection of words called a *mantra*. *Mantra* represents *chaitanya* (active principle of *Shakti*), as the group of words comprising the *mantra* is the outer body of *Shakti*. For this reason chanting of a *mantra* is the main source of awakening *Shakti*. Chanting a *mantra* for a specified number of times awakens the *Mantra-Shakti*. After the awakening, *sadhana* (spiritual practice) goes within to the "active Chaitanya", and then *sadhana* continues automatically. The initiate's "sense of doing" vanishes and is replaced with the "sense of witnessing" whereby the person witnesses the inner active *chaitanya*. At this stage the *sadhan* (tools) of *sadhana* are said to be God-propelled.

Chanting *AUM* or any name of God, such as Rama, Krishna, Hari or Shiva connects the *prana* of the initiate to *Atman*. The chanting should be carried out reverently and with feeling. It is possible to make mistakes when chanting *mantras*, so care must be taken. Sometimes chanting of *mantra* is missed; sometimes its meaning is forgotten; sometimes the right feeling slips away; and sometimes attention on the deity associated with the *mantra* is lost. It is difficult to be careful of all these aspects of chanting together. That is why care and practice are required. When the initiate chants the *mantra* with these precautions and with connected *prana*, then the secret hidden in the *mantra* or its Godliness or *Shakti* awakens in his *chitta*, when *mantra* is mastered. For example, a *mantra* with the deity of wisdom in its seed will make the initiate wise, and he may have the vision of the deity. Thus there are *mantras* with various goals and different deities as the seed. *Mantras* leading to liberation are considered to be the best. However, where the *mantra* is not chanted properly and appropriate care is not taken then there are no results even if he chants for a lifetime.

There are three levels of *mantras*: unconscious, conscious and *mantra-chaitanya*. An unconscious *mantra* is where its *Shakti* or Godliness has not been awakened; it is simply a collection of words. This *mantra* is given by the Guru to the initiate but neither the Guru nor the initiate have any idea about how to awaken *Shakti*. Hundreds of thousands of times the *mantra* may be repeated mechanically without anything happening. When the attention of the initiate is drawn to the fact that the *mantra* is unconscious and he awakens the *Shakti* or Godliness in the *mantra*, then the *mantra* begins to work and the satisfaction of desires begins. When this happens the *mantra* is conscious. At this stage the gross or outer chanting stops because *Shakti* has become active. *Mantra-Shakti* begins to act in the body and mind of the initiate, and all accumulated *karma* is thinned out. The "real form" or *Atman* of *mantra* is the *chaitanya* hidden in it, while the set of words is only its outer body; just like the *Atman* and gross body of an individual.

Chanting an "unconscious *mantra*" for a long time to achieve its conscious form, and then chanting the "conscious *mantra*" for a long time to achieve its *mantra-chaitanya* level is one of the methods to awaken. One feels the power of *mantra* when it becomes conscious. *Mantra-chaitanya* is the awakening of the *kundalini*. The *mantra-chaitanya* can be wakened from the beginning by receiving the grace of a true Guru who will give the *mantra* to the initiate as a donation or gift. Receiving the grace of the Guru connects the *Chit-Shakti* of the Guru to the *Chit-Shakti* of the initiate, which activates the *mantra* in the *Chit-Shakti* of the initiate when his own power awakens within.

The *chaitanya* in the *mantra* awakens in the body and *chitta* of the initiate, which causes *kriyas* in him. The *sanskara* or accumulated *karma* is the base of the *kriyas* while *chaitanya* is the power (*Shakti*) behind the *kriyas*. *Shakti* produces *kriyas*, not the initiate. As a result the initiate is a witness and not a doer. Physical *kriyas* can be seen but mental *kriyas* where the consciousness of the *mantra* remains all the time are not always seen. The large number of times a *mantra* is repeated is aimed at making an unconscious *mantra* conscious. Repetition brings this about. However this takes a great deal of time. That is why receiving grace and a *mantra* from a Guru early saves time and effort.

Having reached the stage of automatic chanting through mental *kriyas* all attempts to chant using individual effort should be resisted, since this can stop the *kriyas* within and the initiate can revert back to the lower state. Where the initiate continues to use effort, *karma* at the same level as the forced chanting begins to accumulate, and past *karma* stops thinning out, which reduces the level of *sadhana*. No chanting or religious singing should be done after the awakening of *Shakti*, which can interfere with the automatic process. A *mantra* given by the Guru can be chanted any time, but it should be stopped if the *kriyas* begin in the presence of non-initiates.

After the activation of *Shakti* a *mantra(s)* may emerge within the *chitta* of the initiate. This may be due to the chanting of those *mantras* in former lives, and may now be required to help the thinning out of *karma*. The *mantra* thus emerged should not be stopped, and *Shakti* should be allowed to continue with a sense of surrender on the part of the initiate.

During *Shaktipat* initiation, the will (determination to help) of the Guru is associated with the *mantra* or touch or sight, whatever the method of initiation. It is this will, which is important and is for the benefit of the initiate. As soon as the *kriyas* begin, the initiate has gone beyond the chanting of *mantra*. *Mantra* in the initiation has its own importance. Sometimes the *kriyas* may stop and then the initiate can chant the *mantra* given by the Guru. It can be chanted while sitting, lying, walking or doing anything else; and there is every possibility that the *mantra* will re-start the *kriyas*. Without *mantra* the initiate may feel without help or shelter. It is therefore recommended that the *mantra* should be passed to the initiate during initiation. Initiation without *mantra* is inadequate.

Some people attach greater importance to chanting of the *mantra* than the *kriyas,* and may stop the *kriyas* and start chanting the *mantra*. However, *kriyas* are more important and replacing *kriyas* with *mantras* can prove harmful. Activities of the *kriyas* are the real chanting of the *mantra*, and one should take recourse to the *mantra* only when the *kriyas* are not taking place. The *mantra* being left behind and *kriyas* beginning is the true aim of the chanting of the *mantra*.

Sometimes following *Shaktipat japa* or chanting takes place automatically without effort. The *mantra* may be the one given by the Guru or it may have emerged by itself, and be one which the initiate may or may not be familiar with. The seed of this *mantra* was already sown in the *chitta* of the initiate, sometime in the past. It is that seed that germinates in the form of *ajapa-japa* or chanting-without-chanting.

There are different levels on which *ajapa-japa* can manifest:

1. It may be loud and uncontrollable. The initiate may feel that some unknown force is causing it.
2. The chanting may not be heard externally but the movement of the lips can be seen. The chanting goes on within and it is subtler than in the first case.
3. The movement of the lips also stops and the initiate feels the chanting going on within. One's attention is on the mouth. This state is yet subtler than the first two.
4. The attention is taken away from the mouth and the chanting goes on in the *chitta*, as the initiate feels it. This form is even subtler.
5. The initiate hears the sound of chanting within his mind, and hears the chanting going on within, without effort. This is the subtlest form of chanting-without-chanting. Whatever the form may be it is a part of the *kriyas*.

The initiate should remain unattached with *ajapa-japa*, remaining as a witness, and should not worry if it does not happen. It has its own timescale, and may start and stop according to *karmic* requirements. All the *kriyas* are meant to thin out the *sanskara* or accumulated *karma*; and, when the process of thinning out is complete, *kriyas* stop by themselves.

**Layayoga**

The word "laya" means "absorption". In this case it is absorption of *chitta* in a thing or a thought and is called "Layayoga". In spirituality *Layayoga* implies absorption of the mind in the "Cosmic Sound" that is heard inwardly by yogis or initiates. This Sound is also known as *anahata-naad* or "unstruck sound" since it is produced without two things striking against each other. Since the aim of the initiate is to stay in *Atman*, there is no attachment to this sound. The person hears it as a witness with a feeling of renunciation and non-attachment, just as one is not attached to the activities of *Hathayoga* and *Mantrayoga* or *ajapa-japa*. However, the Sound is heard with concentration, and the *chitta* of the initiate transforms according to the Sound. One's oneself becomes void, the state of no mind. This state is known as *Layayoga*, a state of absorption also known as *sampragyat samadhi*, as the *chitta* exists though in association with the naad or Cosmic Sound. In *asampragyat samadhi chitta* stops working completely, and with it the sense of the world and related knowledge disappears. The emergence of the *Naad* or Sound and absorption of *chitta* in it are subtle *kriyas*, and are there for the benefit of the initiate.

At a certain point the initiate hears the inner sounds loudly and in different forms. As spiritual practice becomes more advanced the sound becomes more and more subtle. In the beginning one may hear sounds like drums, clouds, waterfalls and the roaring of a lion, while towards the end the sounds are softer like a flute, violin and the buzzing of bees. In this way the Cosmic Sound is heard internally in different ways, becoming subtler every time. The initiate may alternate between loud and soft sounds and should become absorbed in the sound that most appeals spending time contemplating on it. As dissatisfaction grows towards the outer world, there is absorption in the inner sound, just as water becomes absorbed in milk. Leaving behind all interests, hopes, disappointments and pleasures of the senses the initiate should ponder on the inner sound and become absorbed in it. Becoming absorbed without being attached is difficult.

Just as the bee collecting honey does not care for the smell of the flowers, in the same way the initiate contemplating on the inner sound should not be concerned with the sense objects of the outer world. The flickering and restless mind that normally searches for different objects of pleasure outside can be easily controlled by the inner sound since the sound takes the mind away from the senses. The benevolent inner sound acts like a net that catches deer running freely in the forest, and acts like the bank of the ocean that stops all waves. Constant hearing of the inner sound thins out the attraction for sensual pleasures, and the mind and *prana* become absorbed in formless *Brahman*. When the sound becomes subtle the activity of *chitta* also reduces in direct proportion. As *chaitanya* disconnects itself with *chitta* and becomes reabsorbed in *Atman*, the individual and inner sounds also become absorbed in *Atman*. Finally only *Atman* is left, which is a part of *Paramatma*, and that too eventually loses its individual identity and becomes one with the Absolute.

For individuals, whose intellect has not grown properly, the path of "inner sound" is simple and practicable. The ears are closed with the thumbs. With this the *chitta* of the yogi becomes concentrated and absorbed in the sound, which opens the way to *asampragyat samadhi*. However, one should not only depend on the *kriyas* but also observe the rules and regulations of yoga for final success.

A yogi who has achieved freedom from the three states of waking, dreaming and sleeping, and has given up all the worries of the world and appears like a dead person is actually *mukta* or liberated. At this stage the inner sound holds no attraction, and the yogi appears without emotion although the physical body is still present. This kind of yogi is not affected by the dualities of heat and cold, respect and disrespect. His consciousness is in *Atman*. The sight is still and concentrated, even though there is nothing to see; and, *prana* (inhalation and exhalation) is stabilised. Such a yogi is unaffected by good or bad events, cannot be moved by the fear of death, no kind of black magic can effect him, dualities like happiness and sorrow have no effect, neither does taste, smell, touch or sound. *Chitta* is neither awake nor asleep and there is no forgetting in him. Activities take place in *chitta* only when *Shakti* is associated with it. When the connection with *Shakti* is broken, because of absorption in *Atman*, *chitta* becomes completely inactive. Such a yogi, although in good health and being awake, looks like being asleep. Inhalations and exhalations are nearly stopped. Liberation has been achieved.

A person whose *chitta* has been stabilised without any shelter or dependence on any thing or person, should be taken as residing in "inner Cosmic Sound" or *turiya-avastha* or the "state of *Brahman*", which are synonymous.

*Chaitanya* once lit is everywhere and it remains with the unstruck sound in the knowable form; and the *chitta* or mind remains there too, that is, the mind is absorbed in the knowable. When all kinds of auspicious and inauspicious tendencies of *chitta* come to an end, then what remain is the "knowable *Chaitanya*", and that is the highest level of Absolute God. This may also be known as the highest position of Infinite *Atman* or *Paramatma*. It is for this reason that initiates are advised to absorb themselves in the unstruck sound, which thins out accumulated *karma* and allows the highest spiritual position as *Atman* to be achieved. Going beyond mind and unstruck sound after their absorption into one another is arriving at *Paramatma*. Unstruck sound is energy, which helps the elements of the universe, i.e. earth, water, fire and air, to dissolve and then what remains is inexpressible, attributeless and formless *Brahman*, since all elements vanish in *Brahman*, like the waves on the ocean which return to the ocean. This state of absorption

is also known as *unmani avastha*. A yogi who
concentrates on the unstruck sound looks like a log of
wood, because both *chitta* and *prana* are absorbed in
*Atman*, and he hears nothing else. A yogi in *unmani
avastha* has transcended all states of being, is free from
all worries, looks like a dead person and is certainly
liberated. The five states of being—waking, dreaming,
sleeping, trance and dead—are transcended, and because
all tendencies have been quietened, the yogic state is
firmly established.

All methods of *Hathayoga* and *Layayoga* become
successful through *Rajayoga*. *Chitta* is the seed that is
sown in the field of *Hatha*. Through the union of *prana*
and *apana*, it is watered through the water of *vairagya*
(renunciation of material and sensual pleasures). This
yields the fruit of *asampragyat samadhi* (absorption with
dissolution of *chitta*).

### Rajayoga

*Rajayoga* normally means "natural meditation". Since
each kind of yoga eventually turns into natural
meditation, its practitioners address each yoga in its
developed form as *Rajayoga*. Whether it is *Hatha,
Mantra, Laya, Naad* or *Dhyanyoga*, each aims to bring
the concentration of the practitioner to a single point.
This allows entry into *sadhana* where there is automatic
concentration. Also *sadhana* thins out *sanskara,* which
cleanses and purifies *chitta*; and then *chitta* achieves the
natural state of desireless concentration, known as
*unmani avastha*.

There are certain states of meditation which can be
arrived at through regular effort and practice. Those
states are reached automatically after the awakening of
*Shakti* because of the emerging of past *sanskaras,* and
the initiate seeing them as a witness and not a doer.
*Yogadarshan* was the first to mention the activities
following *kriyas* that are described here in some detail.

*Shaktipat* initiation generates *kriyas* that produce three kinds of results in the initiate:

1. With the activation of *Shakti*, *chitta* becomes transformed; there is renunciation towards material and sensual pleasures, and *sanskara* of attachment becomes thinned out. An interest is taken in pure and auspicious activities; *sadhana* becomes regular which thins out ignorance and unwise *sanskara*. This is known as *nirodh parinam* or "prophylactic result".

2. Withdrawal from lust, attachment and sensual pleasures gradually reduces fickleness (fluctuations) in *chitta* and helps the person to focus on a single thought, scene or past experience. There is a gradual thinning out of interest in the affairs of the world and single-pointed concentration towards a single goal. This is known as *samadhi parinam* or "absorption result".

3. While concentrating one loses the sense of time, similar to being deeply absorbed in some activity and not realising that the time has gone. In the same way, an initiate involved in *sadhana* is so absorbed in the activity that the external world is reduced to a void, as the attention turns inward. Thus the knowledge/wisdom from the past, present and future (in trance or otherwise) become united in "one". This is known as *ekagrata parinam* or "unification result".

When a person has *kriyas,* knowledge of past lives may arise. However, when the awakened *Shakti* introduces *kriyas*, the aim of *Shakti* is to thin out the *sanskara*, which may or may not involve experiencing past lives. By sustained effort with a goal of knowing the past in mind, one is led to the knowledge of past lives if this is what is desired. But, the aim of *kriyas* is solely the thinning out of *sanskara*, and not knowing the causes of certain *karma*, one may not know past lives. Nevertheless, one's *chitta* is purified towards spiritual perfection. If the initiate wants to know the past and this is his goal then this knowledge will come, but it is not advisable as it can be an obstacle to further development. If for some reason the all-knowing *Shakti* wants the initiate to know the past, then this will happen. The initiate should not worry if the experiences of past lives do not enter into his *chitta*.

Patanjali's *Yogasutra* talks about *dharana, dhyana* and *samadhi* as the three final steps of the eightfold path of *Rajayoga*. When one tries to concentrate on an object, sometimes *chitta* concentrates and sometimes it flickers. This is called *dharana* and happens where the concentration is not stable. When one achieves continuity in concentration at the same goal, and the seer, seeing and seen remain separate, it is said to be *dhyana*. When the trinity vanishes, and the three merge into one so that the seer, seeing and seen become one, then this is *samadhi*. If the attention of the initiate shifts before the state of *dhyana* has arrived, the person has lost *sanyama* or control. But, if concentration is maintained on the same object until the stage of *dhyana* is reached then *sanyama* or control is present, which the initiate is strongly advised to have for success. This is why focused awareness on breathing is such a powerful tool for achieving *samadhi*. With *sanyama, siddhis* may emerge as an experience, which should be witnessed by the initiate, without any attraction or attachment to them.

*Siddhis* or paranormal powers are *kalpita* or "imagined", if one engages in practices aimed solely at achieving those powers, and achieves them. Paranormal powers that come voluntarily to the initiate as a by-product of sadhana are *akalpita* or "unimagined". After the awakening of the *kundalini, siddhis* may appear by themselves. If the initiate takes an interest in them, or tries to achieve mastery over them, or begins to worry if they are not repeated, then the *kriyas* are stopped and spiritual progress is arrested, and he returns to the material world eventually. Thus the initiate is advised not to give attention to *siddhis,* if and when they take place, to just witness them without feeding them with attention.

One of these *siddhis* is the disappearance of the body. This happens because the reflection of light from an object makes the object visible. The greater the "receiving power" of the object, the more luminous it appears to others. If a yogi reduces the "receiving power of light" to zero or does not receive the light through yoga, then he may disappear for onlookers.

As virtuous *sanskaras,* e.g., friendliness and compassion emerge and become more dominant in the *chitta* and the initiate concentrates and exercises control over them, they become stabilised and internalised in the consciousness of the initiate. Having concentrated with *sanyama* or control on the strength of animals, such as an elephant, the initiate can acquire the strength of those animals. However, *sanyama* does not develop in many practitioners, and hence this *siddhi* is not easy to achieve. As the initiate continues with *sadhana* and has faith and surrender to the inner *Shakti, sanyama* can be achieved. And then, there is access to all experience and knowledge. Will and meditation alone cannot achieve this kind of *siddhis, Sanyama* is necessary. With the development of "natural one-pointed concentration" or *sanyama,* that is, control over fickleness and fluctuations of *chitta,* experiences of divine forms, taste, smell, words and touch—all kinds of *akalpita* or unimagined *siddhis*— are experienced. The *siddhis* are there as subtle tests for the initiate to choose whether attention is given to *siddhis* or turned towards *Atman.* Not all initiates have the same experiences. There are special ones, which are experienced by some and not others. One example of these is experience of *Siddhis* or yogic-powers or paranormal powers. There are also subtle *kriyas* that are so fine that the initiate or onlookers may not feel that these are *kriyas* at all. Both these experiences are of higher level and deserve special reference. They are discussed in more detail in Chapter 8.

Concentration with controlled *chitta* on the outer sun leads to the stability of *chitta* on the inner sun within *sushumna*. That is why the entrance to *sushumna* is known as the sun-gate. At this stage the person receives knowledge about the universe. *Sanyama* on the moon results in knowing the star system, and that on the star Dhruva results in knowing its speed. Since the world within is akin to the world outside, the sun, moon and stars are all seen within oneself. However, seeing them confirms that the journey is going in the right direction. There should be no attachment to the experience or longing for it to be repeated. This applies to all kinds of *siddhis*. There is nowhere in the script of *Yogadarshan* where it is advised to concentrate efforts on developing *siddhis*.

In the course of *sadhana* when the *chitta* of the initiate concentrates on the *prarabdha* (current) and *sanchit* (accumulated) *sanskara* then knowledge of happy and unhappy events resulting from *prarabdha* arise. By knowing what desires are emerging in the *chitta* one knows the state of *chitta*. The whole future appears before the initiate like an open book. One knows in advance when one's life will end.

The first five steps in the eightfold path of the great sage Patanjali are: (1) *Yama,* meaning moral conduct, such as non-violence, non-stealing, truthfulness, continence and non-covetousness; (2) *Niyama,* meaning religious observances, such as purity of mind and body, contentment, self-discipline, study of scriptures and devotion to God; (3) *Asana,* meaning postures to keep the spine straight and body fit for meditation; (4) *Pranayama,* meaning control of breath and regulation of *prana* and

(5) *Pratyahara,* meaning the withdrawal of senses from external objects. These five steps directly confront the mind with the aim of breaking through the veil of illusion, and suppress the vicious thoughts of the *chitta* by fighting its tendencies. Some rare people will achieve success through this route, but most will get tired of the consistent fight, lose patience and become opposed to the whole practice. With the awakening of *Shakti* too one has to confront the inclinations of the *chitta* to some extent, but the main goal is to have faith and surrender to the *Shakti.* Gradually She increases one's will, thins the *sanskara* out, and with determination the vicious thoughts of *chitta* become weaker and weaker automatically. In this way the first five steps of Patanjali's path become automatically successful, without conscious fighting and confrontation with the *chitta.* These five steps are essential for *sadhana,* and are difficult to achieve by force, which, the *Shaktipat* initiation and surrender to awakened *Shakti* achieve naturally. Purification of *chitta* in this way prepares the ground for witnessing the *Atman.*

**Intellect and *Atman***

Intellect works through the power of *Atman,* and hence is not capable of receiving the knowledge of *Atman,* just as the computer cannot know its own programmer. When the *chitta* is purified, the knowledge of *Atman* begins to reflect in it. Just as a clean mirror is required to see oneself, in the same way a clean *chitta* is required by *Atman* to see itself reflected in the *chitta.* Witnessing "purified ego" in the *chitta* is known as *atma-sakshatkar* or the witnessing of "Pure *Chaitanya*" or *Atman.*

After having the above experiences the *sanskara,* desires and vicious thoughts of *chitta* are thinned out. Enjoyment of pleasures through a balanced *chitta* vanishes the *prarabdha* and the heart of the initiate becomes clean and pure like a mirror. *Chaitanya Shakti*

of *Atman* can be seen reflected in the heart. The activities
of the initiate now show the presence of *Shakti* within,
just as the working of the refrigerator shows the presence
of electricity. When the *chitta* has been purified the
presence of *Shakti* is not seen through the *kriyas* but
through the reflection of *Atman*. I-ness (identifying
oneself) in the *chitta* is also because of the *Shakti* of
*Atman*; and, seeing in pure *chitta* one sees the *Atman-
Shakti* in pure form of I-ness too. This is known as seeing/
witnessing of *Atman* by *Atman* itself. None of the sensual
organs, mind, intellect or ego can reach to *Atman*. *Atman*
sees its own reflection in the mirror of *sattva* or purified
*chitta* alone.

Just as twilight spreads all over the sky before dawn,
in the same way *chitta* is flooded with all kinds of
experiences with light, sound, *siddhis* and others before
the direct knowing of *Atman* takes place. This is known
as *pratibh-jnana,* meaning, the knowledge of the virtues
of *Atman*. This is the highest stage of *sampragyat
samadhi* and it is also known as "dwelling in *Atman*".
The real knower is *Atman* although intellect is the
instrument through which such knowing takes place.
After the purification of the *chitta* the subtle insights
possessed by the intellect is *sanyama*. There is a stage
when the initiate can exercise *sanyama* on *Atman* when
it is reflected in the *chitta*. However, it is difficult to
arrive at such a stage by individual effort since this
cannot happen before the purification of *chitta* and
thinning out of the material has run its course. Before
this, *chitta* cannot concentrate on *Atman*. It is through
*kriyas* that the cover of *maya* thins out and the
knowledge of *chaitanya* or *Atman* begins to be reflected
gradually in *chitta*. *Shakti* is recognised through the
*kriyas*, which work on the *sanskara* present in *chitta*; but
when the *sanskaras* are thinned away then the *kriyas* of
*Shakti* are also quiet. Then the presence of *Shakti* is
known through *chaitanya* or *Atman*.

Intellect and *Atman* are different from each other and have opposite natures. *Sanyama* with Absolute God as one's goal leads to the knowledge of *Atman*. Intellect is unconscious, inert and leads to some results, while *Atman* is conscious and is a result in itself. Although they can never be united, yet the two are difficult to separate, because of their inter-relatedness. Knowledge of both of them remains inclusive. Due to the synchronisation of *chitta* with *Chaitanya Shakti* of *Atman* it is difficult to know *chitta* independent of *Atman*. This synchronisation itself is why there is desire and interest in sensual pleasures. If this synchronisation were broken there would be a loss of interest in sensual pleasures. This is why purification of *chitta* and the removal of the cover of *maya*, while having separate knowledge of *Atman* and *chitta* is the spiritual goal. To remove this synchronisation the subject of *sanyama* should be *Atman*. *Sanyama* on reflected *chaitanya* on *chitta* or intellect results in the knowledge of *Atman*, which is different from intellect or *chitta*. This is the yogic method of Vedanta, which opens the "knot" between the inert (*chitta* or intellect) and conscious (*Atman*). Individual effort cannot open this knot. It is the continuity of *kriyas* that brings the stage where the "inert" and "conscious" can be seen as different and separate from one another. Then *chitta* automatically turns towards and concentrates on divine touch, taste, sound and light; and the desires and inclinations emerging in *chitta* are constrained.

**Summary and Application**
The four elements of *Mahayoga* have different aims and applications for initiates. *Layayoga* and *Rajayoga* transcend duality so that the *Atman* of the initiate can easily connect and unite with *Parabrahma Paramatma*. Thus the four kinds of yoga are suitable for different types of initiates.

Initiates who are not so zealous, who are ignorant, who look for defects in the Guru, who are greedy, sinful, big eaters, interested in and influenced by the opposite sex, clever, desperate, suffering from disease, under the control of others, very cruel, slow in action and lacking insufficient vital fluid (semen for men and vaginal fluid for women) belong to the category of "mild practitioners". These practitioners need to practise *Mantrayoga*. If they can obtain the grace of the Guru and if they can pursue their *sadhana* seriously and sincerely, then they are likely to realise the Self or *Atman* in about tuelve years.

An initiate whose intellect is balanced, is compassionate and engaged in auspicious activities, is sweet spoken, and remains neutral in most situations and who has equal interest in everyone is a "medium practitioner". Such an initiate can reach the same goal through *Layayoga* in about nine years.

An initiate who is proficient in *Layayoga*, who has a stable intellect, is rich in vital fluids and strong enough to act independently, is charitable, compassionate, forgiving, truthful, brave, and has reverence for *samadhi* and the Guru, and is interested in the practice of yoga is called an *adhimatra* or advanced initiate. Such a person should be initiated into *Hathayoga*, which can lead to Self-realisation in about six years.

The most advanced initiate is the person who knows scripture, who is zealous, brave, hard-working, free from attachments, free from restlessness, who looks and behaves like a young person, is a small eater, has control over the senses, is free from fear, has good moral character, is expert in most activities, is charitable, gives shelter to everyone, is deserving, whose *chitta* is stable, who is intelligent, contented, forgiving, humble, a person who observes the rules of society and religion, is a serious and sweet speaker; who believes in scriptures, worships the deity and his Guru, avoids wasting time with people who are not interested in spirituality, and who is always ready to practise yoga, such an initiate with dedicated efforts positively realises the Self in about three years. This type of person is suitable for all four kinds of yoga, and the Guru does not have to worry about his success.

It is important to note here that although the maximum time for any initiate to realise Self is twelve years, some people do not attain realisation, not even in forty years or even in lifetime. Why is this? The reason is that the above timespan has been estimated for those practitioners who engage in *sadhana* with feelings of surrender and reverence. Whatever the vices or virtues they may have, they leave behind everything and engage in continuous *sadhana* with one-pointed-concentration, dedication and surrender. Most of the initiates lack feelings of surrender, and they cannot maintain the flow and continuity of *sadhana* either. These practitioners may not only take more years than prescribed but they may even continue to oscillate between various paths for several lifetimes.

### Another Way

There is another way of yoga, which is highly effective. For this the initiate stabilises the eyes and looks at a chosen object in bright sunlight. When one begins to see that object in the empty space, then the object can be seen in the sky when the eyes are open. Gradually there is a seeing of the object within oneself, which produces experiences of immense bliss. Practising this when worshiping deity, time of danger, thinning out of sin or gathering of virtues one certainly achieves honours. With this practice a person can see own image within himself. This kind of practice is known as *pratikopasana,* which means worshipping the goal.

Closing the nine doors of the senses opens the tenth door of spirituality. The nine doors are the two ears, two eyes, two nostrils, mouth, urinary and stool passages. The ears are closed with the thumbs, the eyes are closed with the first fingers, the nostrils are closed with the middle fingers and the mouth with the small fingers. By enclosing *prana* in this way and practising regularly the reflection of *Atman* can be seen within oneself. This is another way of witnessing oneself as *Atman*. One who can see the *Atmic* flame within oneself and concentrate on it for even a moment achieves freedom from sins and achieves the highest spiritual position. Maintaining the clarity of one's *chitta* and engaging in witnessing the reflection of *Atman* within, the initiate dissociates from the body and sees him as different from the body and its activities. He becomes stabilised in the element of *Atman* and receives the knowledge that, "I am Atman."

# 8

## SIDDHIS AND SUBTLE KRIYAS

**Siddhis or Yogic Powers**
Sometimes the initiates may realise they have unusual powers of yoga during their *sadhana*. These powers do not help achieve *samadhi;* in fact, they work as obstacles. Their only advantage, when they take place automatically through *kriyas,* is to indicate the state of mind of the initiate and his spiritual development. In this regard they are essential and important, and should be acknowledged. But the initiate is advised to keep the attention focused on performing the *kriyas* and to ignore the yogic powers if and when they appear. The overall importance is the goal of acquiring the state of *Atman* by entering into *samadhi.*

When the *chitta* expands from the body into the world outside it is known as *kalpita* (imagined) *videh dharana.* Expansion of the *chitta* without consideration of a body is called *akalpita* (unimagined) *videh dharana.* Once success has been achieved in *akalpita videh dharana* one can enter the body of another through *chitta* and behave as one likes.

Whether the *siddhi* is *kalpita* (imagined and worked for through spiritual practices) or *akalpita* (never imagined but appearing automatically through *kriyas*), its display and use is an obstacle to achieving the Supreme *Siddhi* of *samadhi.* Just as a man who has been born poor may be lured by the gain of little money, practitioners who are only interested in worldly things do not have strong characters and may be lured by *siddhis*. Just as a mature man will ignore small gains and continue to work for bigger gains not from greed but from wisdom, in the same way an initiate who has a balanced and purified character will ignore common *siddhis* and continue with his *sadhana* until the greatest of *siddhis* in the form of *samadhi* or Self-realisation is achieved.

Attention to *siddhis* prolongs involvement in the materialism of the world or *maya*. Bondage into *maya* is weakened with the thinning out of *sanskara* and worldly desires, which purifies the *chitta*. And then the powers of *Atman* appear automatically and in sequence. The control on *Prana-Shakti* by the initiate is one of these powers. Through request to *Shakti*, the initiate can activate *Shakti* anywhere and transmit it to another. With the control on *Prana-Shakti* the initiate also controls *prana, apana, samana, udana* and *vyana*, which result in the following:

When *udana* is controlled the initiate can walk over an ocean, river, pond, loose mud and thorns, without touching them. Such an initiate may also fly. The *chitta* with all its components can be taken out of the body and enter another body. All of these powers are available to the yogi but are never used.

When *samana* is controlled the yogi's body can be lit like fire.

*Prana* controls different activities throughout the body and is called life-force. Due to the five different activities the one *prana* is given different names: The life-force that enters and exits through the mouth and nose, and is active between the front portion of the nose and the heart is *prana*. The life-force that takes the juices of the material eaten or drunk to their respective places, and is active between the heart and the navel is *samana*.

The life-force that is responsible for excretions and propelling of the womb and related material, which is active between the navel and the soles of the feet, is *apana*. That which is responsible for taking the juices above the throat-pit, and which is active between the front portion of the nose and the crown of the head is *udana*. The life-force that is distributed over the whole body is *vyana*. Important amongst the five kinds of life forces is *prana,* which is the principle life-force, since the working of all others depends on it.

Through *sanyama* (control without fluctuations) the divine faculties replace the sense organs. The distinction between sound and hearing is one example where sound that arises from the physical sense of hearing is forgotten and divine hearing takes over. Sound is temporary and impermanent whereas hearing is unchanging and permanent. The two are not the same thing as hearing continues when sounds have ceased. Thus single-minded control/concentration on the relationship between the "faculty of hearing" and *akash* (sky) can enable hearing without using the ears. Control over the "faculty of touch" and air leads to divine touch; control over the relation between eyes and light leads to divine seeing; control over the "faculty of taste" and water makes one taste divinely; and, control over the faculty of smelling and earth makes one have divine smell. Thus, in the absence of any word, touch, light, taste and smell in the outside world, all these experiences are available through inner/subtle organs.

*Sanyama* on the relation between the body and *akash* makes the initiate's body weightless, so he can walk on water without getting wet, or travel through the rays of sun into the sky. Nevertheless, the yogi does not give importance to these powers, and ignores them deliberately.

Five *maha-bhutas* or basic elements—earth, water, fire, air and *akash*—have their corresponding gross and subtle forms. The gross forms are solidity in earth, liquidity in water, heat in fire, distribution in air and universality in *akash*. The properties and duties of the five elements are known as their forms. The subtle forms of the five elements are smell in earth, juice in water, sharpness in fire, touch in air and word in *akash*. In Sanskrit these subtle forms are known as *tanmatras*. These subtle forms construct the five elements through gradual distortion of inert nature. This process in Sanskrit is known as *anvaya*.

*Anvaya* can be understood in the following way. First nature creates *akash*. Then half *akash* and half air combine to make air. Next half air and half fire combine to make fire. This means that the fire has a quarter of *akash*, a quarter of air and half fire. Water is created from fire and earth is created from water. Nature gives pleasure and pain, bondage and liberation. This is the essence of *maha-bhutas* or basic elements. When *Shakti* provides *sanyama* or control over the "gross forms" of the five elements, their subtle *anvaya* and essence, the initiate 'knows' the forms of the elements and gains power over them. This is known as *bhootjaya ka ashvarya,* meaning "glory of the victory over elements". At this stage the nature of the elements changes according to the will of the yogi, and the following *siddhis* resulting from this can be made to happen:

*Anima:* This *siddhi* reduces the size of an object from big to small. Due to this power the yogi, gods, *gandharva* or beings of the heaven assume a very minute form and can travel everywhere, without being seen.

*Mahima:* With this power small objects can become as big as an elephant, city or mountain.

*Laghima:* This yogic power reduces the weight of an object so it can become small, and fly in the sky like straw.

*Garima:* With this power the yogi can become as heavy as desired.

*Prapti:* With this comes the power to have anything that is desired in the world.

*Prakamya:* Here the yogi does not face any obstruction to whatever he wants to do. Whatever one desires, it comes to pass. For example, one can enter the earth and return.

*Vashitva:* With this power any/all elements, things, beings and circumstances, can be subjugated by the yogi, without the yogi being subjugated by them. The natural properties of the physical elements are changed according to the will of the yogi. For example, one can pass through fire without being burnt, cross water without drowning, a sword can pierce through the body without cutting it and poison is converted into nectar.

*Ishatva:* One acquires the power to create, sustain and destroy the world.

If and when any of these *siddhis* appear the initiate whose aim is to enter into the state of *Atman*, must ignore them without becoming involved or attached to any of them. When successful the body acquires beauty, lustre, strength, and is firm like steel. The same effects are seen when the five elements have been controlled. Next comes victory over sense organs.

There are five "forms" of properties of the sense organs. The first form is the power to receive by the organs, and is called *grahan*. Enlightening knowledge of things and situations, which is the cause of pure ego, is the second form, called *swarup*. The cause of the sense organs is ego, which is the third form known as *Asmita*. The fourth form, known as *anvaya* comprises enlightening knowledge, action, state of being, humility and virtue. And the fifth form of organs known as *arthvatva* is the capacity through which the yogi can use the organs to interact with the world. When he acquires *sanyama* (control) over the five forms in order, then the corresponding property of the organs is subjugated by him. This is known as victory over the organs. *Sanyama* enables the breakthrough of limitations which lack of control over the sense organs imposes. When these limitations are dissolved their true and limitless potential can be experienced.

Three kinds of results emerge from victory over the sense organs: *manojyatva, vikaranbhav* and *pradhanjaya*. *Manojyatva* is the power by which the body acquires the same speed as the mind. This happens because limitations on the body are released. So desired distances, no matter how far, can be reached in a fraction of a second. *Vikaranbhav* is the power to enjoy sense organs without the body, irrespective of place and time, so that the sense organs would work in whatever country and at whatever times the yogi desires. For example, while sitting in New York it would be possible to see what is happening in London. *Pradhanjaya* is the power of subjugating the unseen work and cause or, victory over the formless part of nature. This triune of powers is achieved through the *sanyama* of organs and elements on the path of yoga, and is known as "madhupratika."

There is a specific purpose for which Mother *Kundalini* induces these *kriyas* that result in various kinds of *sanyama*. All things which are either inert or conscious, and which can be generated through the triple virtue of *tamogun* or inertness, *rajogun* or activity and *satogun* or purity present themselves before their master *Atman*, visible and available to be used. All things that are created by the five elements work as servants to their master *Atman* (represented by the yogi with purified *chitta*). The yogi, through the vestiges of knowledge/ wisdom, knows the past, present or future results. He becomes free from grief. He remains unconcerned with *siddhis* and turns the attention to the highest good of *samadhi*.

*Siddhis* arise by surrendering to the *kriyas* induced by the benevolent *Shakti*, and not through individual effort. When ignorance in the form of attachment, ego and desires disappears, all grief is eliminated and the yogi receives the *kaivalya-phal,* meaning the fruit of *kaivalya.* Knowledge through wisdom is the religion of intellect. Intellect, which does not belong to *Atman*, is ignorable, and *Purusha* or *Atman* is different from intellect and is a result in itself— this is the experience received when *karma* dies. The yogi who has been freed from all grief—spiritual, physical and heavenly—enters the stage of *kaivalya*. This is also known as "freedom from *maya*," and it is the highest or climaxed stage of yoga.

Other *siddhis* involve visions of heavenly beings who bring different invitations. Yogis are warned not to take notice even if they come with beautiful ladies who promise all kinds of enjoyments. One should neither be lured by such attractions nor should there be pride at being invited; otherwise grief in the form of repeated incarnations will remain. There are four stages of yogis: *kalpita, madhumati, pragyajyoti* and *atikrant-bhavaniya.* One has to see at what stage one is likely to face such obstacles from the gods.

A *kalpita yogi* has just acquired *sanyama,* and is about to face the related *siddhis*. One who achieves victory over elements and organs through *samadhi* is *madhumati yogi*. A yogi who has conquered the elements and organs through *sanyama* and is going to face higher *siddhis* is *pragyajyoti yogi*. A yogi who has only to dissolve the *chitta* through *asampragyat samadhi* is *atikrant-bhavaniya yogi.*

A *kalpita yogi* is at the beginning stages of yoga and hence he has no chance of being tempted by heavenly persons. The third, *pragyajyoti yogi*, has acquired important *siddhis* and also will not be interfered with by the gods. The fourth, *atikrant bhavaniya yogi*, is so deep in renunciation that nothing affects him. It is the second category of yogi called *madhumati* who is most at risk of being allured by the gods. This is because a yogi at this stage has neither acquired *siddhis* such as *aishvarya* nor has taken deep and strict renunciation yet. It is to test the purity of *chitta* of the *madhumati yogi* that the gods and beautiful ladies/men from heaven request the yogi to enjoy all kinds of pleasures and sports of heaven. The yogi should not be surprised by such requests, and he should try to keep a distance from the attractions and desires of alluring things. These visions can be realised as the activity of the ego, which through desire creates form to sabotage spiritual progress. He should avoid the company of beautiful ladies and tell himself that it is through great effort that he has come to such a stage after suffering for many many lifetimes in this world of miseries. He should think that the flame he has just lit can be put out by the enjoyment of sensual pleasures, and he would be thrown back into the world of *maya* to suffer again. Thinking in this way he neither should disrespect the heavenly beings nor should he feel proud of the invitation and accept the offer. He should never think that he has become such a big yogi that even the gods are coming to request him. This thinking is a sign that the ego is still active. He should pay respect to the heavenly beings, including the beautiful ladies, and request them to leave him alone. He should tell them that only they are fit and qualified to enjoy all these things in the heaven. Bidding them goodbye he should once again engage in the pursuit of *samadhi*. Female yogis should do the same with regard to heavenly men who may appear to lure them away from the ultimate goal of *Atman*.

Universality and all-knowingness come from knowledge gathered through wisdom after the *sadhan* (means) of *sanyama* has been perfected. Through *sanyama* everything comes at the right time and in the right order. Just as an atom is that part of matter that cannot be divided any further, in the same way a moment is that part of time that cannot be divided any further. Time is neither an object nor a reality, it is an imagination. Similarly the moment and its flow are imaginary but it has a deep effect on the life of humans. During the course of *sadhana,* when the initiate achieves concentration and *sanyama* on the moment and its order of flow, then knowledge is received through wisdom. The main use of this knowledge is to attain the state of *kaivalya.*

The difference between any two objects can be known through the factors of division (they belong to), symptom and country (they come from). However, if two objects have the same division, symptom and country, it is not easy to differentiate between them. With the knowledge gained through wisdom the wisdom-insight of the yogi is so subtle that he is capable of understanding the difference between two such objects immediately, without making a mistake. As an example, from a heap of tomatoes looking similar if one tomato is picked up and mixed in the heap again, it is not normally possible to find the same tomato again because all tomatoes look alike Nevertheless, a yogi with "knowledge through wisdom" can find the same tomato again. At this level knowledge is intuitive which is how the yogi can find the tomato. But he ignores this power too and proceeds towards the attainment of *samadhi.*

*Viveka-jnana* or "knowledge through wisdom" is achieved through experiences without the need for external teaching. It relates to the knowledge pertaining to past, present and future on one hand and to the gross and subtle on the other. This is known as complete knowledge. After receiving it the yogi transcends religious duties and is situated in *Brahman.* He is known

as *jeevan-mukta* or liberated while living in the world.
Such a yogi is in the world but not of it. Through the
medium of *kriyas* induced by *Shakti* this "knowledge
through wisdom" comes by itself. If the initiate develops
any pride for having it, the knowledge thus received
reduces to the proportion of the pride. He should exercise
much care with regard to pride and should be a constant
witness over everything. All efforts and pride should be
dissolved in the *kriyas* of *Shakti*.

When balance is achieved between *buddhi* (intellect)
and *Purusha* (*Atman*), that is, when *chitta* is purified to
the same extent as the purity of *Atman* itself, then
*kaivalya* is reached. All kinds of *sanskara* in *chitta* good
or bad, and all kinds of impressions on the intellect are
washed off. The lighted chaitanya of *Atman* reflected on
*chitta* becomes absorbed in *Atman*, and then there is
entry into *nirbeej-samadhi* or seedless-absorption. Having
achieved this stage all properties and virtues become
dissolved in their causes. *Chetan-Shakti* has nothing
more to do, and that too dissolves into *Atman*.

**Subtle *Kriyas***
Normally through *kriyas* it is possible to understand the
purpose of jumping, rotating, laughing, crying or singing;
and, the person worries if he is not experiencing what
others are. But this is normal because no two initiates
have the same *chitta*. Therefore, the nature and
frequency of the *kriyas* necessary to thin out the
*sanskaras* and purify the *chitta* will be different for
everyone. *Kriyas* are proportional to the accumulated
*sanskaras* of each initiate. Some initiates may experience
sweating or sitting at one place or staring at a point for
months after *Shaktipat* initiation. Even though they are
not as intense as other *kriyas* they have their own
importance. There could be a link with past-life activities
and a continuation of the incomplete practices that were
performed in a past life. Since the bodily *kriyas* are gross

and easily visible to onlookers, the initiate is attracted to them and desires to experience them.

Some people may write prose or poetry on subjects that are not connected with their present life. Some people may begin to speak effectively and influence an audience. Others may demonstrate unusual performances in classical dances that were not learned in this lifetime. Some initiates may sound like animals, and it would appear to listeners that some animal is speaking. One explanation for this is that the seeds of interests that were pursued in the past life remain in the *chitta* of the initiate, and with the extra energy supply given through *Shaktipat* initiation those seeds germinate and sprout. The awakening of *Shakti* reverses the order of *sanskara*. Instead of *sanskaras* being accumulated from outside to inside (from activity by the sense organs), the accumulated *sanskara* within come out. Activities similar to what the initiate was doing at the time the *karma* was being accumulated take place at the time of *sanskaras* coming out.

### *Kriyas* and *Kundalini*
The movement of the *kundalini* takes place in four distinct ways, from the slowest to the fastest, and resembles the motion of an ant, snake, frog and bird, in that order. The slowest is the ant. Just as an ant crawls slowly towards its destination, in the same way the *kundalini* appears to be crawling in the *sushumna* towards its goal. The reports from some people about feeling a sense of crawling is indicative of the *kundalini* travelling at this slow pace. Some initiates feel that a fine and sharp small snake is rising in the spinal column. The movement can be slow or as quick as lightning. I can never forget the feeling of a sharp snake, which suddenly rose from my root to the navel centre like an electric spark, and moved along a curve. Some initiates experience the energy jumping upwards like a frog. And

the fastest motion one can feel is like a bird flying from
one point to another along the spine.

Just as life energy rises upwards in the stem of a
tree, in the same way *Shakti*, on awakening, becomes
active, grows and rises upwards on the *sushumna* nerve.
Different initiates feel this rising energy in different
ways, which can sometimes be accompanied by sounds.
Although any part of the body can have movements,
which may be related to *Shakti*, the main movement takes
place when *Shakti* rises in the *sushumna*, and the initiate
feels it. Not all initiates feel the movement of *Shakti*, but
that does not mean that it is not taking place. Some
people feel the movement at a later stage.

Some initiates experience a feeling of divine
intoxication in their body, as if they have drunk alcohol.
It becomes difficult for them to behave normally, and
onlookers judge the person to be drunk. Others do not
understand that it is the intoxication created by the love
of God through *sadhana*. The intoxicated state may also
include bodily and mental activities such as dancing,
vibrating, rotating and singing. As the spiritual state of
the initiate becomes higher and higher, the gross physical
and mental activities calm down and become normalised.
It is only in the middle of *sadhana* that the intensity and
frequency of such movements is noticeable. With the
dissolution of *sanskar* the renunciation of worldly
interests increases, and the *chitta* of the initiate becomes
absorbed in the *kriyas*.

Many initiates feel their body hot like fire and some
feel it cold like ice during *sadhana*. Some feel that their
body has been enlarged and some feel it has been
shortened during *sadhana*. There is no basis for this. In
fact, they are just feelings. However, I remember my back
burning like fire for a few days, and there was constant
itching along the spinal column. I would rub my body
against the corner of the wall for a long time to get

temporary relief, but the itching would not fully subside. After about a week both the burning sensation and the itching disappeared. As far as enlargement or shortening of body is concerned, it may be just a sensation, and in some cases it may really take place. We have recorded the case of Scottish physical medium, Daniel Dunglas Home, who was born on March 20, 1833.[1] Home could stretch his body up to 11 inches and contract it by a similar measurement. As far as the feeling of enlargement is concerned I can say with my experience that sometimes the feeling of expansion is so great that it feels like my consciousness is filling the whole room or even touching the sky.

Sometimes the initiate may find the body separate from himself, as if there is a reflection in the mirror. This is known as seeing one's double. At times one may see one's double while doing some activities. All this is normally experienced during a trance with closed eyes. Some initiates become afraid and open their eyes, which stops the experience. Instead, they should simply witness the event and realise that it is all a play of the unconscious mind—a kind of game, acknowledge it and then let it go. This is known as *swarup-darshan* or seeing one's own form/reflection, which is a sign of spiritual progress. In fact, it is the subtle body that has separated from the gross body. Many initiates travel to subtle or higher realms in their subtle body. For more than a decade I have had such experiences that have been described in *Kundalini for Beginners*.[2] All spiritual journeys are remembered, which is perhaps a natural and necessary part of the training for the initiate. However, attachment to such experiences and wishing them to be repeated should be shunned, otherwise one can remain a spiritual traveller without ever attaining *samadhi*.

Some initiates sweat soon after the initiation or in the middle of *sadhana*. One may not think that this is a *kriya* and may look forward to other *kriyas,* which are

experienced in time. Sweating is one of the subtle *kriyas*
that has its own cleansing process, and is a sign of
spiritual advancement like internal seeing and hearing,
happiness of *chitta*, creation of prose or poetry and
receiving intuitive answers to questions.

Subtle *kriyas* have their own place in *sadhana*.
Sometimes the initiate may not experience any noticeable
*kriya*, but may sit somewhere and not want to get up. It
may be difficult to explain the reason for sitting so, but
there is inner happiness or bliss, and the person may say
that he likes to sit. This experience of sitting may take
place before or after more intense *kriyas*, and one may
feel surprised at it. There may be fear that the gross
*kriyas* have stopped but the person should know that this
is an important milestone in the chain of experiences. If
the *sanskaras* for intense *kriyas* are still in balance, these
may begin again after a while. One should know that the
process of going from grossness to subtleness indicates
achieving higher states on the spiritual journey.

Some initiates report feeling heavy after initiation,
and don't have any *kriyas*. Feeling heaviness in the body
or mind is a *kriya* that stops other *kriyas* from taking
place. Heaviness is the result of *Shakti* trying to remove
some blockages from the *sanskaras* of the initiate and
convert them into proper *kriyas*. In doing so the only
outward effect felt is one of heaviness while inwardly
*Shakti* is doing its work. As soon as the blockage is
removed the mind and body become light and *kriyas*
begin. If this heaviness is not understood medication may
be used to treat it, which may hamper the natural work
of *Shakti*. With the advice of the Guru one should
understand this fact and let the heaviness take its course
for clearing itself.

Some initiates find they think about renunciation
towards the world, and they think of leaving all activities
or *karma*. This feeling of renunciation is temporary and

is a result of *Shakti* fighting with *sanskara* to convert them into *kriyas*. Initiates have several desires and attachment towards the pleasures of senses and related *karma*. The temporary feeling of renunciation is unnatural, and it does not produce real results. However, as *Shakti* continues her work of thinning the *sanskara* and inducing *kriyas*, the initiate comes out of the involvement in *karma*, and the attraction for sensual pleasures and renunciation fades away. The initiate gains firmness on the spiritual path, and makes gradual progress. It is not necessary to give up *karma* by force or by one's efforts. With the purification of *chitta* one attains natural renunciation in time.

Love emerges on various levels according to the *sanskara*. There is love between mother and son, between brother and sister, between two friends, between husband and wife in the pure form and love towards the creation of God. According to the seeds of love in the *chitta* from the past, a particular kind of love emerges and engulfs the initiate. True love is love for God, which is of two categories: devotion for some worldly returns, and devotion with faith and surrender without imagining any return. The former love is not real, and it increases one's attraction towards the world and its activities. Devotion to God with expectations is not love. The latter that is love for loving only, without expecting any return from God, is real love. When this love emerges, it overflows from within, tears begin to flow, and, one may sing, dance or express love through other bodily gestures.

When the average person sees something attractive he looks at it with astonishment and desires it. This accumulates *sanskara* in *chitta*. Another person who is a real devotee of God sees a *sattvic* (natural and pure) scene or an attractive form of the deity, which astonishes him, and as a result corresponding *sanskara* are accumulated. *Shakti* on activation brings these *sanskar* out and correcting activities are induced, which may be *sattvic* (pure), *tamasic* (inert) or *rajasic* (active). These representations, whether good or bad, result in goodness since all *kriyas* are intended to purify *chitta*. Both good and bad *sanskaras* have to vanish from *chitta* as both of them cover the *chitta*. All kinds of *sanskaras*, desires and vices have to disappear from the *chitta* to render it pure. Accordingly any kind of activity resulting from the activation of *Shakti* is good because all activity is working for the good of the initiate.

Some initiates experience strange activities that are related to wisdom and knowledge. There is a feeling of internal questioning and answering where one person is asking questions and another is answering them. One listens to them carefully, and notices the sounds clearly and one's own doubts are resolved by the resulting knowledge. Even this *kriya* is related to past *sanskaras*.

Some initiates have been concentrating and doing *sadhana* in past lives or earlier in this life, and have the related *sanskara* in their *chitta*. *Shakti* brings them out and the person concentrates on the same thing as before. As a result of former *sanskaras* there is interest and concentration on philosophy and bliss, even when one is thinking and working on other things. If there has been concentration on the ego then when *Shakti* is activated this process will continue which may result in the object of meditation, process of meditation and the one who is meditating becoming unified. Then the object of concentration shifts from the seen and seeing to the seer himself. Again all these states of meditation take place by themselves; the initiate does not have to make any effort.

In the *chitta* of the initiate there are many experiences of living in different countries, practices of different faiths and traditions, and several life forms that include animals and birds from several lifetimes. With the awakening of *Shakti* vast accumulations of *sanskaras* over time manifest as *kriyas* and thinning of *sanskaras* begins. A Hindu initiate may suddenly shout the names of Jesus, Allah or Buddha reverently if he has been a Christian, Muslim or Buddhist in a previous life. Understandably Hindu listeners may not like this but the Guru understands since he knows the possibility that the initiate belonged to another religion in some lifetime. The Guru would know that it is the annihilation of *sanskara* for purifying his *chitta*.

The initiate may speak in languages that neither he nor the listeners understand. Sounds of animals such as a lion, dog, cat, cow or frog, or that of a bird such as a parrot, pigeon or peacock, or some other life forms may be produced. Sometimes the initiate may hear new poems being recited within himself. Sometimes new poems emerge from within and the person may write impressive poetry, although there has been no connection with poetry earlier in his/her life. Essays on subjects, which have not been known to the initiate, begin to be written. An initiate may produce fine musical tunes or play an unfamiliar musical instrument, although there was no earlier musical connection. It is like a farmer suddenly turning doctor, or vice versa. Certainly, the initiate has lived a life earlier with these interests and these interests were accumulated as *sanskaras* in the *chitta*, which are now emerging for annihilation. Annihilation of all kinds of experiences, tendencies and interests has to take place before the *chitta* can merge into *Atman*.

### References

1. Guiley, Rosemary Ellen, *Encyclopaedia of Mystical and Paranormal Experience*, San Francisco: Harper, 1991, pp. 266-7.
2. Kumar, Ravindra, *Kundalini for Beginners*, St. Paul, MN: Llewellyn Worldwide, 2000.

# 9

# SUBTLE EFFECTS OF *SHAKTI*

There are certain subtle activities that are of the utmost importance, and which when attempted through effort alone would take up much of life. Activities such as concentration, origination of *siddhis*, balancing *karma* and annihilation of *sanskaras* are swiftly and automatically accomplished in a short time when *Shakti* is awakened and inwardly active. These are important milestones on one's journey to *samadhi*.

**Concentration**

Practitioners try to concentrate on opening the *Ajna-chakra* or eyebrow centre, but are unable to achieve it for long in spite of using a variety of techniques. This is due to a mind that is still involved with the world and unclean nerves, especially *sushumna*. *Prana* can pass through *sushumna* only when it is clean enough. And once cleaned it becomes unclean again because of irregularities in the lifestyle and eating habits of the initiate. Therefore, it is important that this nerve is cleansed regularly. There is a tried and successful method of *pranayama* for cleaning the nerves that is outlined here. The initiate can do this *pranayama* for 20 minutes every day, until *Shakti* takes over and *kriyas* are onset. Firstly, close the right nostril and inhale for a count of four through the left nostril (*ida*), then hold the breath (inner *kumbhak*) for a count of 16, now close the left nostril and exhale completely through the right nostril (*pingala*) for a count of eight, then hold the breath outside (outer *kumbhak*) for a count of eight, and finally inhale slowly to restore normal breathing. The process is repeated by alternating the role of left and right nostrils, and then starting again with the left nostril. *Pranayama*, while sitting in *Siddhasana*, which is cross-legged sitting with two heels pressing the *mooladhara* or root and *swadhishthan* or sacral *chakra* firmly and keeping upper half of the body straight, gives fast results. Three locks, e.g., root lock (*moola bandha*), navel lock (*uddiyan bandha*) and chin lock (*jalandhar bandha*) can be introduced gradually. With this process not only will the nerves be cleaned but also concentration will begin at the eyebrow centre. For details of *asanas* and *bandhas* refer to my book, *All You Wanted to Know About Hatha Yoga.*[1]

Concentration is achieved after coming out of *tamo-guna* (state of inertia) and *rajo-guna* (state of action), and living in *sato-guna* (state of purity). The *chitta* (mind-stuff) then arrives at a spontaneous state of one-pointedness on some subject or goal of interest. When the state of purity and one-pointedness in *chitta* is present concentration is effortless. Objects on which *chitta* finds it easy to concentrate are nature, image or statue of a saint or deity, temple, flower, a particular colour, an inner *chakra* or *akash* (sky), provided the initiate has stabilised on a particular goal. This concentration of *chitta* allows *pratyahar* (withdrawal of *chitta* from the outer world) when *dhyana* or concentration begins. With the awakening of *Shakti* the thinning of *sanskara* begins to take place, which arrests the fickleness of *chitta*. And then concentration on a spiritual matter takes place spontaneously, which is otherwise not possible through one's efforts.

Attention in *sadhana* can be fixed on an outer or inner object. The tip of the nose and the centre of the eyebrows are examples of outer objects. Inner objects are normally the six *chakras* within, the seventh *chakra* called *sahasrara* or crown centre is outside the body. Concentrating *chitta* on an inner *chakra* results in spontaneous concentration on some spiritual subject/ object related to the *chakra*, e.g., the deity, form, colour or sound. Inner *akash* (sky) has five forms: first *akash* is like a big white flame of light, within it is the subtle *akash* that is like a blood-coloured flame. Within the subtle *akash* is *mahakash* that is smoke-coloured flame, within *mahakash* is elemental-*akash* as blue-coloured flame and within elemental-*akash* is *suryakash*, which is like a flame having the colour of lightning. As the initiate surrenders to *Shakti* and the *kriyas* of *Shakti* work on him, concentration on any subject/object or one of the *akash* is possible. At this stage all knowledge of the outer world vanishes, and there is an experience of immense bliss. There is a disconnection with the body, and as a result *chitta* becomes more concentrated.

In addition to the above concentration points there are 16 other points in different parts of the body where *chitta* can concentrate. All concentration is enabled through *kriyas*, and not through individual effort. Therefore, the initiate should enter into *sadhana* with faith, and surrender to *Shakti* and abandon all efforts to fix attention on one specific point. These other points are: toe of the foot—where the initiate's eyes become fixed externally and the *chitta* is fixed internally; *mooladhara* or root-centre—which is spontaneously pressed by the foot which internally concentrates on *chitta*; anus—which contracts and expands causing *apana* life-force to travel upwards in *sushumna* to meet *prana,* which results in *chitta* becoming concentrated there; seminal/vaginal fluid—which travels upwards to the brain where *chitta* concentrates; *uddiyan bandha* or navel-lock—which is accompanied by concentrating on one of the *akash* or the chanting of a *mantra* or the appearance of Cosmic Sound; at the base of the heart—with increasing attention of *chitta anahata-chakra* goes on opening more and more, and concentration increases accordingly; throat-pit— *jalandhar bandha* or chin-lock can be applied spontaneously to stabilise *prana* in *ida* and *pingala*. This results in more concentration; *uvula* in the throat like twin *lingam*—the tongue reverts back in the throat and touches the flesh, a gesture known as *Khechari mudra*, *chitta* achieves spontaneous concentration and the nectar that flows rejuvenates the body; rotation/squeezing of the base of the tongue—this is the cause of *Khechari mudra* and increases concentration; the front half portion of the tongue—attention on this part results in creative poetry and more concentration; the base of the teeth in the upper part—which results in concentration; the tip of the nose— attention here removes the flickering nature of *chitta* and brings about concentration; the base of the nose— attention enables the seeing of the Divine Flame which results in concentration; centre of eyebrows—constant attention here opens the *ajna-chakra* or eyebrow centre, which is recognised by seeing the morning sun's colour internally, and concentration follows automatically; and, the base of the eyes—attention here results in seeing a flame with colours of the rainbow and concentration follows. These are the 16 bases of concentration.

Even though there are 16 identified points where *Shakti* can focus to induce *kriyas,* She can concentrate on any part of the body to bring about concentration. There are innumerable types of *kriyas* and concentrations, and it is not possible to describe them all. The procedure varies with each initiate, and two initiates will never report having the same experiences. Scriptures have recorded only those activities and *kriyas* that have been more common. Accordingly, there are *kriyas* and ways of concentrating that are not mentioned in scriptures.

**Origination of *Siddhis***
*Siddhis* are important indicators of the level of spiritual development. *Siddhi* means the creation of a natural

state in *sadhana,* which results in various yogic or paranormal powers. As long as the initiate is not surrendering and is using individual effort and thinking that he is the doer, a natural state in *sadhana* cannot emerge. When *Shakti* awakens through faith and surrender *kriyas* happen naturally. According to the nature of the *sanskara,* physical, mental and intellectual capacity and circumstances around the initiate the *kriyas* manifest spontaneously. The natural state in *sadhana* originates in five different ways: by birth, medicine, *mantra, tapa* and *samadhi.*

*By birth:* If the initiate had an active *kundalini* in his past life and had achieved a natural state in *sadhana* then this is recorded in the causal body, and it will manifest from birth in the next life. For example, such people from early childhood experience travel to higher realms in dreams, which is an actual soul-travel occurrence. The causal body of the individual remains the same in each lifetime and results from previous lives are stored therein. In this way *Kundalini Shakti* awakened in a particular lifetime continues to be awakened in all subsequent lifetimes until liberation takes place.

*Medicine:* Scriptures mention specific medicines that induce *siddhis.* Although no *siddhis* are seen in the present time through the use of medicines there have been medicines in the past, which brought about *siddhis.* This may be because the science of medicines is lost or the effect of medicines has vanished with time. A distorted form of such medicines is seen in opium, LSD and marijuana, which give an artificial spiritual kick, but have proved harmful in the long run. There must be freedom from these influences to maintain a natural flow in *sadhana.* Intoxicating medicines are not the right solution, and anyone who is controlled by them will have disturbance and grief in his life.

*Mantra*: Chanting of a *mantra* when its meaning is known and with reverence awakens the *kundalini* and produces natural *sadhana*. *Japa* or chanting of *mantra* is in fact the main means of *sadhana* in India. Chanting is included in most of the other disciplines, such as *bhakti* (devotion), *jnana* (knowledge), *dhyana* (meditation), yoga and others; because of this it is the leader of all disciplines. All disciplines of *sadhana* that include *mantra* are represented by the single word "mantra."

*Tapa*: Withdrawing from *chitta*, sense organs and intellect is known as *tapa*. With increasing renunciation one's *chitta* becomes detached from desires and pleasures of the world and the sense organs turn inward. In the end *Shakti*, which operates *chitta* and the sense organs, withdraws from them and turns inward. When this happens there is understanding of the separate existence and working of *Shakti*, and this is the start of real *tapa*. The initiate has nothing to do but to observe as a witness the waves of good and bad *sanskara* emerging and subsiding through the *kriyas* of *Shakti*.

*Samadhi*: *Sadhana* is represented by the state of *chitta* turning towards the goal of inner concentration. Achieving this stage involves the development of *satvaguni vrati* or purified tendencies/inclination first and then a concentration on the spiritual goal. Until and unless the mind and sense organs transcend fickleness and turn away from sensual pleasures, *chitta* cannot concentrate on pure goals. *Chaitanya Shakti* has to give up working with the mind and the organs and turn inward, which happens when the *kundalini* awakens. With this comes the natural state of *sadhana*. The eight steps of Patanjali yoga, all other kinds of spiritual procedures, and even obtaining the grace of the Guru are only intended to achieve this natural state of *sadhana*. After the awakening of *Shakti* when the initiate gives up the attractions of *siddhis* and remains alert towards his spiritual development *Shakti* begins to work on the basis of accumulated *sanskara*. This is the working of the natural state of *sadhana*.

Even after the destruction of the physical body (on death) the subtle body continues to exist along with its five subtle elements, and adopts a new physical body (on rebirth). The flow of nature in this way is possible only because of the synchronisation of *Chaitanya Shakti* with the nature. According to the accumulated *sanskaras* one is given the new body by *Shakti*. When the person resides in *Atman* then there is neither the activity of *Shakti* nor the appearance of any *siddhi*. When *Chaitanya Shakti* of *Atman* flows outwardly then the manifestation of *siddhis* takes place, while when it flows inwards it induces the natural state of *sadhana*. When the subtle body passes from one physical body to another (death and rebirth), the awakened state of *Shakti* goes with it, and one is given a physical body in accordance with it.

In the same way as the farmer does not carry water on his head to irrigate fields, but removes the barrier and allows the water to flows, the initiate can make *Shakti* turn inward through different spiritual practices. Like the water in the field *Shakti* is present in the initiate but because of *sanskaras* and worldly desires the attraction is towards outward objects, via the physical senses, and is wasted. When the flow is turned inward it proves benevolent. Those who have their *Shakti* awakened since birth continue to achieve higher spiritual goals. Others have to use various spiritual techniques, not to obtain the state of *Atman*, but to remove obstacles on the way to the state of *Atman*.

**Balancing *Karma***

There are three kinds of *karma*: *shukla* (bright or virtuous), *krishna* (dark or sinful) and *mishrit* (mixed). Acts that are performed in accordance with *sato-guna* (property of purity), religion and scriptures are said to be *shukla karma*. Acts that are performed in accordance with *rajo-guna* (property of activity) or *tamo-guna* (property of inertia), desires and the pride of doership are called *krishna karma*. And acts that are a mixture of virtue and sin are *mishrit karma*. Every act that an individual performs falls into one of these three categories, and all involve the "desire for the fruits of action" and a "feeling of doership". However, the yogi acts without any desire for results or the feeling of doership and hence his *karma* is neither *shukla* nor *krishna*, and his *chitta* does not accumulate any *sanskara*. This is the difference between worldly people and yogis. There should be change in how *karma* is thought about. Desire or attachment to fruits should be replaced by duty in one's *chitta*, and then no *sanskara* would be accumulated. There is more discussion about *karma* in Chapter 11.

After the arousal of *Shakti*, when the initiate is conscious of it working inside and outside, then the responsibility of events in the world rests upon *Shakti*. There is a feeling that the sense of doership was false and with this insight the yogi is reduced to being an observer. There is intuitive knowledge of God's energy lying behind everything in the universe. The belief that things are happening according to his will or against it vanishes. There is complete acceptance of whatever is. Such a yogi looks like others externally, and does everything as others do, but his *chitta* is balanced and unaffected by the fruits of action. Consequently the accumulation of *karma* ceases for him. There is no *krishna karma* and doing *shukla karma* does not create *karma* because of non-attachment to its fruits or desire for results. Thus the yogi is free from the accumulation of *karma* but those who perform actions wanting to have a particular result continue to accumulate good and bad *sanskaras*.

Due to the accumulated *karma* from many lifetimes desires emerge in individuals. When good desires emerge pious acts such as worshipping, studying scriptures or acting without wanting a particular result are performed.

Spiritual practices are done for the love of them, not because of where they might lead. When bad desires emerge non-positive actions are performed and the person acts in mixed ways. Desires emerging in *chitta* never vanish. According to *Yogadarshan* scripture, even after many incarnations in different bodies and in different countries, accumulated *sanskaras* in *chitta* and the desires that emerge out of them never vanish. *Sanskaras* becomes accumulated in the subtle body, and pass from one physical body to another in each incarnation. Due to these *sanskaras* desires manifest and once the desires enter the *chitta* they never leave it. Thus *chitta* remains the same wherever the person may go. Furthermore, passing a long time in several incarnations does not thin the desires, which emerge whenever situations trigger them. At what point the desires first became attached to the individuals cannot be known. Long before the availability of history, desires existed, so one cannot point out when they began. And since their time of ending is also not known, the desires are classified as *anadi* or timeless. Thus the desires/tendencies are timeless, continual and infinite in number.

Desires in *chitta* are so vast that they never end. This can be seen in the constant desire to live for ever, because of enjoyment in the sensual pleasures of the world. To confront desire one should find the factors, for its existence, and remove them after enjoying all pleasures in a balanced state. Although desire cannot be eradicated completely, it can be reduced so that it does not obstruct spiritual progress. One should become such that desire does not germinate when one comes into contact with the world and the cover of *maya* on *chitta* does not gain more weight. If desire can be constrained to such a level then its presence in *chitta* will not harm the initiate. When desire thinned so much that there is no chance of its escalation, it is known as *vasana-kshaya* or the "demise of desire/tendencies".

Desire/tendencies can be analysed in four ways: the "cause" of it, in what form the "fruit" of desire is tasted by the initiate, "where" the desire comes from and "who" keeps it going. Knowing these four factors and then reducing them so that they are ineffective or powerless will automatically result in desire dying.

*Sanskara* is the cause of desire/tendencies and should be thinned out. If the initiate can withdraw himself from the enjoyment of these fruits and keep the *chitta* balanced and if a person can stop it being influenced by pleasures, then further accumulation of *sanskaras* will stop and future desire/tendencies will die before being born. Desire or tendencies live in *chitta*. When the *chitta* is in a state of *tamo-guna* or property of inertia and *rajo-guna* or property of actions then desire/tendencies will be present. The initiate should prepare the *chitta* so that desire cannot enter. Desire depends on speech, touch, beauty, taste and smell, which give it strength. Hunger for these things results in craving for these sensual pleasures. Sensual pleasures increase desire rather than reduce it. Therefore, the initiate should maintain a constant check on the mind and sense organs, and should keep away from the enjoyment of pleasures, which can stop this cycle.

Desire or tendencies live in the *chitta* in four states: *prasupta* or asleep, *udar* or awakened, *vichhinna* or dismantled and *tanu* or powerless. Desire not acting is asleep. When a desire/tendency becomes active as a result of favourable/unfavourable events it is awakened. When desire/tendency gives up its activity and becomes quiet it is dismantled. The situation is comparable to the seed which when sown in the ground (asleep), on germination and with time, grows into a tree or a plant and bears fruits (awakened), and then the plant is cut down and thrown on the ground (dismantled). When a new desire/tendency awakens the former one is dismantled. This cycle of awakening and dismantling continues. When the desire is asleep, by doing yoga like *bhakti, jnana* or *karma*, or *japa* (chanting) or meditation, the desire can be made so much weak that it has no strength to be awakened, in this state the desire is *tanu* or powerless. The situation is comparable to a grain being roasted, so although it has the original shape it does not have the strength to germinate. In the same way when desire is rendered powerless it cannot awaken even when the initiate comes into contact with the outer world. This is known as the "demise of desire/tendencies".

When *Shakti* awakens and induces *kriyas* in the initiate, it strikes against the *sanskaras* and desire/tendencies, making them powerless and incapable of awakening. Desires live in *chitta* but at the *tanu* or powerless state; they are so weak that they cannot trouble the initiate. Thus *kriyas* are responsible for weakening the *sanskaras* and with it desire/tendencies. *Tamo-guna* and *rajo-guna* in the *chitta* become weak and *sato-guna* awakens and keeps growing. Mind and sense organs stop attending to the outer world and turn inward. In the end when *Shakti* breaks away from *chaitanya* and inertia, and becomes merged with *Atman*, desires/tendencies live in the *chitta* but are in such a powerless state, that their presence or absence does not make any difference. This is the importance of *sadhana* and the resulting *kriyas*.

### *Chitta*

Shakespeare said, "Nothing is good or bad but thinking makes it so." How true it is! No person is either good or bad. Everyone acts and presents his view of the world before others, which is seen differently by different people according to the kind of worldly glasses they are wearing. *Chitta* acts as a pair of glasses by which a person appears and is judged by others to be good or bad. These differences do not exist in reality; they are only in *chitta, sanskara* and desires/tendencies. So there are different states of different *chitta*, and hence there are different beliefs, different thoughts and different experiences towards the same object. The same person, situation or scene may appear good or bad, friend or foe, virtuous or vicious, sin or good deed, fair or unfair, auspicious or inauspicious, according to the background of the *chitta*. Jesus was loved by some and hated by many. If ten people are at the scene of accident, for example, all of them will describe the scene differently, although the scene is the same. The details of their writings will never be the same. Everything in the objective material world comes into being through interpretation. *Chitta* interprets the material world through the glasses of the *sanskara*. When the *sanskaras* have been thinned out and dissolved, the *chitta* is quiet and the objective world dissolves leaving the state of *Atman* or Absolute Reality. Thus the real knowledge of an object is uniform but different people see it differently according to the background of their *chitta*.

If there is disinterestedness towards an object, then real knowledge about it can be gained. This disinterestedness is the absence of desire/tendencies and makes available such knowledge. The real knowledge of the world can be obtained only when accumulated desires/ tendencies, distortions, thoughts and viewpoints are kept away, and objects and events in the world are viewed in a neutral and subtle way. Otherwise everything in the world will appear according to the state of *chitta*, i.e., clouded by desire/tendencies. Inclinations and intentions in the *chitta* can be seen through subtle seeing as scenes, and the seer is the *Purusha* or *Atman*. All determinations, desires, distortions and thoughts are seen by the changeless *Atman*.

Everything in the world, as well as the state of *chitta* keeps changing. Desires, tendencies, distortions, planning and dissolution of plans, everything keeps changing in *chitta*. *Chitta* is an inner thing when seen from the world outside, but the *chitta* and everything happening in it is external from the point of view of *Atman*. Dwelling in lust *chitta* becomes lustful, dwelling in greed it becomes greedy and dwelling in anger it becomes angry. Tendencies and inclinations are the currency of *chitta*. A *chitta* that has no desires/tendencies loses its existence. Thus neither the *chitta* nor the world with all its objects like mountains, rivers, cities and stars is permanent; it is only *Atman* that is permanent and stable. *Atman* and the world belong to different categories and there can never be a real relationship between the two. The whole aim of yoga is to recognise and know *Atman* in its pure form.

*Chitta* contains mind, *sanskara*, tendencies or inclinations and it is related to *Atman*, sense organs and the world. Therefore we can say that yoga has been developed on the basis of *Chitta*.

*Chitta and Atman*: *Chaitanya Shakti* of *Atman* runs *chitta*, which is part of inert matter as well as the living world. Just as electricity is needed to run a motor, in the same way *Shakti* of *Atman* is needed to operate *chitta*, and then the inert *chitta* becomes *chaitanya* or alive and active. However, with the association of its own *Shakti* with *chitta*, which it does to experience the material world, *Atman* begins to see the world as different from itself. In this way *Atman* enters duality, although originally it was non-dual, and *chitta* is covered with ignorance or *maya* – the illusion of the material and objective world. To maintain the illusion, ego develops in *chitta* and it thinks that it is the one that witnesses everything. Ego thus becomes associated with the phenomenal changing self, called *Jivatma,* and the real Self or *Atman*, which is permanent and unchanging, retreats into the background. *Jivatma*, which was at the secondary position, assumes the primary position; and, presumes it is the doer of everything. It then swings between pleasure and pain. The real *Chaitanya Shakti* of *Atman* reflects upon *chitta* and becomes *Chit-Shakti*. *Chaitanya Shakti* is the link between *Atman* and *chitta*.

*Chitta and Desire / Tendencies*: When the ego establishes itself as the doer, *chitta* attempts to get the fruits of *karma* according to what it likes, and hence, accumulates good and bad *sanskaras*. Depending on the quality of the accumulated *sanskaras*, certain desires/ tendencies are awakened in *chitta*. Desires/tendencies feed *chitta* and result in it being attracted to particular feelings such as *kama* or lust, *krodh* or anger, *lobh* or greed and *moha* or attachment. Desire lives in *chitta*, creates interest in sensual pleasures, awakens various tendencies, drives *chitta* and creates attachment with the world. Thus recognising and controlling desire/tendencies is vital for experiencing the bliss of *Atman*.

*Chitta and Mind*: Mind is the process of *chitta* that has thoughts and counter-thoughts, likes/dislikes. Desire creates tendencies in *chitta* and the mind works to achieve these. So once the *chitta* has been awakened by desire, the mind then plans how these desires can be experienced. Desire towards the world is inauspicious and the one towards *Atman* is auspicious. Auspicious desire gives rise to *sattvic* or pure plans, and one becomes involved in worship, prayers, *japa* and *tapa*. Inauspicious desire creates *tamo-guni* (inertia) and *rajo-guni* (active) plans and one experiences lust, anger, greed and attachment. However, all mental planning happens through *Chaitanya Shakti* without which mind has no existence. In general mental planning involves some activity with the world, which is why saints criticise it and encourage people to suppress the mind. But the mind is not easily controlled and it reverts back strongly, becoming difficult for the initiate to control it. This can be seen most in meditation where the effort and difficulty of controlling the mind is most evident. No sooner has the meditation started when out of nowhere will come the thought about the credit card bill that needs to be paid, or some other trivia. In this way the mind takes the attention away from the meditation and control of the mind is lost.

*Chitta and Intellect*: The process of thinking in *chitta* is known as *buddhi* or intellect, and is of two kinds. The first is the thinking that follows the mind. Its job is to see how the planning of mind can be carried out; it does not concern itself with whether the planning is right or wrong. The second kind of planning is that which makes the mind follow it. This intellect being sharp and wise decides whenever a plan arises in the mind whether the proposed action by the mind is virtuous or vicious, or whether it is good for others or not. The wise decision of the intellect is accepted by the mind. Whenever the mind and the intellect act with synchronisation, the action taken is benevolent for the initiate. Whenever mind dominates the intellect, the action is not good for the initiate.

Purity of intellect is necessary for *sadhana*. When the intellect is pure it can make quick and right decisions, which are acceptable to the mind. When the intellect is not pure it becomes incapable of seeing what is right or wrong, and it doubts the rightness of its own decisions. Purity of intellect is achieved through reading, writing, thinking, contemplating and being in the company of saints. In proportion to the purity of intellect the initiate's inclination towards renunciation becomes strong.

*Chitta and Waves*: *Vrattiyan* means "waves" that arise in the *chitta*. If *chitta* is quiet like the sea, then yoga is complete. But when it is not, waves arise in it, according to whatever desires are present. Hence to make *chitta* quiet it should be desireless. Desire awakens according to the *sanskara*; hence desirelessness depends on thinning *sanskara*. *Sanskara* is accumulated because of pleasure of the senses and contact of *karma* with ego. Thus thinning *sanskara* depends on purifying behaviour. It means that "eradication of waves" includes "demise of desire", "thinning of *sanskara*" and "purification of behaviour".

*Chitta* has four main activities: mind, intellect, ego and *sanskara*. It is only when waves arise in *chitta* as a result of old and ripened habits from the past that *sanskara* is accumulated. This awakens craving for the desire to be satisfied, usually expressed by the words 'I want.' Then the mind begins to plan how to experience the desire that is related to the wave, and then the intellect decides what to do about it. Strength from the waves gives the ego pride and temporary relief once the desire has been fulfilled. Unfortunately once this desire has been satisfied the *sanskaras* are not dissolved because there is more desire and so the endless cycle of craving-satisfaction continues. But if the waves of desire are controlled then all activities related to *chitta* become quiet. This is why *Yogadarshan* centres around waves in the development of the subject of yoga. Eradication of waves is yoga because waves arise in *chitta*. *Atman* also appears to be in the form of waves or fluctuations. It is only after the eradication of waves that *Atman* is said to be in its unalloyed and pure state.

*Chitta and Sense Organs: Chaitanya Shakti* originating from *Atman* interacts with inert *chitta*, from which arise the activities of *chitta*, i.e., mind, intellect, ego, *sanskara* and *vrattis* or waves. *Shakti* acting on the base of *chitta* is called *Chit-Shakti*. It passes over the *chitta* and contacts with the sense organs. As a result the sense organs wake up and respond towards the outer world by giving sight, hearing, smell, taste and touch. The level of active *Shakti* in the sense organs is known as *Chetna*. *Chit-Shakti* activates *chetna*, which in turn activates subtle organs, and then the gross sense organs come into action. Thus the root of everything is in *chitta*. When the physical body dies the sense organs are still present but they are not acting because *chetna* is absorbed in *chitta*, which is no more.

Pleasures of the world and the mind are connected through the sense organs. When *chitta* in association with the eyes sees something, this information is passed from the eyes to *chitta*. In this way all other sense organs turn towards the outer world and carry out the orders of the mind. For spiritual progress it is important to turn the attention of the sense organs inwards. As long as the organs are involved in sensual pleasures of the world, spiritual progress is not possible. When the sense organs no longer seek sensual pleasures and they stop, this is known as *dama*. When the connection of organs with mind is broken it is known as *shama*. *Shama* and *dama* together are known as *pratyahara,* which means that organs have given up the food (*ahara*) of sensual pleasures, so that the physical senses and mind are controlled. Without this mind cannot concentrate. When the *kundalini* rises through the body the sense organs withdraw their attention from the outer world and turn inward, which makes the mind comfortable and willing to concentrate internally.

*Chitta and Sensual Pleasures*: Pleasures of the world are inert like the inert world itself. It is only when *Chit-Shakti* interacts with the sense organs through *chetna* that pleasure gives happiness to the phenomenal Self or *Jivatma*. The same thing applies to grief experienced by *Jivatma*. The importance of renunciation or turning from the outer to the inner is to prevent external pleasures affecting the *chitta*, because this accumulates *sanskara*. It is not only that the accumulated *sanskara* should be thinned out, but further accumulation must also be prevented. With renunciation the individual does not desire pleasures and becomes disinterested in them, which stops the influence of sensual pleasures on *chitta* and the further accumulation of *karma*.

*Chitta and Vices*: Vices like lust, anger, greed, attachment, pride, jealousy, envy, and selfishness grow and live in *chitta* because of desire/tendencies. Similar to the four stages of *sanskara* and desire the vices too have four stages: asleep, awakened, dismantled and powerless.

All the vices remain asleep in the *chitta* until one or more of them are awakened when favourable circumstances are available. It is because of the vices that one is unable to perform one's duties, that life becomes miserable and there is an inability to break free of one's web. As the vices become stronger, desire becomes stronger, *chitta* becomes more flickering, intellect is diminished, interest in sensual pleasures increases and an unending chain of miseries continues.

*Chitta and Negative Forces*: There are five negative forces or *klesha* affecting humans—*avidya* or ignorance, which is the opposite of intellect, *asmita* or unification of *Atman-Shakti* with *Chit-Shakti*, *raga* or attachment to some sensual pleasures, *dwesha* or hatred towards some pleasures and *abhinivesha* or the fear of death and desire to live. As *Chaitanya Shakti* contacts *chitta, Atman* changes from non-duality to duality, since it now thinks the world is separate from it. This is the beginning of *klesha* or negative forces. Influenced by the *klesha, chitta* acts with a sense of doership or ego and accumulates *sanskaras. Sanskara,* desires/tendencies and vices are nothing but the children of *klesha.*

King of the five *kleshas* is ignorance that expands and grows in the form of the five negative forces of greed, hatred, anger, attachment and ego. Once ignorance is well established the negative forces are not eradicated easily. They too have four stages of existence like desire and vices, and they are rendered powerless through regular *japa, tapa* and spiritual activities. Ignorance separates *Jivatma* or phenomenal self from *Atman*, and then *Jivatma* searches for pleasures in the outer world. Eventually there is the realisation that such pleasures cannot bring experience of *Atman* and then spiritual practices are performed until the veil of *maya* or illusion is taken away. And then *Jivatma* dissolves or unites with *Atman*. Accordingly, the goal of all kinds of spiritual practices is the removal of the veil of *maya*.

Initially it is individual effort that attempts to remove the veil of *maya*. But there will come a time when the person will get tired. At this point there is a fatigue, a letting go of effort and an attitude of surrender. It is only at this point that the grace of God eradicates ignorance. This is the only way.

*Chitta and Ego*: Due to ignorance or the reversal of intellect, basically "inert" *chitta* begins to think erroneously that it is "active" *chaitanya*. Consequently real *chaitanya* disappears and this illusion of *chitta* remains. This is why *Atman* is known as primary witness and *Chitta's Chaitanya* as secondary witness. *Chitta's Chaitanya* is also known as *Jivatma* or *ahankara* (ego). When desire/tendencies and vices have been thinned the ego is also thinned and weakened because it needs the power of desires and vices to exist. Finally desire, vices and *klesha* are eradicated and *ahankara* or ego is reduced to its weakened but purified form. Awakening of *Shakti* and turning the attention inwards is essential for the dissolution of *ahankara* or ego, which is the false pride of *chitta* and generates *sanskara*.

## References

1. Kumar, Ravindra, *All You Wanted to Know About Hatha Yoga*, New Delhi: Sterling Publishers, 2000.

# 10

# ADDITIONAL FACTS AND ADVICE

## Guru

The importance of having a Guru has been emphasised from the beginning. Finding a knowledgeable and renunciate Guru, and pleasing him with gifts and respect, and doing *sadhana* according to his instructions bring success quickly. There are many signs of success. Taking a Guru as a parent and deity; serving him through body, mind and speech; and believing in the guidance of Guru is the first sign of success. If the Guru is pleased then all auspicious fruits come through. The second sign is having faith in the Guru and scriptures. The third is worshipping him and the deity. The fourth is not being attracted to or repelled by anything, seeing all in balance. The fifth is gaining control over the sense organs, and the sixth sign is a restrained diet.

## Fasting

Fasting is an obstacle in *sadhana*. Some spiritual disciplines advise fasting on specific days for draining out certain juices in the body. However, yogic practices and *pranayama* remove harmful juices automatically so fasting is not required. Yogis normally have a prominence of air in their body, and fasting can make the body very dry. Fasting is also linked with austerities and self-sacrifice, but *pranayama* is considered better in this regard too. *Pranayama* washes off physical and mental dirt and enables the emergence of knowledge. When all fruits are available through the single practice of *pranayama* why should one go for several practices or *karma*? Fasting may be useful for those who are not attracted to the path of yoga.

**Retaining the Seed**
It is important to preserve the vital fluid (semen for men, vaginal fluid for women) during the period of *sadhana*. Continual loss of semen increases flickering and instability in the *chitta* and *prana*. With this it becomes difficult to control the mind and maintain concentration. The main strength of the mind is *ojas-shakti* and it is this that is destroyed when vital fluids are lost.

**Food**
Foods that are sour, dry, hot and spicy, and cooked in mustard oil should be avoided. Green vegetables and butter and milk are recommended. Half to one kilo of milk every day is good to maintain natural fluids in the body. Too much milk and butter can be harmful. According to medical reports vegetarian food helps spiritual progress, while non-vegetarian food and alcohol retards spiritual growth. Whatever one eats it should be in a balanced quantity, neither too little nor too much. Over-eating destroys mental concentration and can upset the stomach, which will affect spiritual practices. Relying on vegetarian meals, especially during *sadhana,* increases *sato-guna* or property of purity, while non-vegetarian food increases *tamo-guna* or property of inertia, and *rajo-guna* or property of action. In particular, giving up non-vegetarian meals because of an awareness that meat is obtained by killing animals helps the initiate to grow spiritually since it involves compassion.

Any kind of food, which is not easily digestible, should be avoided. Food should be pleasing and give the body strength. Food cooked a day before loses its spiritual value and is therefore not appropriate for a yogi. Food left by the Guru has *Chit-Shakti* in it that flows through the tips of his fingers, and it is customary and useful for the initiate to eat that food. Eating from the same dishes as the Guru helps. It would be good to site the example of Swami Vivekananda here. The vessel containing the spit and cough of his Guru, Swami Ramakrishna, Paramahansa, was not liked by some visitors one day, and they wanted it removed. Seeing this Vivekananda picked up the vessel and drank the liquid in it before anybody cleaned the vessel and put it back. Special energy pervades in anything that is used by the Guru. By drinking the liquid Vivekananda proved his faith in and devotion to the Guru and was energised by the *Shakti* present in the liquid therein, which helped in raising his level of consciousness.

A strong and diseaseless body is at the root of religious, financial, sexual and physical strength, and strength is required to achieve liberation. Accordingly, yogic exercises and properly chosen food are necessary for the initiate. One should eat food until the stomach is half-full, should drink water a quarter-full of stomach and a quarter space in the stomach should be left for air to circulate. If a person feels that his stomach is still empty then more food can be eaten, taking care not to overfill it. Eating to the stage of a full stomach brings inertia and laziness. *Sadhana* should not be done either soon after eating or when hungry. Eating little and often is better than over-eating and at one time. If there is real hunger then one can eat a small amount of food and then engage in *sadhana*. Concentration is not possible when hunger is present.

When one is inhaling and exhaling through the right nostril (*pingala* or sun nerve), it is the right time to eat food, as it is the day of the mini-universe that is represented by the body. When food is eaten at this time no fluid is created in the body and food is digested properly. When one is inhaling and exhaling through the left nostril (*ida* or moon nerve), it is not advisable to eat since it is the night of the mini-universe of the body. Eating at this time may result in fluid spreading in the body and food may not be digested. If one is breathing through the left nostril then one should put a pillow between the left arm and body and lie down on one's left side on the bed. Inhalations should be through the left nostril and exhalation through the right nostril. After some time the person will notice that both the inhaling and exhaling is through the right nostril.

Just as a sick person has to take medicine and observe rules prescribed by the doctor until he becomes healthy again, in the same way the initiate should observe all rules until the knowledge of *Atman* has been received. Otherwise success can be delayed. For the person who has achieved the knowledge given by yoga and has become *siddha* or successful in yoga, no rules are prescribed. There are also no rules for the person who is in possession of *tamo-guna* or the property of inertia, and who is attached to the world, and is happy with this attachment without feeling the desire to change.

**Time for *Sadhana***
There are four periods in which spiritual forces are naturally active. Performing *sadhana* during these four periods produces good results: morning, noon, evening and midnight. In the morning between 3 am and 6 am or between 4 am and 6 am according to different schools of thoughts are most auspicious. According to medical reports and drawing on my own experience, the period between 9 pm and 12 midnight is best for sleep. One hour of sleep before midnight is equivalent to two hours after. Then between 12 midnight and 3 am one hour of sleep is equivalent to one-and-a-half hours. Between 3 am and 6 am it is normal, and after 6 am one hour of sleep is equivalent to half-an-hour only. Therefore, if a person can sleep between 9 pm and 2 am or 3 am, then he has

rested enough and is fresh for all activities. I can positively certify this with my experience when I used to do *sadhana* between 3 and 6 in the morning. Then one receives wonderful concentration for *sadhana* that is not possible at other times during the day.

Other good times to achieve *sadhana* are around noon (say 11.30 to 12.30), evening (6 pm to 7 pm) and 12 midnight to 1 am. Spiritual practices carried out in these periods result in a *mantra* becoming automatic and little effort is needed to concentrate. One experiences peace and bliss at these times during *sadhana*. When starting beginners should stick to these times so that later they can be more flexible. Those who are working during the day can choose from the other periods of time or use all of them according to the situation.

**One-Pointedness**
Practitioners normally complain that the mind runs in many directions and it is difficult to keep it directed on a single thought or object. Due to this scatteredness, the thought energy does not concentrate and there is no meditation taking place. Just as a "lens" brings all the rays of sun together and lights the fire, in the same way a "lens" is needed to bring all thoughts together to make meditation possible. Scriptures say that a mind without outward attractions is meditative. Therefore, one needs a "lens" to remove all attractions and bring thoughts together, so that the knowledge of *Atman* is lit within.

Saint Kabir said that instead of using the rosary of wooden beads to meditate with one should use the rosary of respiration. While exhaling there appears the sound of "ham", and, while inhaling the sound appears to be saying "sah", if you notice carefully. This is the automatic chanting of the *mantra* "ham-sah" by nature, which on reversal becomes "so-ham" that means, "I am That." "Ha" represents Shiva and "Sa" represents *Shakti*, and is a natural and complete *mantra* that can be capitalised to one's benefit. One should concentrate on the sound of "so" while inhaling and on "ham" while exhaling, with natural and effortless attention. In time both "so" and "ham" will disappear and *AUM* will emerge within the initiate. This is the well-known Vedic method, called *vipasana,* through which yogis have been successful in producing the holy unstruck sound of *AUM* within them. Once this sound is manifested, it can be traced back to its source, *Brahman,* and the result is Self-realisation. Anyone can practice this method while sitting, walking, lying so that it becomes a natural habit. This is one of the lenses.

Another lens is to believe with constant practice that the deity that is remembered for worship is within oneself. Begin to believe that the "I" with whom you address yourself is really the deity within. The same deity is Shiva for the worshippers of Shiva, Krishna for the worshippers of Krishna, Christ for the worshippers of Christ, and *Brahman* for those who travel the path of knowledge. Anyone calling you by whatever name, believe that your *chaitanya* or fully awake *Atman* is being called. There is one and single deity within known as *Atman,* who is being addressed in all possible ways and by all possible names. In time the Self within will replace the phenomenal self, meditation will become successful and you will be able to see and understand God in your cherished form. Thinking constantly about one's deity one assumes the form of the deity.

At times there may be confusion about where in the body concentration should be directed. The practitioner should not worry about this because the awakened *Shakti* will automatically take the attention to where it should be. *Shakti* within is the Guru within. Just surrender to it and follow its direction. Whatever *Shakti* wants you to do you should do and not do anything by your own efforts. Even if there is not much gain in a few days, one should not be disappointed. In time you will be pleasantly surprised to see the activities of *Shakti.*

## Obstacles

According to Patanjali's *Yogasutra* there are nine obstacles on the path of yoga. *Vyadhi* or disease is imbalance in the natural state of *dhatu* (*vata*, *pitta* and cough in the body, according to Ayurveda), *rasa* or juice (resulting from the food eaten) and *karana* or the group of sense organs. *Styana* is the non-activeness of *chitta*. *Sanshaya* or doubt is an indecisive state of mind. *Pramada* is the inability to follow the methods prescribed for *samadhi*. *Alasya* or laziness is lack of effort in removing heaviness in the body and mind. *Avirati* is the greed for sensual pleasures in *chitta* or the inability of the mind to withdraw itself from attractions. *Bhranti* or confusion is not understanding something in reality and taking it to be another thing, for example, a rope being taken to be a snake. *Alabdha-bhumikatva* is non-attainment of the state of *samadhi*. *Anavasthitatva* is the inability to maintain the state of *samadhi*, once it has been achieved. Unless the last obstacle of *anavasthitatva* after achieving *samadhi* has been removed, it cannot be said that the initiate is successful in achieving *samadhi*.

After beginning *sadhana* pain may be experienced in the body, cold, an upset stomach, loss of vital fluid (semen or vaginal fluid) unwillingly. These are not real obstacles and are not a cause for worry. They are symptoms of defective elements coming out of the body for purification, which results in rearranging the body. Seeds of hidden diseases emerge and subside by themselves. When these obstacles appear attention should be withdrawn from outside and effort concentrated on the navel while chanting a *mantra*. Chanting for some time will bring more comfort after which the urge to engage in *sadhana* begins again.

The only person who will be successful in *sadhana* is he whose present incarnation is the last one. Others are known to take time proportional to the number of

lifetimes they are lagging behind. This is why different
practitioners experience different symptoms and *kriyas*.

## Doubt

It is well known that the awakening of the *kundalini* is
not easy, and initiates sometimes experience doubt about
the awakening that has taken place within them. There
is a story in the famous scripture *Yoga-vashisht*. Once
there was a *brahmin* who began *sadhana* to acquire
*chintamani* or the touchstone. Due to his sincerity and
dedication the touchstone appeared before him after a
short time. The *brahmin* could not believe that such a
rare thing could appear before him so quickly, and cast
doubts with many arguments that it was not real. He did
not touch it and entered into *sadhana* again. The
touchstone also disappeared after a while. While he was
meditating some children who were playing nearby threw
a piece of glass towards the *brahmin* by mistake. When
the *brahmin* opened his eyes he was glad to see the glass
and thought that he had got the real touchstone after
long *sadhana*. He took it and sold everything and went to
a far country where he wanted to settle. When he
discovered that the piece of glass he had could not give
him the riches, there was no limit to his miseries. He
realised that it was not the touchstone he expected.

Getting a rare thing easily creates doubt in the mind
of the person who receives it. When this happens
comparisons should be made between the wisdom which
is given to such a person and those described in
scriptures, and then a decision made as to whether real
awakening has occurred or not. If the saying of the Guru
and statements of scriptures agree with one's experiences
then it is a real awakening of the *kundalini*. Experience
oriented knowledge leads one to *siddhi* or success in yoga.
Doubting the Guru is also detrimental to spiritual
progress. If one has reverence for *sadhana* then there is
also reverence for the Guru, and vice versa. Sometimes

doubt appears in the form of a friend to cheat the initiates, leaving behind misery. As such one has to be careful and vigilant if and when a doubt is created in the mind. It is doubt that removes the initiate from the path of *siddhi* or success in yoga. One who does not have *Atman* as the goal, reverence for the Guru and scriptures, and is doubtful, is heading for destruction. A doubtful person is neither happy in this world nor in the other world. Thus doubt is a dangerous thing.

**Restlessness and Disturbance of Mind**
With the awakening of the *kundalini* the accumulated *sanskaras* from several lifetimes emerge on the surface and disturb the mind, consequently the mind becomes restless. Steadiness of mind cannot be achieved until the mind becomes quiet and restful. There is a story in the scriptures that runs as follows.

A poor *brahmin* wanted to become rich by invoking a ghost. He approached a well-known *siddha* who had control over ghosts. The *siddha* told him that problems also arise from the ghost as well as riches, and advised him to give up his desire. But the *brahmin* continued to press and so the *siddha* told him what to do. After some time the ghost appeared before the *brahmin* and asked him why he had been called. The *brahmin* told the ghost that he should live with him, follow his instructions and fulfil his demands by his powers. The ghost replied that he would do so but he too had a condition, which was that he couldn't sit without doing any work, not even for a moment. The ghost continued to say that the moment he was not told to do something he would take away all that he had provided through his powers and destroy the *brahmin*. The *brahmin* said that he had unending work and agreed to the condition laid down by the ghost. Immediately after receiving the instructions from the *brahmin*, the ghost prepared a magnificent house, a beautiful pond, plenty of money, clothes and other things. In a little while the ghost had provided the *brahmin* with everything of this world. Then he asked for more work but the *brahmin* had nothing more to give him. So the ghost reminded the *brahmin* of the terms of the agreement and moved towards him angry and red-eyed. The *brahmin* was afraid and he ran to the *siddha* for help. The *siddha* told the *brahmin* to go home and fix a pole in the ground, and then ask the ghost to go up and down the pole without a break until further orders. The *siddha* said that the ghost would soon get tired and would leave him unharmed. The *brahmin* did what *Siddha* told him. The ghost had to follow the instructions and began to go up and down the pole. He was soon so tired of doing the same thing over and over again without a break that he requested the *brahmin* to release him promising that he would do no harm. The *brahmin* then released the ghost and enjoyed the rest of his life without losing any comforts.

Our mind is like this ghost, it wills and does things here and there, and cannot be quiet and stable for a moment. Restlessness and agitation are the property of the mind, just as heat is the property of fire. It cannot rest for a moment and continually creates *karma* through its activities. Therefore, whenever the initiate sits for *sadhana* after leaving behind all other activities, in that moment where the mind has nothing to do, like the ghost, it attacks the initiate with comments and criticism. To destroy the ghost in the form of the mind the initiate should ask the mind to go up and down the *sushumna* nerve, which can be taken as a pole running up through the backbone. The initiate should move the attention from *mooladhar* or root-centre to *sahasrara* or crown-centre and then back. This to and fro motion will make the mind tired and it will beg for release. This will destroy the elements of *chitta*. With the destruction of the elements of *chitta* the "light of *chitta*" or the experience of *Atman* emerges. Destruction of *chitta* is known as liberation.

Worrying about steadying the mind makes it even unsteadied. It is best to follow the instructions of the Guru and engage in *sadhana* without putting undue pressure on oneself. It should be remembered that it is the intention that is most important. Control is only possible over intention and not over the result of such intention. This natural way of yoga makes the ghost-mind steady so that it dies its own death with time.

Mind and *prana* are like a kite and thread. Just as the kite is tied with a thread, the mind is tied with *prana*. Regular chanting of a *mantra* given by the Guru tightens the thread that is *prana*, and then the kite in the form of mind is controlled. By chanting at the four auspicious times described earlier, the fruit is received proportional to the time invested in *japa* or chanting. A person, who can associate the chanting with the inhalations and exhalations day and night, will experience benefits in a short time.

The quality of *sadhana* is not always the same. Sometimes *sadhana* becomes well established in a short time and one finds happiness and bliss, while at other times it seems impossible to achieve. This is because the state of mind and body are not always the same. Until and unless one becomes immersed in *Atman*, this difference will continue. One should not bother about happiness or bliss, and should continue with the *sadhana* with faith and optimism. At the right time one will achieve peace in the inner *Atman*.

Through this process the body may also become thinner, smarter and more eager to work. This is because the earth and water elements keep the body strong and irrigated with juices just as rainwater keeps the mud soft. *Pranayama* makes the body thin, and strong and capable of work, just as the sun makes the soft mud dry and strong. This is a symptom of success in *Hathayoga*. Other symptoms of being successful in *Hathayoga* are a thin body, a smiling face, the appearance of unstruck Cosmic Sound internally, depth and beauty in eyes, an absence of disease, victory over seed or power to hold ejaculation, cleansing of nerves, lustre of the body, absence of greed, clarity and sweetness in speech and a pleasant bodily smell.

## Shakti is Always Awake

*Shakti* is never dormant, it always awake, but normally it is directed outwardly and is "spiritually dormant". When its flow turns inward, we say that the *kundalini* is awakened (spiritually). The outward flow of *Shakti* represents the involutionary cycle called *prasava-krama,* and the inward flow represents the evolutionary cycle called *prati-prasava-krama.* The outward flow of *Shakti* enables worldly accomplishments called *riddhi* and the inward flow enables spiritual developments called *siddhi.* Lord Ganesh, the elephant-headed son of Shiva and Shakti, is the benevolent god who provides both *riddhi* and *siddhi.* When *Shakti* completes its outward and inward duties it merges with its source *Atman.*

## *Yoga* Philosophy of Patanjali

Patanjali, in his classic work *Yogadarshan,* describes *Ishwara-pranidhan* as the most important method of Self-realisation. *Ishwara* means God Absolute. *Pra* means "direct evidences", *ni* means "certain" and *dhan* means "to comprehend". That is, when the initiate perceives the divine power within, directly and with certainty, then he is known as *Ishwara-pranidhan.* As explained in Chapter 9 it is *Atman* who witnesses itself, without the aid of any intermediary in-between. This is *Ishwara-pranidha* of Patanjali.

When *Shakti* is directed outwards it is known as *Chetna* or Consciousness. When *Shakti* turns inward with the awakening of the *kundalini* after *Shaktipat* or otherwise, it is called *Pratyak-Chetna* by Patanjali; and, *Chaitanya* or Conscious Being is the fundamental level of energy which generates the whole universe with everything living and non-living. *Chaitanya* carries the life energy called *prana*. *Prana* moves *chitta*, which is originally inert. When the *Shakti* reflects on the inert *chitta*, it collects the imprints of good and bad *karma* from the past, called *sanskara*; this reflected *Shakti* on *chitta* is called *Chit-Shakti*. *Sanskara* and the five afflictions, namely, ignorance, I-ness or ego, attachment, aversion and the fear of death, settle around *chitta* as concentric layers. The living being called *Jiva* or *Jivatma* erroneously assumes the role of the doer and thus accumulates *sanskaras* in one's *chitta*. *Pratyak-Chetna* or inwardly awakened *Shakti* begins to thin out these accumulated layers around *chitta* and purifies it.

Patanjali describes *Kriyayoga* as the combination of *tapa* or penances, *svadhyaya* or self-study and *Ishwara-pranidhan* or surrender to God. According to him the merger of individual consciousness with Universal Consciousness called *samadhi* takes place through surrender to God. Gradual annihilation of *sanskaras* and the five afflictions in *chitta* by *Pratyak-Chetna,* which is awakened by surrender to God, leads to the attainment of *samadhi*. However, the state of surrender to God is automatically attained with the awakening *kundalini*, which is most easily done through *Shaktipat*.

*Yogadarshan* talks about the combination of *japa* or chanting and surrender to God, which clean the *chitta* in time and awaken the *kundalini*. However, the process is slow and long, which can frustrate the practitioner so that he is not regular and steady in his practice. He may not be able to identify evidence of spiritual growth and so may be discouraged from continuing. Patanjali suggests another way, which is to concentrate on the picture of an elevated soul, reading the biography of that person and meditating on him to tune the mind of the practitioner with the mind of the elevated personality. He recommends becoming the disciple of an elevated soul or

Guru, and to approach him with humility and then receive *Shaktipat* from him. The *Chit-Shakti* of the Guru extends to the *Chit-Shakti* of the practitioner, who sits in front of the Guru, and the state of surrender to God is automatically obtained.

Having obtained the state of surrender to God, the initiate should practise *japa, tapa* and self-study, which will awaken the *kundalini* in time. It is important to practise without desire or expectation. Expectation blocks spiritual experience. This is the *Kriyayoga* of Patanjali, which is a preparation to the actual *Kriyayoga,* that is the yoga of automatic movements. *Ishwara-pranidhan* is then characterised by *japa* initially and later with the awakening of the *Shakti* of *Mantras*. The initiate now begins to experience *kriyas* over which he has no control, and that is why the process is called *Kriyayoga*.

*Shakti* is of three kinds: *Jada* or inert, *Chetna* or consciousness and *Chaitanya* or Universal Consciousness. *Jada Shakti* is the one that manifests in non-living things, such as hydrostatic force, the power of wind, electricity or lightning. This form of energy is raw, and has no capacity to regulate itself. For example, an electric bulb cannot turn itself off even when the light is not required. *Chetna Shakti* or consciousness regulates the senses, mind, intellect and ego of the initiate as the "discriminating power of intellect", and it can distinguish between right and wrong. *Chaitanya Shakti* is universal and creates all living and non-living things. It is the power that acts through the senses of the initiate and through which worldly acts are performed. It is the vibration of this high level energy, which is responsible for everything we see or hear. *Chetna Shakti* (consciousness) on awakening purifies *chitta* and becomes *Shakti* itself. *Kundalini Shakti* in humans is the *shesh* or residual of the Universal *Shakti*, which awakens from its spiritually dormant state when a touch of Source Energy comes through the Guru on *Shaktipat*. Since *Kundalini*

*Shakti* transforms the initiate through its action and discrimination, it is conscious or *chetan* and not inert or *jada*.

## Actions by Mind, Intellect or *Shakti*

At times one may not be clear about why certain actions are being performed. Mind, intellect and *Shakti* each give directions for action. Mind is the emotional part of one's nature and is easily impressed by dualities such as happiness and sorrow, love and hatred or pleasure and pain. When dominated by emotions actions are motivated by anger, passion, greed, delusion or lust, and are directed towards obtaining some favour, or the removal of something unfavourable. When dominated by the intellect, social and religious obligations, rules and traditions, and discriminates between right and wrong, just and unjust, and good and evil are taken into account. In such cases actions are balanced and may not be harmful to others or oneself. One is normally peaceful and steady while performing such actions. When dominated by the awakened and active *Shakti* within, the direction is marked with purity of mind, desirelessness and concern for right actions. The initiate can mistake the direction of the mind to be the voice of *Shakti* and act accordingly. One has to be careful to understand the nature of directions, which is better understood with personal experiences.

## Group Meditation

*Kriyas* in group-meditation develop usefully for most initiates according to their needs. One is not experiencing movements while practising alone may start and another may find that the movements are more intense in a group. However, more developed initiates who have reached the state of *dhyana* or meditation may find intrusions into their peaceful states because of laughing, crying, jumping, singing or shouting activities of other initiates. Nevertheless, a higher state initiate is generally not

affected by any activity when engaged in meditation, and
may be benefited as a result of his advanced spiritual
requirement. The initiate may decide after a few
occasions whether to meditate alone or in a group. This
is discussed further in the next chapter.

# 11

# PHILOSOPHICAL DISCUSSIONS—I

**Where in the Body is the Mind?**
Mind can be defined as the state of fluctuations caused by waves of desires in *chitta*. These waves or *vrattis* change from one object to another according to what a person is concerned with at that time. Thus, if there is pain in the stomach, then this is where the mind is at that moment. It is the same for someone with a headache. Here the mind is in the head. Where a thorn pricks the foot, then the mind is in the foot. The mind enables a person to be aware of pain. Therefore, the mind expands throughout the human body. There is no particular centre in the body that it can be confined to. The mind can reach an object several thousand miles away from the subject and unite the two at any time or place. This is why telepathy is a real phenomenon. There are no restrictions or limitations on the mind. It functions equally in giving awareness of pleasure and pain, yet it cannot be identified with any specific part of the body.

Mind is how the conscious self associates itself with the senses, which results in hearing, sight and so on. As soon as this association of self with senses is broken, *chitta* becomes restrained and inactive, and, the mind is freed from fluctuations caused by desires. In this way a state of deep contentment is achieved through the awakening of *Shakti* and the *kriyas* work to break the association in the mind of the initiate.

## Is it *Shakti* or Emotions that Direct Body Movements Outside Meditation?

*Shakti* on arousal converts *sanskaras* into *kriyas* or movements before they change into a passion or emotional drive. But, the awareness of *Shakti's* working comes only when the mind is attentive to the process, although the movements (*kriyas*) continue in all states of consciousness that is waking, dreaming and dreamless sleep. The initiate becomes aware of the *kriyas* taking place as a dream on awaking from sleep. Onlookers may also notice movements in the initiate.

Even after *Shakti* awakens the accumulated seeds of past tendencies continue in the *chitta*. This results in the ego reappearing and more *sanskaras* accumulated. It is possible from observing the daily activities of the initiate to see how much *Shakti* governs him. The initiate has to attain the state in which *Shakti* directs all affairs and there is conscious awareness that *Shakti* is the 'doer' in all working both spiritual and non-spiritual.

## Should *Sadhana* or Spiritual Practices be Continuous?

Spiritual practices should always be maintained; even in the midst of difficult times, such as when a member of the family dies, the arrival of guests, some function taking place in the house or when a woman is menstruating. Nothing should affect one's *sadhana* or practices, although alternatives might have to be found. Since the activities of *Shakti* take place at the level of the mind, outward cleanliness is of no consideration.

## Some Do's and Don'ts When Doing *Sadhana*

The initiate should not consciously concentrate on one part, such as, at *ajna-centre* between the eyebrows, the root of the nose, solar plexus or root-centre. *Chitta* with its elements of mind, intellect, *prana* and the senses should be left free to act without interference. It is also not necessary to sit in any particular posture. It is best to be comfortable. The sitting position can be changed if it is uncomfortable. Thoughtless awareness leads to heightened experiences, which are proportional to the passivity in the initiate. That is, the more indifferent and unconcerned one is, the greater are the chances of subtle experiences.

At times during *sadhana*, passions, giddiness or falling asleep may all be experienced. These are natural consequences of the *kriyas*. *Sanskara*, both good and bad, come to the surface for annihilation and are finally converted to passionless *kriyas*. Any increase in passions is temporary and changing. Accumulated seeds from the past cause giddiness. These seeds try to withhold the manifestation of certain *kriyas*. They should not be worried, as the *kriyas* will soon find their own way to emerge. Falling asleep is no ordinary sleep but "yogic sleep" known as *yoga-nidra*, which leads to a pleasant state of consciousness. The difference between ordinary sleep and yogic sleep is that in ordinary sleep a person takes about 10 to 15 minutes to wake up and be alert, while in yogic sleep awakening and alertness are immediate. Initiates have reported having several kinds of pleasant experiences during *yoga-nidra*, such as receiving instructions from the Higher Souls.

Sometimes, the initiate may experience some *pranayama* and *kumbhak*, *asanas* and *mudras*, and feel sick with fever. Again the initiate is reminded not to be concerned and to let things happen naturally. The person can sit or lie down if feeling feverish. A *mantra* can be chanted if the desire arises to do so but the person should not concentrate the mind on it. If the initiate experiences the *kriyas* immediately then chanting is not necessary. The purpose of chanting is over when the *kriyas* begin to take place. One should remain passive and watch the movements without any worry. Some particular experiences may precede a certain movement in the initiate. One may even find the way or the "key" to unlock heightened experiences. Surrender and passivity are the password.

Routine activities are performed with some desires, and these create *sanskaras*. Automatic movements that result from *kriyas* do not accumulate further *sanskaras*. *Kriyas* become subtler with time and finally disappear, leaving the initiate in a state of permanent bliss. Therefore, any reduction in *kriyas* should not worry the initiate.

## Internal and External Spiritual Disciplines
The initiate should not divide daily activities and spiritual discipline. He should remain absorbed in spiritual activities continuously. This is the only way to reach the apex of spirituality. Routine activities are taken care of automatically while dedicated to spirituality.

There are internal and external spiritual discipline. Internal discipline includes *japa* (chanting of *mantra*), *tapa* (observance of austerities), study of scriptures and religious books, worship and yogic exercises. External discipline includes the performance of worldly duties without passion and desire, and without interest in gaining reward for actions. Disciplining the mind in this way eradicates the further accumulation of *sanskaras*.

There are three kinds of *karma*: (1) *kriyaman karma* or the action in progress, (2) *sanchit karma* or accumulated effect of actions in the past in one's *chitta* and (3) *prarabdha karma* or fateful action. To understand them one can look at the three kinds of results which arise from an action: first—there is an experience of pleasure or pain; second—each experience is imprinted and stored as an invisible seed in *chitta*; and third—these accumulated seeds then have their effects in the future. The store of accumulation becomes so huge that it directs future actions without the person being aware. This is known as fate. Habits formed over several lifetimes become tendencies that compel a person to act to satisfy the cravings produced by these habits. The chain of cause and effect, which appears to have no beginning or end, forms a vicious circle. One has to accept and face these consequences, whatever amount of spiritual progress one might have made.

Breaking the chain of cause and effect means that the factors that created it, that is, attachment and involvement, must be replaced by non-attachment and non-involvement. This is the application of the external spiritual discipline. In addition to that the sense of *ahankara* or ego of being the doer, has to be given up which then enables freedom. It is the attachment of mind to the action and not the action itself that binds the individual. This done, there is no further *sanskara* accumulated. To achieve this requires internal spiritual discipline, to gradually make the *chitta* pure and tranquil. One way of achieving this is to seek the company of holy people. Such company is effective in two ways: first—one receives their blessings and direct energy that can transform *chitta*; second—it might be easier to follow both kinds of spiritual disciplines when there is guidance and advice from people who have experienced different stages. On realising this state of tranquillity one is not affected by any kind of misery and remains absorbed in eternal bliss.

The results of spiritual discipline can be effected by whether there is attachment or involvement. All acts should be done with non-attachment and non-involvement with fruits of action. If this is not possible then all acts should be carried out with a sense of duty. If this cannot be done all acts should be done as worship to God. Even if there is not total conviction about the hand of God behind all activities, the idea can still be nourished in the mind and heart. The idea that God creates everything and all acts are for God can be nourished. The fire of internal and external spiritual disciplines roasts the seeds of *karma* to the extent that they cannot germinate any further, and this stops the further growth of bondage. Finally, one lives with divine grace and eternal bliss.

## Constant Communion with God

When *Shakti* is awakened within and experienced by the initiate directly, the sense of doership is lost and the initiate becomes the seer. Now the initiate experiences the Divine as independent of himself and is in communion with Him. As soon as the aspiration and communion has ended, the ego comes back in the place of seer and the association with God is no more. Thus, uninterrupted remembrance of God means that the initiate is aware of the divine presence both when experiencing *Shakti* acting within and when involved with the activities of the world. Chanting of *mantra* is one way to achieve this goal. When the chanting becomes automatic as *ajapa-jap* then the divine power is felt directly and there is a permanent  connection with God. The constant presence of the Divine is also felt when inner Light and inner sound are awakened. Then the spiritual light within is seen permanently and the Cosmic Sound is heard through the inner ears constantly. Light and sound are the twin pillars of God. After some time the blue light or blue pearl is seen with closed and open eyes. This is a constant reminder of God.

The initiate now becomes the seer of the divine presence in everything living or non-living all the time. There is now direct knowledge that the movement of wind, flow of water, lightning and shining of stars are all working through one divine power. The initiate as a witness perceives all kinds of good or bad happenings in the world as acts of God. It is not through arguments or philosophical discussions but through systematic spiritual progress that the initiate arrives at the state of being constantly aware of God.

**True and False Inward Instructions**
Initiates receive two kinds of inner instructions. Active
*Shakti* within and *chitta* under the influence of *sanskara.*
Instructions from *Shakti* are for the benefit of the initiate,
while those from the *chitta* maintain suffering. In general
it is not easy to discriminate between the two. It is down
to the competence of the initiate to discriminate correctly.
Instructions from *Shakti* come when *sanskara* has no
influence, and the mind is free from all feelings and
attachments. When the initiate has advanced far enough
spiritually then the message comes through dreams,
visions, and automatic writing or hearing as *Shakti*
continues her work. *Atman* reflects clearly in the *chitta*
when it is pure. Hence, the trueness of the inward
instructions relates directly to the purity of *chitta.*

**Where is God in the Human Body?**
All faiths and traditions have declared that God resides
in each hair of the human body and every particle of the
universe. Nevertheless it becomes necessary to pinpoint
Him at one place so as to experience Him everywhere.
This can be understood using the example of a cow who
has the raw material for milk in its entire body but the
milk only comes though the udders and not through any
other part of the body. In the same way God is first
experienced in the heart when the heart *chakra* awakens.
However, as the *kriyas* become manifested God's
activation is experienced in different parts of the body. It
is the ego part of *chitta* in the heart that experiences
singing, laughing, crying, hearing or having visions. In
the same way the reflection of God is first felt in the
heart.

　　With spiritual advancement the initiate becomes like
a *ghata* or jar that is full of water, and the touch of water
is felt in every part of the jar. In the same way the initiate
too feels the presence of God in every part of the body and
in every creation outside of the body. The whole universe
is seen as consciousness and the play of *Shakti.*

**Vision of *Ishta* or Aspired Form of God**

When *Shakti* is awakened and activated, the "form of the desired aspect of God" may appear during *sadhana* or spiritual practice in the same way as the *kriyas* are manifested. Forms of Shiva, Krishna, Christ or Buddha may be stored deep within our subtle consciousness as *sanskara*, and emerge when the *kriyas* churn consciousness. The image of a deity may appear during a trance or as a vision seen when the eyes are open. This is not the realisation of God, as no one knows what God is like.

Our beliefs are based on social upbringing and family surroundings. Many faiths and traditions prescribe the method of concentrating on the image of your *Ishta* or aspired form of God, which is one of the techniques for meditation and Self-realisation. However, this method is for practitioners in whom *Shakti* has not awakened yet. Such a vision may increase one's concentration, which may bring joy, but then there is the risk of losing the seer within and stopping the thinning of *sanskara*. The energy of desire will always create form, and where there is desire there is *sanskara* even if it is at its most subtle level. So no attention should be given to visions of form.

For those initiates whose *kriyas* are already flowing freely no concentration is needed. Concentration should not be a goal anyway for these initiates, which will come as the *chitta* is purified. The *kriyas* should be given a free hand to thin out *sanskara* and lead the initiate towards *samadhi*.

Sometimes when adverse circumstances affect the purity of *chitta*, the *sadhan* or spiritual practices may become irregular. At such times the *mantra* given by the Guru should be chanted and/or traditional method of prayer and worship may be adopted until the finer state of experiences returns.

## Is Suffering Because of Separation from God?

There is no separation from God nor is there any suffering that is real. When *Shakti* interacts with the inert and inanimate *chitta* where the *sanskaras* are active, *chitta* thinks that it is conscious and is the doer of everything. To the inert *chitta* the transitory appears permanent and the unreal world appears real. It takes, the responsibility of everything that happens onto itself and when things do not happen the way they are expected then this is viewed as suffering, which in reality it is not. *Jivatma* or living-being in association with *chitta* undergoes (unreal) suffering and forgets the real *Atman*, which is pure, permanent and full of knowledge. In this way suffering is taken as real by the "living being", and because of this perception of suffering which is due to *avidya* or ignorance there is the thought of separation from God that is *Atman* within.

Destroying ignorance removes the veil of *maya*, and results in the end of (assumed) suffering and the restoration of the natural state of permanent happiness. The veil of *maya* becomes thicker with every incarnation because of the accumulation of *karma*. The moment one lifts oneself, the veil of *maya* is dropped, nothing remains hidden and the two (*Atman* and *Paramatma*) are found to be one. The removal of ignorance means extinction of ego or I-ness, which happens with the awakening and conscious recognition of *Shakti*. This recognition causes the consciousness to dissociate from *chitta* to become free to associate with *Atman-the-Brahman*, which is the demise of suffering and unification with God.

## Does the Guru Lose Power While Initiating Others?

Gurus belong to two categories: first, a Guru coming from the authentic lineage of Gurus, who is empowered as Guru by his Guru; second, a teacher who is not empowered in the tradition of Gurus and is not sufficiently awakened. In addition to one's own spiritual power, the empowered Guru represents the collective force of the entire clan, being the last in the line of Gurus. Such a Guru has unlimited power and performs the duty of multiplying the spiritually awakened ones bearing fruit after fruit. This kind of Guru is never proud of himself and he works solely as the instrument of *Shakti*. A genuine saint of this kind does not lose his power while initiating any number of disciples. The power remains unaffected, neither increasing nor decreasing. Generally teachers develop their own techniques of passing power in the course of their experience, although the basic rule remains the same.

A Guru of the second category, who is not empowered in the tradition of Gurus, may not be sufficiently awakened in the cult of spiritualism, and hence he might lose some power while passing grace to others. Egotism is a real danger for a Guru in this category, and may reduce his power, though not necessarily.

Some people think that by sitting with initiates in the course of spiritual aspiration *Shakti* will come to them automatically and a formal initiation is not necessary. And yes, *Shakti* is always present everywhere, but the aim is to kindle the dormant power of someone by an awakened one. It is like lighting an unlighted candle by the lighted one. Or to use an earlier example, the electric switch is ready and the current available but the switch needs to be turned on. The Guru regulates the power by assessing the well-being of the initiate, and then the transmission takes place, which is no ordinary transmission of energy. The Guru as a person is not so relevant, the physical form being only a vehicle of the Divinity. It is the Divine Grace that is present in him, which is important, and which is unlimited and irreducible by any number of initiations.

## Use of *Ashramas*

The main difference between an "ashrama" or "Centre for Spiritual Training" and a normal house is that the main objective of an initiate in an *ashrama* is *sadhana* or spiritual practices, while *sadhana* is just one of many things done in a house. While in an *ashrama* the initiate learns that life outside was totally different, and now one has to put all attention towards purifying *chitta* by dissolving greed, lust, anger and pride. Gradually one has to learn to dissolve *ahankara* or ego and all attachments. Such goals are more likely to be achieved in an *ashrama* where every activity and person is focused on this purpose alone. Both intention and practice are more intense, and one-pointed concentration is easier to achieve in an *ashrama*, and for this reason can be more effective.

When the number of initiates with the Guru increases, alternative arrangements have to be made so that proper training can be given to the larger group. Since staying with the Guru for longer periods of time helps the initiates to develop, and because the atmosphere of the *ashrama* cannot be found elsewhere, some initiates like to stay longer, and some want to stay permanently. In addition there are others who come to get answers to questions. It is through this process of enquiry that some people decide to become initiates. Lodging and boarding arrangements have to be made for them too.

A Guru plays the role of God on earth in the sense that his primary objective is to raise the consciousness of all of his initiates without discriminating between them. Like the divine father, the Guru brings up his children in the most loving way without getting attached or lost in the involvements. A real/advanced initiate does not need an *ashrama*, as much as a beginner, who is certainly benefited by the atmosphere of the *ashrama* for spiritual growth. It is not necessary that the Guru resides in the *ashrama* all the time; some duly authorised person(s) can represent him round the clock. Normally there are trusts and committees that run the *ashrama* according to the rules and regulations set/approved by the Guru.

Rules and regulations are framed in such a manner that there is required discipline for the spiritual growth of initiates. However, initiates must recognise that the comforts of home are not possible in an *ashrama*. The *ashrama* provides the basic requirements only. Where an initiate finds that his needs are more than what the *ashram* provides, then he can arrange such things himself. One should maintain cleanliness, safeguard the property and not get involved in the differences and quarrels of others. Fair relations should be maintained with others and greater understanding, tolerance and forgiveness of others. The courses, if any, should be attended properly.

The articles of the *ashrama* should be used properly with minimum use and a feeling of sacrifice for others. Rooms should be left clean after leaving, keys and other items returned. Books and manuals should be used carefully without marking them in anyway, so that others can use them again. Some people are in the habit of keeping the books and manuals in their possession to pass them to others unofficially, without the knowledge of the keeper. Such habits are not good, and they should be curbed. When irregularities of this kind occur the rules have to be tightened which affects the interest of genuine people who have to suffer the consequences.

## Solitude versus Company

Both solitude and contacts with people are necessary for the spiritual journey of the initiate. Solitude is necessary at the initial stages only for *sadhana* or spiritual practices, while later it is important to live in the world and yet transcend it. Whatever one has achieved in solitude should be solidified and tested so that it is not affected by events in the outside world. The initiate should remain aware of the effects of *sadhana,* and should be able to help others by solving their problems and guiding them on the spiritual path.

Although solitude can be found in the corner of one's house or in the jungle, real solitude lies in the mind itself. A person who is not affected by life lives in solitude even when amongst people. Once this virtue of solitude has been acquired it does not matter whether the person lives in the jungle or in the crowd or at home. A story told by Swami Vishnu Tirth is appropriate here. Once there were two friends pursuing the spiritual path. One of them got married and the other gave up the world and meditated in the Himalayas for about 20 years. The married friend fathered about half a dozen children while the other friend who had renounced all this talked at length about his spiritual attainments. The married friend appreciated the penance and *sadhana* of his recluse friend and talked politely about his own limited spiritual practices at home. In the evening the prostitutes living behind the house of the married friend began to sing and dance. The recluse friend was disturbed by the melody of songs and enchanting sound of the dances and said that he cannot live there as his heart was being carried away by those attractions. The householder then declared that his friend had learnt nothing in those 20 years of *sadhana* in seclusion.

The initiate should monitor his behaviour from time to time to make sure that the passions and attractions of the world do not affect him. Most of the Gurus in the tradition of *Shaktipat* have had *ashramas* but were in constant touch with people from the outside. This served the double purpose of testing himself as well as teaching and guiding the deserved ones. Outside attractions will always invade the mind but the *chitta* must be kept unaffected by them by observing them and not acting on them. Once the purity of *chitta* has been attained and realisation of the Self or *Atman* has taken place then living in the world or in seclusion does not make any real difference.

While practising in solitude the initiate should sit in groups to see whether calm can be maintained or whether it requires effort. If effort is required then there is still more for the initiate to learn and experience. Thus neither solitude nor contacts is sufficient on its own for spiritual perfection. The two complement each other and make the initiate complete. Training or *sadhana* in solitude makes the initiate strong enough to live an effective practical life. This helps to achieve the spiritual goal more quickly.

## *Sadhana* for a Married Woman Who is at Home

Married women have to play a double role at home: Looking after their husband and children, and taking care of domestic duties. They are more sensitive and emotional than men, so that when they show any spiritual interest, they can progress faster than men towards *samadhi*. According to the traditions, especially in the East, a woman's life is one of sacrifice. If she can devote herself to her husband and others selflessly and without desire, then she can redirect her attitude of love, service and devotion easily to God. In orthodox Indian tradition the husband represents God for her, and if she takes it seriously and sincerely, she can rise to the highest spiritual peak in a short time. Two points need to be mentioned here: firstly, that this reverence for the husband may not exist in other faiths and traditions, where male and female are seen as equal; secondly, the husband has to have the qualifications and behaviour that qualify him to be a representative of God. This said, there are innumerable examples of women, especially in India, who have reached spiritual heights through sincere service and devotion to their husbands, whether their husbands deserved it or not. Everyone has to choose an ideal or deity to worship as a representative of God, and women can have this spiritual arrangement naturally, which can lead them to being a saint. However, I caution here that I am not advocating that all women adopt this system. Where the husband is not sensitive or perceptive to what his wife is trying to achieve through him there is a danger that the ego will take over, and what once had the potential for a beautiful and pure spiritual relationship changes into one of abuse and exploitation. The method is given here as one of the methods that can be adopted by a woman if it suits her.

Both the feminine nature of women and the masculine nature of men are so fixed and strong that they are born as the same sex in their next incarnation. Many people can remember their several past lives lived both as men and women. I have described some cases in my book, *Secrets of Kundalini Awakening* (2002).[1] A woman medium in USA remembered her past seven lives, four as a woman and three as a man. Even when one is born with different sex, or when one transmigrates to an animal or other form of life, the basic nature of masculinity or femininity remains the same. This might account for a woman who is born as a man but who is aware of having had a feminine nature in the past and who looks for a relationship with another man, known as homosexuality. And in the same way a man who has been born as a woman looks for another woman for a lesbian relationship. However, the purpose of living both sexes in different lives is to balance the feminine and masculine natures, or between sentimentality and intellectuality, to arrive at Self-realisation.

A natural relationship is of that between a man and a woman who are living as husband and wife. The woman represents *Shakti* who is Goddess in higher/subtle realm and mistress in physical realm. She creates the universe as female energy of God, and even God cannot function without her. If a woman understands this important aspect of her, and lives as mistress with an attitude of surrender and service, without a sense of doership or ego and full of sacrifice, she can rise to the level of goddess in one lifetime. However, having understood and practised devotion and surrender within the marriage, she should take a Guru for further emancipation, since a husband cannot replace a Guru. There is no harm if both husband and wife take the same Guru. Old orthodox beliefs that disciples of one Guru are brother and sister does not really apply, since all souls are independent and unique, irrespective of the relations they have on the physical plane. When I talked with my father through a medium eight years after his death, in 2000, he told me that we are not father and son, and that we should talk as two fellow souls. So any two people can take the same Guru, whatever their relationship. In fact, having different Gurus and living in the same family can bring controversial discussions and discord between the members.

Leaving the house and family for spiritual purposes is not advisable for either the wife or the husband. From a woman's point of view it is good to purify her *chitta* through selfless service to the family, and to follow the instructions of the Guru in *sadhana* at the same time. There is no need to wait for a favourable time; any time is favourable and practice can be done without giving up the family, since this will amount to duties being neglected. If she waits, then this waiting may be indefinite. Many who left their families before the time was right suffered and repented later. God or Self can be realised right where you are under all existing conditions.

It is appropriate here to quote the example of three famous saints. Saint Eknath, Saint Tukaram and devotee poet Narsingh Mehta arrived at the same time in the temple of Pandharpur, Maharashtra, India. As Tukaram was entering the temple, Eknath was coming out. He had just been praying to God saying, "God Almighty, you have given me a wife who is according to my liking, and that is why I could devote myself to you. If you would not have given me such a wife, I could not have found you. Oh God your compassion is endless." Just when Eknath came out, Tukaram entered and kept on looking at the image of God, his heart full of devotion and tears flowing from his eyes. He prayed to God saying, "Oh God, how compassionate you are! By giving me such a quarrelsome and rough-natured wife you have acted so kindly to me. If you had given me a beautiful and obedient wife, then maybe I would have devoted myself to her rather than to you. By giving a fighting woman to me you have attracted me towards you. Instead of being involved in the love of my wife, I am involved in your love. It is only because of such a woman that I am drawn towards you. I am so grateful to you."

Just after Tukaram came out, devotee poet Narsingh Mehta entered with his sound instrument, singing songs of devotion with every part of his body dancing with the love of God. His wife had died sometime ago. He prayed with the following words, "Oh God, my wife has left me, it is so good. Now I am free of all worldly involvements and I can devote myself to you completely. You have removed the worldly obstacle from my path, I am so grateful to you."

All three saints experienced God differently and in different circumstances. Outside conditions will keep coming and going in different forms. If one can keep the attention inclined towards God and always remain thankful then one can be happy and satisfied, and travel on the spiritual path successfully.

## The Place of *Sadhana*
The proper atmosphere is of great help in advancing spirituality. After practising regularly and strengthening the system it does not matter where the practice is carried out. It is found that *prana* or spiritual forces are high on top of hills or mountains and near flowing water such as a river. That is why *ashramas* are normally built at such places. One finds a natural concentration at such

places without extra efforts. Spiritual practice somewhere where activities are full of passions and desires result in the mind being adversely affected. There is little *prana* that can help concentration at such places. In the same way that still water is needed to see a reflection in a lake so a still mind and a quiet atmosphere is needed to see *Atman*. However, it is not so easy to live at such places of quiet and natural beauty and practise because of the duties of the world. In this case, a room in one's house can be fixed where others would not go and where eating, drinking or carrying shoes would not take place. With regular practice the room becomes filled with *Chit-Shakti* and concentration develops automatically. Those who do not have a house like that can find a place in a temple, a garden or some religious centre where the effect of outside atmosphere is minimum.

## Householder versus *Brahmachari* or Celibate

The method of *Shaktipat* is open to worldly as well as unworldly people; so there are no restrictions. As a householder one has to live with all the activities and requirements of daily life, without getting involved with them and work towards minimising needs. All activities are performed with a sense of duty and detachment from the fruits of all actions. By living with pleasure and pain one is in fact above them. This is a preparation for the second stage of *brahmacharya* or celibacy. A celibate is someone who has withdrawn from the activities of the world and has no desire for pleasure or enjoyments of any kind. His life is full of service and sacrifice. There is constant study of scriptures, endurance of suffering, patience, and a rising above dualities such as respect and disrespect. One has to achieve near perfection in these areas before being recognised as a saint. Due to this, practitioners are warned before choosing this spiritual path since it requires much courage and withdrawal from the pleasures of life.

However, the two types of initiates are not completely exclusive of each other. As the celibate can inspire the householder, so the celibate or recluse depends on the householder for some of his worldly needs. Therefore, coordination between the two is necessary. In any case, the life of the recluse is more difficult in the sense that whether one receives help for needs or not, satisfaction has to be maintained under all circumstances.

## References

1. Kumar, Ravindra, *Secrets of Kundalini Awakening,* New Delhi: Sterling Publishers Pvt. Ltd., 2002.

# 12

# PHILOSOPHICAL DISCUSSIONS—II

## The Uncertainty of Life

In spite of much investigation and many theories it has not been possible to predict how long someone will live. We never know when we will breathe our last breath and be summoned back by Almighty. Death is watching us constantly, and the moment we are unguarded it can grab us. In general, the closer one is to death, the more attachment there is to life and the world. Given this it is a pity to waste time by gossip, worldly entertainments and being attached to any kind of work. It is easy to flow with the current of worldly attachments but difficult to stop and think about the purpose of life. It is only human beings, who can discriminate between what is good and what is bad, no other forms of life can discriminate to this level. In other life forms their discrimination stops at either enjoyment or suffering. No one knows in what *yoni* (life form) one lived in former incarnation(s) and what virtuous deeds might have been performed in order to be born as a human in this incarnation. A person might have been a cockroach, a horse, a thief, a beggar or a saint in a past life. To be lucky enough to have been born as a human, it is pitiful if life is only about earning money, and/or gaining power and position. Only a human being can think and act, and only a human can thin out the effects of previous life actions. The fortunate one who can set his eye on the actual goal of his achievement, that is, unmanifested Almighty God, is rare.

*Prana*, mind, intellect and the senses are conscious of the external material world and unaware of the Soul. This is why the unreal world appears real. *Atman* and *Paramatma* are so subtle that awareness about them can only come through realisation brought about by long and untiring observation, guidance and patience. In the past people knew the importance of *satsang* (company of religious or saintly persons) and "spiritual camps". They would stay with such people for a few days after which they would be cheerful and energetic. Gatherings like these also offer the opportunity to ponder over the nature of existence and the goal of life. Advancements in science and technology and fast living have reduced the frequency of spiritual camps, and as a result, hollowness and insecurity have crept in. It is recommended that such camps should be organised from time to time, so that people can break out of routine and receive the chance of taking the first step towards knowing truth. There are yoga camps for initiates, which are advanced since they involve people who have already been initiated on the spiritual path.

**Yoga Camp and Initiates**

Although readers may know what the word "yoga" means, it is good to point out here that by yoga one understands *hathayoga* only, which is a set of *asanas* or yogic postures. *Hathayoga* is only a part/means of "yoga", which means "the union of Soul and Supersoul", that is the goal attained in *samadhi*. In yoga camp different aspects of attaining *samadhi* are discussed and/or practised. Normally initiates would perform *sadhana* two, three or four times a day, according to their routines, and would attend to lectures and question-answer sessions as scheduled. The following conditions are recommended for use in such camps.

1. The camp is open for initiates from the line of Gurus or the defined system of yoga only.

2. Children should not be brought along since they cause interruption in *sadhana* and unnecessary trouble to their parents.

3. Different entertainments and having a choice of delicious or special meals should not be encouraged. Gossiping should be stamped out. An attitude of simple living and high thinking should be maintained. The camps are meant only for earnest seekers of knowledge.

4. Attendees should carry clothing and other articles of use according to the prevailing climate.

5. Attendees should be punctual in attending lectures, discourses, *satsang* and other activities organised in the camp.

6. Attendees should come prepared to stay for the entire period of the camp. People who leave in-between affect the spiritual atmosphere of the camp.

The most common complaint made about the spiritual path is the lack of time available to be committed and serious about it. If a person lives on average between 70 and 80 years, if we then deduct nearly 30 years for sleeping, another 30 years for professional activities and about 15 years for eating, entertainment, travelling or caring for family, there is less than five years left for spiritual pursuits. Most people say they cannot find time for spiritual activities. All kinds of excuses are made, such as a wife or husband or child is sick, it is not possible to get leave from the office, or the need to travel for a particular job; all these will be offered as excuses for not doing so. So an appeal is made here to all readers to find time to attend a spiritual/yoga camp, if and when they come to know about it.

Everyone has work responsibilities and no one can afford to drop out of work. It is not in our nature to sit for long periods without doing anything. Therefore, it cannot be said that one should give up work per se, but should give up the attachment to whatever work one is doing. It is "not the action" but involvement in the action in terms of wanting a certain result that binds a person. If actual work is given up without the attachment to work being given up first then it is wrong. On the other hand, if attachment to work is first given up, and the person continues as a duty or service to God, without caring about what the fruits of this action would be, then this is known as sacrifice, worship or *yagna* (sacrifice in holy fire) which purifies the mind. Initiates attending the camp are fortunate as the "fire of purification" has been lit in them through *Shaktipat* and the purification of *chitta* is taking place automatically through the *kriyas*. All that is now required is for the person to be regular in *sadhana* and have patience. One should have faith that God will certainly help everyone and draw everyone who shows the slightest effort and sincerity close to Him.

**Period for Self-realisation**

It has been mentioned in Chapter 1 that the period of Self-realisation varies from three, six, and nine to twelve years for different initiates depending on which of the four different categories they belong to. Yet some initiates do not progress spiritually even after 20, 30, 40 or 50 years after getting *Shaktipat*.

In fact, three to 12 years is only a rough estimate while in reality no specific period can be set, because variations are so large. This is because initiates are unable to maintain the level of faith, surrender, detachment and continuity of *sadhana* or spiritual practices necessary. In spite of a conscious will to surrender, the ego will not allow real surrender to the Guru and *Shakti*. Although it has been mentioned earlier that surrender is made to the Higher Consciousness in the Guru and not to the physical Guru, yet most people are unable to break free of the ego's confinement. The attachment to pleasures and possessions of the world is too great, and the amount of time being devoted to *sadhana* is not enough. These are the reasons that the spiritual journey becomes so long and uncertain for many initiates. Yet there are initiates who realise Self or *Atman* within a few years, even months, and the profound art of *Shaktipat* will always continue to exist.

## *Sanskara* and Memory

*Sanskara* are the accumulated impressions of good and bad experiences on *chitta*. These impressions are thoughts, mental tendencies and resolves which finally become destiny or fixed events in our lives. *Sanskaras* appear as "memory waves" through one's mental tendencies or inclinations known as *vasanas*. After *Shaktipat* initiation, the *sanskaras* gradually stop manifesting either as memory waves or as mental tendencies and the formation of destiny is also broken. Impressions are converted into *kriyas,* which lead to a gradual demise of *sanskaras.*

## Self-efforts and *Pratyahar*

*Sanyama* or individual controlling efforts by an initiate is helpful only up to the point of detachment from worldly attractions, which removes obstacles from the path of *Shakti*. From here *Shakti* takes over. With its inward progress, the senses dissolve into the causal mind; the mind dissolves into intellect, intellect into ego and ego into *chitta*. Five elements (earth, water, fire, air and *akash* or sky) also dissolve with the purification of impressions, and *kriyas* begin the path of spiritual progress.

When *chaitanya* or conscious self reflects on *chitta*, knowledge about the external world is received by the intellect. But because of *pratyahar* the external knowledge has no influence on the *chitta*. Noises will be heard outside, that cannot be stopped, but they will not affect the *chitta* and it will not become restless. Thus outside awareness continues without affecting the *chitta*. However, it is *Shakti* that brings about *pratyahar* and not one's efforts only.

## Losing External Awareness
External awareness can be lost, when one-pointed awareness of an object arises during *kriyas,* and the mind focuses fully on that, thus losing outside awareness. It can also be lost when the contact between Soul and *chitta* is lost with the completion of *chitta's* modifications. Then *asampragyat samadhi* or thoughtless absorption occurs and all external knowledge is lost. Since external awareness is due to the activity of *chitta*, the moment its working stops, external knowledge vanishes.

## Mind and Intellect
With the interaction of *Shakti* the *kriyas* of mind and intellect take place in the *chitta*. Mind is responsible for *sankalpa* and *vikalpa,* that is, determinations and indifferences or resolves and dissolution of resolves. Intellect, on the other hand, is the process of thinking. Before spiritual perfection is achieved, it is the intellect that controls the mind, whereas later it is the mind that controls the intellect. A worldly person is an example of the first kind while the latter is the case with a *jnani* or wise person.

## Repetition or Changing of *Kriyas*
*Kriyas* take place according to whatever impressions are in *chitta*. When *chitta* has many impressions, *Shakti* has more work to do and *prana* or life energy is more active to dissolve them. When *prana* is extremely active it is known as *vikshipt* (restless) *prana*. When impressions of similar nature exist in bulk, related *kriyas* may continue for several years, without changing. However, if the impressions are few then the related *kriyas* will take place for a day or two, then they will either stop or change

to new ones. Since *kriyas* take place for the purification of *chitta*, the initiate should not worry about whether they change or remain the same. Cooperation with *Shakti* in letting it work without interference is all that is needed.

### *Jnani* (Knower of Truth) and *Yogi*
There are two states of *samadhi*: meditative and awakened. *Samadhi* is attained after following a yogic path and purifying the *chitta*. Intellect is then based on truth rather than on impressions. At this point steadiness in *Atman* or Self is acquired. A stage comes when the events of the world do not affect the mind at all and there is constant experience of *pure consciousness* everywhere. It is then that one acquires the state of "awakened *samadhi*". One experiences the bliss of *samadhi* even in the awakened state. A person living with "awakened *samadhi*" is said to be a *jnani,* who is certainly superior to a yogi who still has meditative *samadhi*. In other words, a yogi with meditative *samadhi* eventually becomes the *jnani* with awakened *samadhi*.

There are seven states of intellect described in *Yogadarshan* by Patanjali. The state of *samadhi* is only the fourth, the other three are higher states that are subsequent to the state of *samadhi*. *Sadhana* is necessary only up to the fourth state; thereafter "surrender" becomes the path.

### Feeling of Another Spirit Entering the Body
There are two situations in which an experience of some spirit entering the body takes place. Commonly it is after the death of someone close that a person mourns and weeps continuously for many days. In such a situation the mind becomes weak and the person thinks about irrelevant things and imagines terrible calamities. He may feel that the dead relative's spirit or some other spirit has entered into him or her. When this happens he loses his consciousness, which can be seen by others.

For those who are involved in yoga and *sadhana* and in whom *Shakti* is active, an outside spirit can do no damage to them. Such a person's spiritual forces are awakened and no untoward spirit can enter into such an initiate. There are times when Mother *Kundalini* may feel like a spirit, when the person experiences activities in various parts of the body. Furthermore, when *Shakti* becomes very gracious she may be directly felt and experienced as talking to the initiate as another spirit, giving advice and protecting the initiate. When this happens, the body is filled with a new charge and there is no need for fear. There is no chance of any harm even if one sees terrible things or bad omens. One should be confident that good is going to take place and one may even have a direct realisation. *Shakti* is always and ever a force for good. There should be no doubts and *sadhana* should be continued uninterruptedly and with full faith. It must be remembered that *sadhana* is self-perfecting and *Shakti* is all knowing. Whatever experience is necessary for the initiate to go through takes place through *kriyas*. Surrender to *Shakti* makes one happy and composed.

**Forewarning and Protection or Punishment by *Shakti***
*Shakti* is the all-knowing and mother of all beings. Her activities are always to better everyone and raise human consciousness, whether the initiate can discriminate between good and bad or not. Some initiates may be forewarned and protected while others may be punished for past actions in order to purify their *sanskaras* and uplift them in this manner. Due to ignorance the initiate does not know what is good and what is bad for him. One may talk philosophically and nurture one's ego but one does not know what has been stored in one's *chitta*. Only Goddess *Shakti* knows everything and it is best for the initiate to have faith and surrender. At times of difficulty one can sincerely pray to the Mother asking for Her

compassion after telling Her about one's limitations. One can ponder about one's worldly involvements and attachment to circumstances, and the grace of the Mother that brought one out of these limitations. In times of doubt and uncertainty the best action is to go within and then say or do what feels right. If one is true to what feels right and is honest in this process then Mother *Shakti* will take care of the rest. The only thing an initiate can be sure of throughout this process is the purity of his intention. *Shakti* then converts the purity of this intention into activities to reduce the remaining *sanskaras*.

God showers the same grace on everyone—men, women or animals; but our experiences differ because of the different capabilities we have to receive this grace. One who is in close touch with the subtle activities of *Shakti*, experiences *kriyas* to a greater extent. Receiving different amounts of grace is like having different eyesight; some can see very well, some only to a degree and others are totally blind. Physical as well as psychical capabilities vary from person to person. Blaming God or *Shakti* for it has no justification.

The pathway to attaining Self or God becomes easier for the initiate who sees the grace of God in every situation and every *kriya,* and who rises above the dualities of pleasure and pain, gains and losses.

**Shaking due to Mental Imbalance**
According to the mode of purity (*sattvic*), activity (*rajasic*) or inertia (*tamasic*), one's state of mind changes from time to time. When the feelings become intense, the mind becomes imbalanced and debased resulting in intensified breathing, trembling or shaking of the body where the hair rises on the body. This shaking is different to the shaking caused by *kriyas*. It is like the kind of intense breathing that occurs from fast running unlike *bhastrika pranayama*, which is the true *kriya*. *Yogadarshan* of

Patanjali warns against this kind of shaking, which is due to an imbalanced mind, which is an obstacle. There are other obstacles mentioned such as doubts, inertness, laziness, lethargy, certain diseases and lack of interest in yoga causing sorrow and weakness of the mind. This in turn may cause shaking, irregular breathing patterns, anger or trembling. Shaking caused by *kriyas* is healthy and results in divine joy, and it should not be misunderstood with the shaking of the former kind.

### Sleep versus *Samadhi*

Sleep in the normal sense is one of the five states of *chitta: pramana, viprayaya, vikalpa, nidra* (sleep) and *smriti* (memory). When one sleeps well one says that "one slept well" and it stays in the memory. Good sleep is a kind of one-pointedness and occurs within an active *chitta. Turiya* state or *samadhi* is the state when all modifications or activities of the *chitta* come to an end. Thus these are two entirely different things.

### Piercing of the *Chakras* and Awareness

There is sometimes doubt about the sequence in which the *chakras* are pierced when *Kundalini Shakti* awakens. Although all *chakras* are pierced simultaneously, some of them could be slow so that the initiate cannot match an experience with its related *chakra. Chakras* that are pierced intensely may result in the *kriyas* associated with them being more intense. The initiate may be surprised to see a particular *chakra* being opened, without experiencing the ones below it opening. One may compare the situation with a fire pot being placed at *mooladhara* or root centre, and the flames rising to new heights from time to time, that is, the different *chakras* showing related experiences according to *Shakti* flowing up and down. *Shakti* may reach the top and the person would then experience a heavy head, one-pointed concentration and bliss, without showing much experience related to the lower *chakras*. This does not mean that the lower chakras were not pierced. In fact, all *chakras* are pierced to some degree.

The state of cosmic consciousness is said to be the awakened state, while the state of worldly involvements is the sleep state. The third is the state of mental modifications, which is known as the dream state. Thus, someone who has introverted awareness is awake, and someone having extroverted awareness is asleep. In other words, when it is night for others, it is day for the yogi. When the yogi is awake the word disappears for him. According to saint Dadu, a *jnani* (knower of truth) finds the whole world asleep; there is no one who is awake. A person who knows the ultimate truth while being physically awake is the awakened one.

## Increased Sensitivity on Awakening

With the awakening of *Kundalini Shakti,* the initiate becomes mentally, emotionally and physically delicate, sensitive and transparent so much so that external factors affect him quickly. For example, having compassion for a sick person one may fall sick oneself. I have noticed these effects on myself for several years. Physically I have become so sensitive that I cannot use very warm or very cold water in the shower, it makes me feel sick for days if I do so. After entering a swimming pool I sneeze many times as if I have a cold. Generally I wear undergarments that are skin tight, otherwise I do not feel comfortable. Emotionally I am easily hurt with the grievances of others, and mentally I have become very sensitive to things that happen around me.

Some practitioners report an increase in their sex drive and increased anger after awakening, and this may apply to other weaknesses as well. However, one has to assess the situation carefully. The rise in sexual desire is not because there is an attractive woman around the male initiate, and anger felt is not because of some circumstances. When passions and negative tendencies arise without an external trigger, it is the stored *karma* or tendencies that are coming to the surface for annihilation. After purification the symptoms vanish gradually. Initiates are advised to live an appropriate lifestyle with proper eating habits to help the working of *Shakti*. If they are not careful and do not give due care and attention their spiritual progress can be hindered.

## Psychology and *Shaktipat*

Mind and *prana* (life energy) are two different things. Psychology is related to mind while *Shaktipat* is related to *prana*. *Prana* is stirred and it moves upwards with *Shaktipat*. It has nothing to do with thinking or psychology. Activities of *prana* are very subtle and they bring noticeable changes in the physiology of the initiate.

## Knot between Gross and Subtle Bodies

The belief that physical body is the self, and "I-ness", is the knot between gross and subtle bodies. *Kundalini Shakti* is Divine Consciousness; its awakening and experiencing by the initiate is direct experience of God's independent consciousness. This is the only way to untie the knot and to transfer consciousness from "lower-gross" to "divine-subtle".

## *Shakti Sankraman* (Exchange) between Two Persons

The coming and going of *Shakti* can be experienced in two ways: one, by having subtle insight and direct experience, two, by the observation of external effects. Well-known examples are the ways in which blessings and curses are known to work. The good and bad effects can be experienced by the self or can be seen in the experience of others. Various faiths and traditions are full of such mythical instances. Compassion towards a person may heal him, but at the same time the healer may inherit the disease himself. One instance was recorded in history a few hundred years ago. It involved the Mughal Emperor Humayun of India. His son was suffering from an incurable disease and all medical practitioners of that time had proved inaffective. Then the father-king prayed to God sincerely and intensely to cure his son and give the disease to him. In the presence of many the son was cured and he lived for many years ruling India, while the father died of the same disease in a few days. This is the *sankraman* or exchange of *Shakti*.

*Shakti* remains active throughout a person's life after it awakens; and, various kinds of *kriyas* keep manifesting according to the state of mind of the initiate. Upsurges and outbursts of anger, love, compassion or devotion take place especially in gatherings where many people are present. Ordinarily the exchange may not take place but during discussions, discourses and lectures both the speaker and the listener can be affected. To protect oneself from this exchange initiates are advised to stay away from crowds and gatherings. There are greater chances of such an exchange when emotional outbursts take place. One should keep a balanced mind and walk away from such situations.

Anger is one of the greatest menaces and it disturbs the balance of both parties who are arguing, the one who is angry and the other who receives the anger. It is caused by weakness and it damages *sadhana*. When things happen contrary to one's wishes anger takes place. The initiate should develop a habit of remaining indifferent towards pleasure and pain. The development of silence and forgiveness counters the upsurge of anger in due time. Prayer to the all-knowing Mother *Shakti*, who is active in the initiate after *Shaktipat*, can remove most of the negative habits.

**Victory over External Influences**
Initiates are normally involved with social and political issues, their job, their family, friends and other attachments, reading newspapers and/or watching news on TV to the extent that their *chitta* is always occupied in

dealing with related matters. Affairs of the world involving gains and losses can disturb the balance of the mind, which affects *sadhana*. This is the reason that living in the *ashrama* is recommended. Most people cannot live in an *ashrama*, but they should develop a nature such that their mind is not affected by the affairs of the world. One can keep a track of the happenings in the world without being influenced by them.

## Three Levels of Attention

The eyes and mind are two functions and seeing can be external or internal. From them there are three different combinations. When the eyes see some external object and the mind also attends to that external object, then both the eyes and the mind have external attention; this is "external level" of attention. When the eyes are looking at some external object but the mind is focused on some object within or internally, this is a combination of external and internal states. If the eyes are closed so that nothing is seen externally but the mind is focused on something external, then this is a combination of internal and external factors and is the "combined level" of attention. When the eyes are closed and the internal eyes are seeing some inner light or vision, and the mind is also inwardly focused on the same object, then both functionaries are seeing inward. This is an "inward level" of attention. Thus there are three kinds of attention: external, combined and internal. The state of a yogi is such that he has open eyes but the mental attention is always on *Atman* or Self within. This is said to be the best state of attention.

## Should an Initiate Remain Celibate or Marry?

This point has been covered earlier when three saints; one married happily, the other never married, and yet another having a wife who fights with him regularly; all received liberation in their own way and thanked God for the conditions they lived with. Here the situation is slightly different when an initiate is following spiritual path already and wants to know whether he can marry without leaving the quest for spiritual attainment.

In *Bhagavad Gita* Lord Krishna says that all spiritual practices have only one aim—freedom from the bondage of the world. This can only happen when one rises above duality and the intellect becomes steady and anchored in ultimate truth. This principle applies to householders and renunciates equally.

Regarding marriage, when someone marries for physical pleasures alone, there may be problems. In Vedic tradition one marries not for enjoyment but to free the Self from worldly attachments. Then there is no problem. A man prays to Mother Goddess for a wife who stimulates his mind, a woman who can follow his mind, and who is from a spiritual family and can cross the ocean of birth and death. A wife chosen in this manner takes on the difficult task of swimming across the ocean of *maya* along with her husband. The same thing applies to a woman when she decides whether she should marry or not.

Marrying for physical pleasures and ignoring morality and education often ends in quarrels, divorces and sometimes in murders. According to the Vedic tradition there is a "celibate period", a "married period" and a "forest dweller" period. The first two stages prepare the ground for spiritual life as a forest dweller. Being in the middle of physical pleasures and worldly activities prepares the path for liberation from *maya* or illusion. There is no harm in being passionate and enthusiastic about events that happen in life and to enter fully into them as they occur but then when they are over one should return again to a state of balance and equanimity. Learning to remain unperturbed between fame and infamy, gain and loss, victory and defeat, union and separation is preparation towards attaining the spiritual goal. On the other hand, becoming attached to pleasures and being affected adversely by sorrow results in being derailed from the path of salvation.

The Soul is always alone and unaffected—this is the teaching from the Vedas and should be remembered at all times. When this teaching is forgotten and the Soul connects to the senses and the mind, it begins to experience things, which forms *karma*. *Kathopanishad* compares the senses with horses, mind with the reins and body with the chariot. When the reins are loose the horses are free to drag the chariot of the body towards worldly attractions. If the reins are kept pulled the horses are in control and the chariot moves towards its spiritual destination. If the mind continues to be pulled towards the Soul the senses remain under control and the intellect becomes steady. Such is the state of a yogi who is not deterred by any debacles or attractions. Finally one finds one's abode on one of the spiritual planes.

## Illicit Relations

Taking out morality and religion from illicit relations, it is the involvement of the mind and nothing else that affects the spiritual progress of the initiate. It is the compassion involved with the killing of animals that makes a vegetarian initiate closer to attaining reality, and not anything else. In the same way a spouse is a natural companion in spiritual pursuits, but extra-marital relations involve an excess of physical hunger that attaches the mind or *chitta* to worldliness and takes one away from *Atman* or Self. Attachment to the body increases with sexual desires and can become the cause of falling from the spiritual path for both partners. When one is out-of-body while living or between two incarnations one finds that there is no maleness or femaleness attached to the Soul. In fact, one chooses to be either a male or a female before going for the next incarnation.

If however, an initiate has sex outside of marriage or under circumstances where there is no attachment to the body and is engrossed in thoughts of God or deity, it does not harm him on the spiritual path. In saying this I am not advocating in favour of extra-marital relations but pointing out that it is the involvement of mind that matters and not the action itself. Any person who is engrossed in thoughts of God and lives from within, who is above dualities and is always contented, and who has realised the Self, is the true Guru even if he is known to have an immoral character in the eyes of the world. Those who think about their Guru's morality will be negatively affected; and others, surrendering to the Higher Consciousness in the Guru will eventually be liberated from *maya*. Such is the effect of mind's involvement with things.

## Vision of Light is the Vision of God

*Brahman* does not have any appearance. Different kinds of lights that are sometimes seen during meditation or after *samadhi* in the twilight zone (half-awake-half-asleep) are visions of *Saguna Brahman* or *Brahmana* with attributes. Orthodox belief talks about seeing God in bodily form, and that happens to some initiates, nevertheless, visions of light are also visions of God. When the seer, the seeing and the seen merge into one, the initiate sees God. This leads to the cessation of all modifications or fluctuations of the *chitta*. According to *Mundakopanishad*, seeing *Brahman* in the golden form of . light liberates one from good or bad *karmas* once and for all. One becomes similar to God, pure light without bodily form. The golden, luminous beauty is *prana* that has risen from *Brahman*. It radiates in all beings. His hands, feet, eyes, head and mouth exist everywhere. One who has known this does not talk about it.

## Experience of *Brahman* and Study of Scriptures

Since the experience of *Brahman* is a matter of personal unfoldment some people may question why is it important to study scriptures? However, studying the scriptures removes doubts, enlightens intelligence and develops deeper interest in spirituality. Study, recitation and contemplation of scriptures are an essential part of *sadhana,* which enables the initiate to have direct and personal experience of Truth.

Scholarly study of scriptures, pondering and working on grammatical details, depths of words and sentences, and a critical evaluation of the subject matter keeps one stuck in superficial knowledge. Without *sadhana* such study is empty of spirituality. It is solely confined to the intellect. The *chitta* of such scholars remains filled with desires of worldly pleasures and affected by the dualities of pleasure and pain. They do not receive the real benefit of studying scriptures, although they might earn a degree for writing their thesis. To know God one's *chitta* must be filled with the qualities of *sattva* (purity) and devoid of *rajas* (action) and *tamas* (inertia). *Chitta* is purified and the initiate is prepared to know God with the simultaneous study of scriptures and regularity of *sadhana*.

## Importance of Faith

Sometimes it is argued that if mechanical *bhakti* or devotion, yoga and *sadhana* can lead to the knowledge of God, what is the need for faith? The first thing to ask here is, why would one do anything to find God if one has no faith in Him?

According to Maharishi Vyas, commenting on *Yogadarshan* of Patanjali, faith protects the initiate as a mother protects her child. There are three things: *rit, sat* and yoga. *Rit* is the intellect gained from *samadhi* and the knowledge acquired from within, *sat* is that truth

which is experienced personally without external aid, and
yoga is one-pointedness of *chitta. Rit, sat* and yoga are
inter-related, and faith provides inspiration and
protection from failing to achieve the spiritual goal.
Intense *faith* becomes *bhakti,* intense *bhakti* becomes
meditation, and meditation becomes *samadhi,* bringing
the knowledge of *Brahman*—this is a natural order. Faith
without discrimination between true and false is blind,
while the one based on *rit* and *sat* bears fruits.

## Different Paths Have the Same Goal

There are different paths such as *bhakti* (devotion),
*karma* (selfless action), *jnana* (knowledge), Vedanta and
yoga. Even yoga has different paths such as *Hatha,
Mantra, Laya* and *Rajayoga.* Followers of one path may
criticise the followers of other paths, but all paths
recommend meditation in one form or another. Some of
them suggest meditation on God with form and some on
God without form. Some suggest concentrating on the tip
of the nose, some on a specific *chakra*, some on a sound
and some on an object. Every path requires surrender to
God and dissolution of their ego into God. Thus the
follower of the path of knowledge (*jnana*) aims at merging
ego in cosmic consciousness to achieve oneness with
Brahman. A *karma-yogi* performs duties without likes
and dislikes and thus acquires a steady intellect and
becomes situated in the Self. In the path of devotion
(*bhakti*) the ego merges in the deity and becomes one
with it. Whatever the path, there are three essential
steps: *dharna* (withdrawal from outside world and
concentration), *dhyan* (meditation) and *samadhi* (inner
absorption). So while there may be some variations in
approach, the final goal is the same—peace and
tranquillity of *chitta.*

At one place Lord Shiva has suggested 125,000 ways
to purify *chitta.* Therefore, a discussion about the
superiority of any one path over the other is only

applicable to external *sadhana*. Once *Shakti* is awakened, by whatever method, all external methods stop and internal *sadhana* takes over. Then whatever has to be done by the initiate is guided by *Shakti*. *Shakti* is omniscient and knows the *sanskara* and spiritual needs of the initiate. From then on the responsibility of selection of spiritual practices is taken over by *Shakti* and there is nothing left for the initiate to decide.

## Precautions after *Shaktipat*

Only the initiate who is fully prepared (having awakened the *kundalini*) will receive liberation upon receiving initiation, while for others being initiated will first get their *kundalini* awakened so that internal *sadhana* begins from then on. The flaws in one's *chitta* will still be seen after *Shaktipat*. *Shakti* will first remove the *sanskara,* and then pacify the three *gunas* or modes of living. And thus the purification and annihilation of *chitta* continues until *samadhi* is attained. During this process the initiate must be as watchful as a pregnant woman. Like the signs of pregnancy, the initiate receives indications that some spiritual progress has started within. Then like the development of a foetus, the initiate experiences *kriyas* and has the feeling that the seed of knowledge is growing within. Thereupon the woman guards the foetus to ensure its safety. In the same way the initiate should take precautions and follow the instructions of the Guru to protect the knowledge gained and ensure its further growth. If the woman ignores the rules the embryo may be destroyed. In the same way the initiate may waste the *Shaktipat* received if he does not adhere to the rules or acts contrary to them.

No initiate is above the rules. Until the experience of *samadhi* and witnessing of *Atman* or Self takes place, the guidelines of the Guru and scriptures should be strictly followed.

# EPILOGUE

*Chitta* or psyche, which appears similar to the subject of awakened *Purusha* or *Atman*, is the subject or goal of discussion. *Atman* who is the master of *chitta*, knows all tendencies because it is not result-oriented since it is an end in itself. Tendencies of the *chitta*, its determinations and thoughts are always result-oriented and have a separate existence from the beginning; *Purusha* watches the tendencies of *chitta* as a witness. The average worldly *jiva* or living-being imagines the form of *Atman* according to those tendencies of *chitta*, because at the arousal of tendencies in *chitta*, *Atman* appears according to them. But *Atman* does not become like that; it always remains a witness. When the tendencies resolve and dissolution of resolves are completely annihilated, *Atman* appears established in its own form.

Just as the sense organs and objects of the world being visible are not self-lighted, in the same way *chitta* being visible is not self-lighted. Statements of the kind, "I am angry," "I am happy," "I am afraid," and "*My chitta* is disturbed," show that there is some entity, other than *chitta*, that witnesses these waves of thoughts. That entity is known as *Atman* or *Purusha*.

*Chitta* is the centre where the outside world and, the light and energetic form of awakened *Purusha* are both reflected. *Atman* is eternal, pure, knowledgeable and free. World is mortal, decaying every moment and changeable. Since both the world and *Atman* are simultaneously reflected in *chitta*, symptoms of both of them are found in the individual. This is why *jiva* does not remember death, which is associated with it in every moment. On the one hand, the individual thinks that he is knowledgeable, wise, pure, free and superior to other beings and keeps forgetting death; while on the other hand, he cherishes the thought of impurity, doubts his intellect, and remains afraid of death, dependability and ignorance.

*Chitta* is thus where the reflections of *Chaitanya Atman* and the mortal world meet. Being turned towards the world *chitta* experiences the world, but it does not experience *Atman* in spite of the *chaitanya* state and virtues of *Atman* which are reflected on it. This proves *chitta* to be different from *Atman*, and its changeability puts it into another category than *Atman*.

This visible world (*Prakriti*, the female principle of God) is for enjoyment by the *Purusha* (*Atman*, the male principle of God) and not by the *chitta*. *Chitta* has an inert establishment, which is separate from the *Chetana Atman*. *Sadhana* or spiritual practices for liberation, and all kinds of auspicious or inauspicious activities by the *chitta* are not for itself but for the *Atman*.

Tendencies or thought-waves and *chitta* are related and result-oriented, while *Atman* stands separate from them and is an end in itself. Birth, life and sense enjoyments are the results of these tendencies under which a person is born and continues to be involved with pleasures, happiness and sorrow till time eternal. Tendencies/desires, *chitta* and their results are influenced by the three properties of *sato-guna* (purity), *rajo-guna* (activity) and *tamo-guna* (inertia), which fluctuate as a part of the nature. *Prakriti* too is sometimes manifested and sometimes unmanifested, and hence its representations also keep changing. Accordingly, the visible world keeps changing all the time. However, *Atman* or *Purusha* and its properties

never change with the changes in the visible world, and
that is why *Atman* is not result-oriented. It is an idea
that *Atman* appears to be changing according to the
changes in the *chitta*. Just as a jewel on coming in contact
with a blood-red flower appears to be red but does not
become red, in the same way *Atman* appears to be
changed but it does not actually change. Thus *chitta* and
changes or results in it are lighted from outside, but
*Atman* is self-lighted. Anyone who comes to realise this
truth about *Atman* or *Purusha*, the outside world
disappears for him and he achieves the highest good.

Such a realised person becomes free from questions of
the kind, "What was I in the past life", "What countries
did I visit and how did I live?", "What is the real form of
me?", "What forms would I acquire in the future?" "Which
countries will I visit?" and "How would I live?" One
becomes free from such questions related to *Atman*.
Queries of this kind appear until one knows the truth,
and soon after the experience of *samadhi* one knows that
such questions are the result of changes in the *chitta*.
Nevertheless, it is the person with such *Atman*-related
questions in mind that deserves the experience of
*samadhi*. Such a person gains recognition amongst the
seekers of truth.

Just as water flows only downwards, in the same way
mind, intellect, ego and sense organs remain turned
towards the outside world before knowing the truth.
Afterwards, wisdom weighs heavily on the *chitta* of the
knower of truth and it turns inwards towards the state of
*kaivalya* or inner absorption without fluctuations.

An important question arises at this stage about the
life of the yogi, and that is, whether or not one's *chitta*
ever turns towards the world so that one can behave in
worldly manner? Although the *chitta* of the knower of
truth flows towards the wisdom, the holes of former lives
keep intruding. Whenever the *sanskara* of wisdom are

stronger, *chitta* turns towards wisdom, but because of the former worldly *sanskara* one behaves in a worldly manner too. Thus both *paramarth* (highest good) and worldliness continue together, but because of worldliness in-between obstacles keep coming in the progress of *paramarth*. One should make the following efforts to remove this obstacle.

One should take this obstacle of occasional worldliness similar to the *kleshas* or negative forces like ignorance, lust and envy. This can be burnt through *sadhana, japa* and *tapa* to the extent that they would not germinate again; their power of germination should be destroyed. With the emergence of wisdom-*sanskaras* their accumulation goes on and worldly-*sanskaras* go on minimising. Later worldly-*sanskaras* can also accumulate and become sizable; therefore, one should not just feel satisfied with the emergence of wisdom-*sanskara*. Absence of the ego of doership in the *kriyas* of *Shakti* stops the accumulation of worldly-*sanskara* and one continues to progress higher and higher in spirituality. The situation therefore demands the inward awakening of *Shakti* and then continued *sadhana* with the sense of surrender, thereafter.

All-knowingness is the fruit of wisdom, just as monthly interest is the fruit of money loaned. When the desire of all-knowingness after acquiring wisdom also vanishes, wisdom-knowledge keeps accumulates in the *chitta* regularly. Continued, uninterrupted and steady *sadhana,* and continued practice of renunciation leads to the annihilation of worldly-*sanskara* and the accumulation of wisdom-*sanskara*. This is known as *dharmamegh samadhi,* which is the highest state of *sampragyat samadhi*. Absence of turning towards the outside world from time to time, and continuous reflection of the natural virtues of *Atman* on the *chitta* is *dharmamegh samadhi*. Even in this state *chitta* is not fully inactive and its connection with *Chetana Shakti* is not broken; and so, a *sato-guna* (pure) tendency turned towards *Atman* still remains. For this reason the present state of *samadhi* cannot be placed under *asampragyat samadhi* (absorption without seeds of intellect); it is defined as the highest form of *sampragyat samadhi* (absorption with seeds of intellect).

*Dharmamegh samadhi* brings freedom from *karma* and *kleshas*. Once the yogi transcends desire and attachment, he does not accumulate *karma* even if involved in the activities of the world. Thus the *chitta* becomes free from all *kleshas* and *karma*. Becoming free from all kinds of negative forces the knowledge of outer world is reduced to a minimum. The cover of negative forces slips from the *chitta* and falls on the outside world.

There are three basic properties of nature: *tamo-guna* or the property of inertness, *rajo-guna* or the property of worldly interest and action and *sato-guna* or the property of pious thinking and action. These three properties are responsible for providing *bhukti* and *mukti*: *bhukti* means the enjoyment of worldly and sensual pleasures, and *mukti* means liberation or freedom from *maya* or illusion. When *dharmamegh samadhi* is attained the double purpose of the three properties is served, and the three properties lose their potency; they do not have the capacity to give a new body to the yogi. For people involved in actions with *paramarth* (highest good) the three properties serve their purpose and disappear, while for others they continue to exist. Thus the chain of further incarnations is broken for the former while it continues for the latter.

There is a natural order in the action by *Shakti*. First is *prasava-krama,* which means the downward flow of *Shakti* from *Atman*, turning towards the outer world. First of all it comes in contact with inert *chitta* or psyche, awakens and activates it and assumes the form of *Chit-*

*Shakti.* Then it comes into contact with inert sense organs
and awakens and activates them, which is known as
*Chetana Shakti.* This is how the world is constructed.
*Jiva* or living being becomes attached to the body, actions
or *karma*, property, family, prestige and popularity. A
sense of doership emerges and one imagines about
pleasures through senses in the world. One now begins to
take more and more care of the body, health and beauty,
earns wealth, gathers comfortable things and becomes
involved in different kinds of constructive work. With this
the accumulation of *sanskara* goes on. As a result of this
desires, tendencies and inflictions such as lust, anger,
envy, and greed find a home in the *chitta*, and one rotates
in the chain of death and reincarnations. This part of the
work of *Shakti* is for *bhukti* or enjoyment of pleasures
and pains.

The next action for *Shakti* is *prati-prasava-krama* in
which *Shakti* turns and activates inwardly through
*sadhana* or grace of the Guru. This inward awakening of
*Shakti* is known as "the awakening of the *kundalini*" and
*chetana* is said to have become *Pratyak-Chetana.* The
same *Shakti* that the *jiva* assumed to be one's own, is
now felt as working on different parts of one's body
independently of one. This is the opposite of the first
action and *Shakti* begins to annihilate whatever was
constructed in the first action. Feeling *Shakti* separate or
independent from oneself the sense of doership begins to
dissolve. As a result one's attachment to action or *karma*
also begins to dissolve. One begins to feel detached from
the family, property, *karma*, body, power and position.
Sense organs begin to give up their food (*ahar*) and get
situated in withdrawal (*pratyahar*). In other words, mind,
sense organs and intellect give up outwardness and turn
inward.

There are various obstacles that hinder this process
but consistent *sadhana* with surrender to Guru and God
gradually provide victory over these obstacles. With the

awakening of *Shakti* a sense of witnessing emerges. *Shakti* converts the *sanskara* into *kriyas*, and resistance to worldliness, one-pointedness and *samadhi* grow in the individual. Desires and tendencies begin to thin away and *chitta* begins to develop equanimity and balance towards the dualities such as pleasure and pain. Further accumulation of *sanskara* stops, and detachment from sensual pleasures begins to take place. Factors that disturb and fluctuate the *chitta* are annihilated and one progresses towards the attainment of *dharmamegh samadhi*. Light of the knowledge of *Atman* begins to spread, bliss increases and one remains satisfied by and through *Atman*. *Shakti* provides concentration to *chitta* at different levels and passing through different kinds of *samadhi* one gets established in *dharmamegh samadhi,* a *samadhi* that has yet the seeds of intellect and thought fluctuations. However, as the progress continues, the flow of *chitta* towards sensual pleasures stops, and as all negative forces are completely annihilated one gets established in *asampragyat* or *nirvikalpa samadhi* (inner absorption without the seeds of intellect or thought fluctuations).

The final goal of yoga is to achieve that state in which worldly as well spiritual activities come to an end. There is nothing more to be done. The three properties of *tamo-guna, rajo-guna* and *sato-guna* are dissolved in the reverse action of *Shakti* and the element of *Atman* alone remains. The outside world disappears completely. This state is also known as *kaivalya* or *swarup-pratishtha,* meaning the establishment in one's original form. There is nothing left for *Shakti* to do any more. She has completed both worldly and spiritual works. She collects all her activities and gets dissolved in *Atman*. It is *Atman* that began everything and the final attainment too is *Atman*. The circle is complete.

# LAST WORDS

It is a privilege to write these last words for this book. My background has been in Mahayana Buddhism. In Mahayana as in all spiritual traditions great emphasis is laid on the principle of surrender, which *Shaktipat* embodies. It is the surrender of the ego self to the higher Self which brings about an enlightened way of living in the world. *Shaktipat* is the vehicle for achieving this.

Stefan Anacker, in his book *Seven Works of Vasubandhu*, speaks of an "enlightenment *chitta*" which is set into motion when *karmic* conditions are right. All of us have this *chitta* within us, but without the intervention of a Guru through the process of *Shaktipat* it can remain dormant. Intense desire for enlightenment can awaken this *chitta* without a Guru but it is more likely that the powerful energy that is transmitted through a Guru at initiation can activate it faster than individual effort.

Awakening this *chitta* is the first step to enlightenment. Its further growth and development depends on mindfulness and for this reason is the basis of enlightenment. To be mindful means to be constantly aware of every thought, feeling, impulse, and action; to continuously monitor everything that is thought or felt; not judging whether these thoughts, actions, behaviours are right or wrong; just observing that they are present without wanting to change their nature in anyway. Too often experiences of bliss and oneness are reported during a meditation and after a while a person says "but it went away." This is because the sense of mindfulness or of continuing contemplation was intentionally or unintentionally forgotten when the meditation ended. The fruits of the spiritual path are the same as in any other path in life in that the more love, care and attention we give to it the greater are the rewards. Cultivation and maintenance of this mindfulness is down to every person who has a deep desire for enlightenment.

*Shaktipat* begins the process of weakening the ego mind. The *kriyas* which Dr Kumar has described at length throughout the book are aimed at purifying the Buddhist concepts of *sanskaras* which are the hindrances preventing the realisation of our Buddha nature or *Atman* in the Hindu tradition. The ego mind covers these *sanskaras*. Since they have accumulated over many lifetimes the ego mind is strong and not easily weakened. It has to be strong because it ensures we do not remember our divine inheritance. The *Shaktipat* with the raising of *kundalini* together with spending time in an *ashrama* is essential to lay a good foundation for weakening the ego mind to allow us to become aware of our divine home. For this to happen the chattering mind has to become still and quiet which is not easy. I have direct experience of the difficulty in stilling and quietening the mind and can vouch for the importance of spending time in an *ashrama* or some other retreat setting.

In 1996 I went to India to track the life of the Buddha. I had been studying and practising Buddhism for many years and it had given me so much that I wanted to give something back in thanks. As part of this journey I enrolled for a ten-day silent meditation retreat in Bodhgaya. Prior to this I had done the occasional weekend meditation retreat but nothing more challenging. Most of my study up to then had been theoretical. The retreat was a Vipassana retreat. Silent meditation or Vipassana meditation is insight meditation and is aimed at quietening the mind to allow wisdom and insight to emerge. There were about 200 people from different nationalities (none Indian) enrolling with me. Accommodation was a straw mat on a concrete floor in a room with six other women. Each day began at 5.30 am with an hour-and-a-half of yoga and then there was 45 minutes of meditation before breakfast. The remainder of the day consisted of different forms of sitting, standing and walking meditation, all in silence and for 45 minutes. In the afternoon there was an enquiry session where one of the facilitators answered any questions retreatants had. In the evening there was a *dharma* talk taken from one of the Buddhist scriptures. The final meditation was at 10.30 pm. There were two meals, breakfast and lunch with tea and fruit in the afternoon. And this by and large was the pattern for those ten days.

Days one, two and three I found easy enough. My mind was pre-occupied with looking at everyone else and deciding who I would speak to when the silence was broken on the last day. Everyone looks interesting when there is no talk. On day four I noticed that I was getting irritable and my mind was giving me a hard time with comments like 'What are you doing here?' But I persevered. The walking meditation was easier than the formal sitting sessions. The weather was beautiful and the grounds of the Thai monastery where we had the retreat were idyllic. Walking among such beautiful surroundings it was easy to feel connected to nature and in these sessions I felt a closeness to something that was bigger than me. When I was walking I wasn't looking at my ego or counting my breaths but was connecting with something immense and powerful through nature. In contrast the sitting sessions couldn't have been more painful. Ten minutes was like an hour. I found it impossible to watch my breath for more than a nano-second and I spent every session hoping that the bell that signified the end of the sitting would ring. At each session I would vow that this was the last time I was going to put myself through this. But then in the next session walking outside in the sunshine and then sitting didn't seem too bad, and the memory of the hard time my mind had given me receded, only to return again with a vengeance at the next sitting session.

I persevered, constantly doing battle with my mind and telling myself that 'I had to stay' and berating myself for not being stronger and saying to myself? 'What kind of person would I be if I gave up half way?' This was an exhausting process and on day seven I thought I was going to have a nervous breakdown. At the end of day seven I had had enough. I reasoned that I was going to be travelling around India on my own for another four months and that if I became ill, I was alone. At that point I decided to leave. There was no self-punishment in this decision, just an acceptance that this was what I would do. In that decision to leave I stopped fighting with my mind. I let go of everything that I thought I should or should not be doing; and in that moment of letting go, I experienced the most wonderful calm and peace. This was a complete surprise, so I decided to stay and continue with the rest of the retreat.

I am convinced that it was the use of reason through which I stopped fighting with my mind that brought forth this breakthrough. Reason is vital for shifting consciousness. The more a person uses reason to think and ponder on spiritual truths, the greater the understanding and insight. It is different from intellect in the sense that intellect is of the mind but reason is of the soul and if something doesn't feel right after reasoning it out then it is not right. Obedience to any doctrine without using reason cannot and does not bring spiritual freedom, only reason can do this. It shows the willingness to think independently. By taking the elements of spirituality and applying reason to establish what resonates and what doesn't and then following whatever resonates through good and bad to its greatest depths, is a sure path to enlightenment. This is the valuable lesson that the retreat taught me as well as showing me just how strong the mind is and how it needs the kind of intense spiritual practice that only a retreat can bring to begin the weakening process. *Shaktipat* and the spiritual instructions from a Guru awaken this capacity to reason. Whether or not it is deepened following initiation depends on how honest and courageous the initiate is in his spiritual quest and on whether or not there is attachment to the Guru.

This letting go didn't result in the sitting meditations being any easier but somehow the constant chatter of my mind with its do's and don'ts had ended and I could sit without agitation. What a difference this made to the meditations! From this I realised that it is not in the fighting but in the surrender that peace and calm is found. *Shaktipat* is a powerful mechanism for this surrender.

Dr Kumar has mentioned how easy it is to fall prey to temptation on the spiritual path. The higher one progresses the subtler are the temptations to remain stuck at a particular stage. The development of *siddhis* or paranormal powers has been discussed in the book and is one such temptation. Another is the temptation to want too much spiritually. I also remember when I finished the retreat being tempted by the opportunity to stay and do a second ten days. I remember thinking 'now that I have achieved this state of calm staying another ten days would be even better' but then I remembered my promise to myself to do only one retreat and I said 'no'. It is easy to become trapped in spiritual experiences which point to another reality but in this is also a trap. Greed on the spiritual path is the biggest hindrance to achieving the Buddhist idea of *nirvana*. For Buddhists the roots which prevent the realisation of *nirvana* are greed, hatred and delusion. *Shaktipat* penetrates to the roots of these hindrances so they can emerge through *kriyas* to be dissolved.

Strong desire and intense emotion awaken the *kundalini*, which is the spiritual energy of enlightenment. But while thousands are managing to raise the *kundalini* few of these have become enlightened. This begs the question why? I believe it has to do with the nature of intention. If a person wants spiritual freedom solely for himself then the process is longer and slower than if a person wants enlightenment to be able to help others and show them the way out of suffering. In the case of the latter the intention to help others galvanises the enlightened *chitta* and gives it such power that it can wipe out the effects of many lifetimes of accumulated *sanskaras* in one go. Wanting any spiritual benefits for others makes sense because at the highest metaphysical level there is no separation between us. We are all parts of the one divine body, so when we are sincere in only wanting the best for others we are ensuring that we want only the best for ourselves. In wanting the best for others we are confirming to the universe that we accept this basic truth.

In Mahayana Buddhism this idea has been elevated by the concept of the *Bodhisattva*. This is someone who has attained spiritual freedom but who chooses to return to the material world to show others the way out of suffering. Great importance is given to this concept and many Mahayana Buddhists believe that being a *Bodhisattva* is the closest one comes to discovering our Buddha nature. One famous *Bodhisattva* is Avalokiteshvara who is the *Bodhisattva* of compassion. If mindfulness is the basis for enlightenment then compassion ensures its continuing unfoldment. Out of compassion comes wisdom and knowledge and all compassion begins from not seeing any separation between others and us. Though many, we are one. Living with others in an *ashrama* provides the opportunity to practice compassion, and no act of compassion no matter how small is ever wasted. In every compassionate act the ego mind is weakened and this is why compassion is powerful because when kindness is shown to another then in that moment the ego self is forgotten which weakens its power and intensity. But this is such a subtle process that it is easy for disillusionment to set in. This is why kindness should be shown without any thought for reward or result. The compassion shown should be a kind of affectionate detachment in that once it has been shown it is forgotten. Only in such unconditional acts can real spiritual progress be made. Where there is expectation attached, the act becomes tainted and instead of working towards *nirvana* adds to *samsara* or what the Buddhists call the world of suffering.

These last words would not have been possible without the invitation from Dr Kumar to write them and to him I express my gratitude. They also would not have been possible without the consciousness, which operates through my right brain, and it is to this that my greatest gratitude and indebtedness lies. Since my own *kundalini* rose four years ago, the connection between what I know in terms of spiritual understanding and how I know it through *kundalini* has pointed unrelentlessly to the connection between *kundalini* and the right brain. When the *kundalini* rises it stimulates activity in the right brain, which enables the transmission of spiritual insights and understanding. To write these words without acknowledging their source is to me to be guilty of spiritual fraud. *Shaktipat* and all the spiritual methods described in this book carve a pathway to the right side of the brain and when this pathway is deep enough and *karmic* conditions are suitable; *kundalini* will rise safely and naturally. Awareness of the link between spiritual practice and this pathway is key to attaining spiritual liberation. *Shaktipat* accelerates this process.

**Margaret Dempsey** (R.N.M.H./B.A.)

Right Brain Institute

PO Box 34424

London W6 0WP

You can read about my experience with *Kundalini* on www.margaretdempsey.com: The Power Within – A True Story of Hope.

Email: dempseym2002@yahoo.com

# WHAT HELP IS OFFERED?

The theory of *kundalini* and the Integral Path of Yoga have been described in some detail, and a practical formula has been presented in the book, *Kundalini for Beginners* (Kumar 2000, 256). Greater discussion with a practical formula has been given in my book, *The Secrets of Kundalini Awakening* (2002) in which the process is described through pictures. In the two books mentioned above I have given details of other worlds. I have discussed the power of Soul and have elaborated on various ways of achieving higher consciousness. Thus, these books have self-help programme, which practitioners can follow and use to prepare them for initiation. We have established centres in New Delhi, Copenhagen, London, Bradenton (Florida), Suva (Fiji) and Sydney for practical spiritual growth. It is advisable for practitioners to practise the integral path of yoga for six months to one year. Depending on the personal progress and wishes of the individual during this period, practitioners are accepted as disciples for *Shaktipat* initiation.

*Deeksha* or initiation to a disciple of another Guru is normally avoided. However, if someone is interested in receiving *Shaktipat* initiation from us, the same is performed taking into consideration under the following:

1. That practitioner may have fallen prey to a false Guru and may have been befooled for money and/or other disadvantages.

2. That he may not be getting satisfaction from the initiation received from the other Guru and he may have got permission to look for another Guru.

3. That spiritual progress of the practitioner may have stopped for some reason or the other and he may have lost faith in the Guru.

4. That practitioner may be happy with the Guru but may be unable to contact him further because of unavoidable reasons and he may find the same *Shakti* working in our lineage of Gurus.

# Glossary

| | | |
|---|---|---|
| *Ahankara* | = | ego, I-ness |
| *Ajna* | = | sixth *chakra* or eyebrow centre |
| *Anahat* | = | fourth *chakra* or heart centre, place of *anahat* (unstruck) Cosmic Sound |
| *Akalpita* | = | unimagined |
| *Akash* | = | sky |
| *Anvaya* | = | construction of five basic elements through subtle forms |
| *Apana* | = | life-force working between the navel and souls of the feet |
| *Asampragyat samadhi* | = | absorption with the dissolution of *chitta* |
| *Asan* | = | mattress or woollen sheet used to sit for *sadhana* |
| *Asana* | = | yogic postures of *Hathayoga* |
| *Asat* | = | impure |
| *Ashram* | = | centre for spiritual practices |
| *Atman* | = | Supreme Self |
| *Avidya* | = | ignorance |
| *Ayurveda* | = | ancient Vedic system of medicines in India |
| *Bhakti* | = | devotion |
| *Bhaktiyoga* | = | path of devotion |
| *Brahma* | = | God as the Creator |

| | | |
|---|---|---|
| *Brahmacharya* | = | celibacy |
| *Chakra* | = | vortex of energy located in the central nerve *sushumna* |
| *Chaitanya* | = | Conscious Self, active principle of *Shakti*, carrier of *prana* and mover of *chitta* |
| *Chetana* | = | Consciousness, level of active *Shakti* in sense organs |
| *Chhaya darshan* | = | seeing one's reflection or the double |
| *Chitta* | = | psyche; storehouse of *sanskara*, mind, intellect and *ahankara* or ego, instrument of knowledge |
| *Chit-Shakti* | = | *Shakti* reflected on *chitta*, Conscious Energy of mind-stuff |
| *Dama* | = | non-involvement of sense organs with pleasures of the world |
| *Deeksha* | = | initiation |
| *Dharana* | = | contemplation |
| *Dharma* | = | religion (literary meaning), duties prescribed through religion |
| *Dhyan* | = | meditation or concentration |
| *Gauni Bhakti* | = | secondary path of devotion |
| *Ghata* | = | jar |
| *Grahan* | = | the act of receiving |
| *Guna* | = | property: *sato-guna* (purity), *rajo-guna* (activity), *tamo-guna* (inertia) |
| *Guru* | = | spiritual teacher/master |
| *Hathayoga* | = | path of yogic exercises, *pranayama* and *mudras* (gestures) |
| *Ida* | = | subtle nerve to the left of *sushumna*, representing moon/coolness |
| *Ishta* | = | one's cherished form of God |
| *Ishvara-* | | |

| | | |
|---|---|---|
| *Pranidhan* | = | surrender to *Ishvara* (God) |
| *Japa* | = | chanting of *mantra* |
| *Jiva or* | | |
| *Jivatma* | = | living being, phenomenal self |
| *Jivanmukta* | = | liberated while living |
| *Jivan-mukti* | = | liberation while living |
| *Jnani* | = | the knower of Truth |
| *Kaivalya* | = | complete inner absorption without any fluctuations |
| *Kalpita* | = | imagined; yogic powers imagined and worked for |
| *Karma* | = | action |
| *Karmayoga* | = | path of selfless action |
| *Klesha* | = | negative forces |
| *Kriyaman karma* | = | action in progress (*karma* in the present) |
| *Kriyas* | = | automatic movements |
| *Kumbhak* | = | cessation of breathing |
| *Kundalini* | = | Dormant serpent power /sleeping spiritual energy at the base of spine |
| *Kundalini-Shakti* | = | Awakened Spiritual Energy; *Shakti* turned inward |
| *Maha-bhuta* | = | basic elements—earth, water, fire, air and *akash* |
| *Maheshwara* | = | another name of Lord Shiva |
| *Manipur* | = | fourth *chakra* or navel centre |
| *Mantra* | = | a combination of sacred words having latent energy |
| *Maya* | = | illusion |
| *Mooladhara* | = | first *chakra* or root centre |
| *Mudra* | = | body gesture |

| | | |
|---|---|---|
| *Naad or Nada* | = | Cosmic unstruck Sound heard internally |
| *Nirodh Parinam* | = | result in the form of a prophylactic towards worldliness |
| *Nirvikalpa samadhi* | = | inner absorption without fluctuations |
| *Parmarth* | = | the highest good |
| *Pingala* | = | subtle nerve to the right of *sushumna*, representing sun/heat |
| *Prakriti* | = | Universe created by *Shakti*, the female principle of God Absolute |
| *Prana* | = | life-force—active between the front portion of nose and the heart |
| *Pranayama* | = | breath control exercises |
| *Prarabdha (karma)* | = | fateful action (*karma* propelled by hardened habits) |
| *Prasava-Krama* | = | involutionary cycle |
| *Prati-Prasava-Krama* | = | evolutionary cycle |
| *Pratyahara* | = | withdrawal of senses and mind from the outer world |
| *Pratyak-Chetna* | = | consciousness turned inward |
| *Purusha* | = | *Atman*, the male principle of God Absolute |
| *Ridhi* | = | worldly accomplishments |
| *Rishi* | = | reputed spiritual practitioner |
| *Sadhan* | = | automatic spiritual practices through *kriyas* |
| *Sadhana* | = | yogic/spiritual practices through one's efforts |

| | | |
|---|---|---|
| *Saguna* | = | God with attributes or manifestation |
| *Sahayoga* | = | natural joining of Soul with Supersoul |
| *Sahasrar* | = | seventh *chakra* or crown centre above the top of the head |
| *Samadhi* | = | inner absorption, superconsciousness, oneness of individual and Universal Consciousness |
| *Samadhi* | | |
| *Parinam* | = | result in the form of inner absorption |
| *Samana* | = | life-force—active between the heart and the navel |
| *Sampragyat* | | |
| samadhi | = | absorption with fluctuations of *chitta* or intellectual consciousness |
| *Samsara* | = | the world of suffering |
| *Sanchit karma* | = | accumulated *karma* from the past |
| *Sanskara* | = | hardened habits and accumulated *karma* from past lives |
| *Sanyama* | = | concentration with control on flicker-ness of *chitta* |
| *Satsang* | = | the company of the devotees of God |
| *Sattva* | = | *sato-guna*, virtue of purity |
| *Savikalpa* | | |
| samadhi | = | inner absorption with fluctuations |
| *Shakti* | = | Spiritual Energy/Power |
| *Shaktipat* | = | Transmission of Cosmic Energy from Guru to initiate, resulting in the awakening of *kundalini*. |
| *Shama* | = | disconnection of sense organs with mind |
| *Shiva* | = | God as destroyer/transformer |
| *Siddhis* | = | paranormal powers or spiritual attainments |

| | | |
|---|---|---|
| *Sushumna* | = | subtle central nerve running through the spinal column |
| *Swadhishthan* | = | second *chakra* or sacral centre |
| *Tanmatras* | = | subtle forms of five basic elements like earth and sky |
| *Tapa or tapas* | = | austerities |
| *Udana* | = | life-force—active between the front portion of the nose and the crown |
| *Unmani avastha* | = | state of thoughtless absorption |
| *Upasana* | = | worship |
| *Vairagya* | = | renunciation of materialism and sensual pleasures |
| *Vishnu* | = | God as the preserver |
| *Vishuddha* | = | fifth *chakra* or throat centre |
| *Vrattis or Chitta-vrattis* | = | thought waves of the mind |
| *Vyana* | = | life force distributed and active over the whole body |
| *Yoga* | = | spiritual practices leading to union with the Self |
| *Yoga-nidra* | = | yogic sleep following *sadhana* |
| *Yoni* | = | form of life in a particular incarnation |

# BIBLIOGRAPHY

Greenwell, Bonnie, 1990, *Energies of Transformation: A Guide to the Kundalini Process,* Cupertino, CA.: Shakti River Press.

Krishna, Gopi, *The Awakening of Kundalini,* NY, USA: Kundalini Research Foundation, 1975.

Kumar, Ravindra, *Secrets of Kundalini Awakening,* New Delhi: Sterling Publishers, 1992.

———, *Destiny, Science and Spiritual Awakening,* New Delhi: Sterling Publishers, 1997.

———, *Kundalini for Beginners*, MN, USA: Llewellyn Worldwide Ltd., 2000.

———, *Secrets of Kundalini Awakening,* New Delhi: Sterling Publishers, 2002.

Muktananda, Swami, *Chitshakti Vilas (The Play of Consciousness)*, Maharashtra, India: Gurudev Siddhapeeth, 1972.

Purushottamtirtha, Swami, *Yogavani or Siddhayogopadesh*, Varanasi, India: Siddha Yogashram, 1938, 1999.

Shivomtirtha, Swami, *A Guide to Shaktipat,* Maharashtra, India: Devatma Shakti Society, 1997.

Shivomtirtha, Swami, *Kundalini Siddha Mahayoga*, Devas, India: Sri Narayan Kuti Sanyasa Ashram, 1984, 1997, pp. 51-52.

Vigyani, Yogendra, *Mahayoga Vigyan*, Rishikesh, India: Vigyan Bhawan, 1938, 1997.